A guide to the official publications of the European Communities

JOHN JEFFRIES

A guide to the official publications of the European Communities

Second edition

MANSELL PUBLISHING

ISBN 0 7201 1590 6

Mansell Publishing, 3 Bloomsbury Place, London WC1A 2QA

First edition published 1978. Reprinted 1979. Second edition published 1981.

© John Jeffries, 1981

Distributed in the United States and Canada by The H. W. Wilson Company, 950 University Avenue, Bronx, New York 10452.

British Library Cataloguing in Publication Data

Jeffries, John
    A guide to the official publications of the European Communities.—2nd ed.
    1. European Economic Community countries—Bibliography
    2. European communities—Bibliography
    I. Title
    016.3091'4'055   Z7165.E8

    ISBN 0-7201-1590-6

Text set in 10/12 pt Linotron 202 Times, printed and bound in Great Britain at The Pitman Press, Bath

Contents

Contents

Preface to the second edition

The opportunity has been taken to bring this work up to date to the end of 1979. The chapter devoted to Eurostat takes account of the many changes in statistical publications which have taken place since the first edition. The work has been completely rewritten and it is hoped that the reader will find that the relationship between different types of publications has been clarified. The basic arrangement of material remains according to the institutional framework of the European Communities and conforms as far as possible with the arrangement of the official catalogues. Moreover, the book remains what it says it is: a guide to the official publications of the European Communities. If it had been a guide to sources of information about the European Communities it would have been a very different work. Official publications are, after all, only one source of information, however important. On the other hand it has become obvious that it would be pedantry to ignore some of the more important publications from other sources where they complement or exemplify official publications. It would have been wrong to ignore mechanized information retrieval and a number of excellent publications in the area of the law of the European Communities. Nevertheless the reader will have to look elsewhere for an exhaustive treatment of other sources of information.

I continue to be indebted to officials of the European Communities and I wish to record my appreciation for the unfailing co-operation of Emma Harte and Carlo Pau of the London office of the Commission. The patience of my family during the revision of this work cannot remain unacknowledged.

John Jeffries

The Library
University of Kent at Canterbury

February 1980

Abbreviations and acronyms

AAMS   African and Malagasy States
          see also AASM, EAMA
AASM   Associated African States and Madagascar
          see also AAMS, EAMA
ACP   African, Caribbean and Pacific States
ACTU   machine-readable file of documents issued by the Secretariat-General of the Commission
AGREP   Permanent Inventory of Agricultural Research
AISE   Archive of Socio-economic Information
AOC   Associated Overseas Countries
          see also AOM
AOM   Associés d'Outre-mer
          see also AOC
ASEAN   Association of South East Asian Nations

Benelux   Belgium, Netherlands, Luxembourg
BLEU   Belgium–Luxembourg Economic Union
BTN   Brussels Tariff Nomenclature

CAMAC   Computer-aided Measurement and Control
CCCN   Customs Co-operation Council Nomenclature
CCT   Common Customs Tariff
          see also TDC
CECA   Communauté Européenne du Charbon et de l'Acier
          see also ECSC
CEE   Communauté Économique Européenne
          see also EEC
CELEX   automated information system for European Community law
CES   Comité Économique et Social
          see also ECOSOC, ESC
CIRCE   Information and Research Centre of the European Communities
COM   Commission
Comecon   Committee for Economic Co-operation
COREPER   Committee of Permanent Representatives

CREST   Comité de la Recherche Scientifique et Technique
CRONOS   machine-readable file of statistical time series
CST   Classification Statistique et Tarifaire pour le commerce inter-
         national

DG   Directorate-General
DIANE   Direct Information Access Network for Europe
DOM   Les Départements d'Outre-mer

EAEC   European Atomic Energy Community
           see also Euratom
EAMA   Les États Africains et Malagache Associés
           see also AAMS, AASM
EC   European Communities
ECDOC   European Communities Documentation
           see ECO1
ECG   European Co-operation Grouping
ECHO   European Community Host Organization
ECO1   machine-readable file of Commission working documentation
ECOSOC   Economic and Social Committee
           see also CES, ESC
ECSC   European Coal and Steel Community
           see also CECA
EDF   European Development Fund
           see also FED
EEC   European Economic Community
           see also CEE
EFTA   European Free Trade Association
ENDOC   Environmental Centres in the Community
ENREP   Current environment research projects in the Community
ESA   European System of Accounts
           see also SEC
ESC   Economic and Social Committee
           see also CES, ECOSOC
ESONE   European Standards of Nuclear Electronics
Euratom European Atomic Energy Community
           see also EAEC
EURODI-
CAUTOM   multilingual terminology data bank
EURO-
FILE   inventory of data bases available in Europe
EURO-
NET   European network

Eurostat   Statistical Office of the European Communities
           see also SOEC

FED   Fonds Européen de Développement
           see also EDF

GATT   General Agreement on Tariffs and Trade
GEONOM   Geonomenclature

HMSO   Her Majesty's Stationery Office

IMF   International Monetary Fund

JET   Joint European Torus
JNRC   Joint Nuclear Research Centre

Maghreb   Morocco, Algeria, Tunisia
Mashrek   Egypt, Jordan, Lebanon, Syria

NACE   Nomenclature Générale des Activités Économiques dans les
           Communautés Européennes
NATO   North Atlantic Treaty Organization
NCE   Nomenclature du Commerce
NCP   Nomenclature Commune des Pays
           see also GEONOM
NICE   Nomenclature des Industries des Communautés Européennes
NIMEXE   Nomenclature Import–Export Europe
NIPRO   Common nomenclature of industrial products
NST   Nomenclature Uniforme des Marchandises pour les Statisti-
           ques de Transport

OCT   Associated overseas countries and territories
OECD   Organization for Economic Co-operation and Development
OSIRIS   mechanized system for the production of statistical tables
OT   Overseas Territories
           see also TOM

PRC   Proposals, Recommendations, Communications

SCAD   Service Central des Archives et de la Documentation
SEC   Système Européen de Compatibilité Nationale
           see also ESA

SEDOC   Système Européen de Diffusion des Offres et des Demandes
         d'Emploi Enregistrées en Compensation Internationale
SITC   Standard International Trade Classification
SOEC   Statistical Office of the European Communities
         see also Eurostat
SYSTRAN automatic translation system

TDC   Tarif Douanier Commun
         see also CCT
TOM   Les Territoires d'Outre-mer
         see also OT
TVA   Taxe sur la Valeur Ajoutée
         see also VAT

u.a.   European Unit of Account
UDC   Universal Decimal Classification
UN   United Nations
UNCTAD   United Nations Conference on Trade and Development
Unesco   United Nations Educational, Scientific and Cultural Orga-
         nization
UNIDO   United Nations Industrial Development Organization

VAT   Value Added Tax
         see also TVA

WEU   Western European Union

CHAPTER 1

Introduction

THE EUROPEAN COMMUNITIES

The origins of the European Communities lie in the political and economic uncertainty following World War II. In fact a number of international organizations sprang up in the immediate post-war years in response to the problems of economic reconstruction and political instability. The benefits of integration are more obvious in the case of small countries and it might be that should the EEC ever collapse the Benelux economic union would remain. The Schuman declaration of 9 May 1950 was said to be a new departure, not only because it involved the big countries. At the instigation of Jean Monnet, Robert Schuman, who was the French Foreign Minister, suggested that France and Germany should pool their coal and steel resources. This would be a limited but decisive step towards European unity and the resulting organization would be open to all European countries. It was felt that the unique character of this proposal lay in the creation of a supra-national authority: in other words the participating countries would relinquish sovereignty in order to achieve common ends.

The European Coal and Steel Community was founded by the Treaty of Paris in 1952. Its success reinforced hopes for political integration but such hopes received a set-back when the French National Assembly failed to ratify the Treaty establishing a European Defence Community which had been signed by the six Paris signatories. As a result, proposals for a European Political Community also collapsed. Nevertheless, the economic benefits of the ECSC could not be denied, and these could provide a more solid basis from which to promote European integration, but the outlook for outright political unification had undoubtedly grown rather less promising.

The executive of the ECSC was the High Authority but it is significant that when the Rome Treaties were signed the name chosen for the executives of the two new Communities was 'Commission', suggesting the delegation of authority rather than the pooling of sovereignty. Nationalism is supposed to be against the spirit of the Treaties but one does not need to be a confirmed cynic to see the pursuit of national objectives apparent in the deliberations of the Council of Ministers.

The Rome Treaties of 1957 were a logical extension of the use of the economic methods which had made the ECSC a success. Of the three Communities the EEC has had the most wide ranging impact. Nearly all the secondary legislation of the European Communities is now EEC business and 'EEC' and 'Common Market' have come to be regarded as synonyms for 'European Communities'.

The attitude of the United Kingdom had been ambivalent. The fostering of greater political stability in Europe was favoured, but the UK did not join the founding countries at the outset and became involved in a kind of trading rivalry by promoting EFTA. News broadcasts came to include frequent references to the 'inner six' and 'outer seven'.

When the UK attempted to join the Communities in the sixties this was opposed by De Gaulle and the membership negotiations came to nothing. And these were the crucial years of Community development. The most severe crisis came in 1965 when the French began a boycott of Community Institutions which lasted seven months. A dispute over agricultural policy caused a rift which became resolved into the question of whether a country could veto a proposal on the ground that a vital national interest was at stake. The crisis ended with the so-called 'Luxembourg compromise' of 28–9 January 1966. Essentially, the outcome of this episode is that the Treaty provisions for majority voting in the Council of Ministers have been overturned.[1] In effect the Council will now continue to debate an issue until a unanimous decision can be reached and no vital national interests are claimed to be infringed. (The text of the 'Accords de Luxembourg' can be found in the *Ninth general report on the activities of the Community* (EEC), pp. 31–3.)

On a more positive note, the Customs Union was completed in 1968—actually ahead of schedule. The Common Agricultural Policy, the first of the common economic policies was implemented in the sixties. The institutional structure was rationalized by the Treaty of Brussels in 1967 in the creation of a single Commission and a single Council. From 1961 Association agreements were made with third world countries.

The accession of the UK, together with Denmark and Ireland took place in 1973 (Norway having failed to ratify the Treaties). British membership was not finally settled until the referendum of 1975.

If the founding fathers were most concerned with a vision of European unity then their aspirations have not been wholly realized. Even the hesitating steps towards monetary union have met with only partial success. Euratom was undermined when France decided to go its own way in nuclear policy and there seems no doubt that any move towards integration will always be circumscribed by the policies of national governments. So far as the European Communities are concerned the question of who wields what power and for what purpose is a complex one but the decision-making body is the Council of Ministers which consists of politicians who are accountable to the governments they represent. Both the House of Commons and the House of Lords were quick to realize the importance of bringing pressure to bear on British ministers when they set up Committees to scrutinize Commission proposals before they had been considered by the Council.

In the British referendum campaign the 'anti-marketeers' made much of the argument that the UK was relinquishing its right to govern itself in favour of the faceless bureaucrats of Brussels. The reality of the situation does not seem to be quite so clear-cut. Perhaps the European Communities will take on a more administrative than governmental character in future. Greece, Spain and Portugal are candidate countries at the moment and perhaps a larger Community will also be a rather looser association than Monnet envisaged.

Moreover, the 'Committee of Wise Men' have drawn attention to what they describe as the *lourdeur* which afflicts the Institutions of the European Communities. Their *Report on European Institutions* which appeared in 1979 draws attention to ways in which

improvements in the institutional arrangements might facilitate
progress towards European Union. The need for such a report
might in turn be taken as indicative of a trend away from
integration. As the report itself concludes:

> the present time seems to us ill-suited to futuristic visions which
> presuppose a profound and rapid transformation of attitudes
> within the Community. The chance of such a transformation in
> the next few years seems to us exceedingly slight.

THE MACHINERY OF THE
EUROPEAN COMMUNITIES

The legal basis for the structure of the European Communities is
complicated because of the number of Treaties in force. It might
be anticipated that at some future date there will be a single
European Community governed by a single Treaty but at
the moment there are three Communities governed by eight
Treaties.

From 1958 the Court of Justice and the European Parliament
were common Institutions of the three Communities but it was not
until 1967 that the executives were merged. The accession of the
new countries in 1973 only altered the composition of the
Institutions; it did not involve any changes of structure or legal
powers.

Commission

In the words of its Secretary-General: 'The Commission is the
guardian of the Treaties; it is the executive arm of the
Communities; and it is the initiator of Community policy and
exponent of the Community interest to the Council.'[2]

The strength of the European Communities is therefore closely
related to the strength of the Commission. However it is far from
being the gigantic bureaucracy that some imagine it to be. Indeed,
by the standards of most Whitehall departments it looks a very

modest operation indeed. In 1979, the permanent staff of the Commission excluding research staff but including language staff was 8,302 but of these only 2,145 had 'conceptional' duties.

'Commission' is also the name of the college of thirteen who are the executive of the European Communities. At the moment there are two members of the Commission from the larger countries and one each from the smaller countries. Article 10 of the Treaty of Brussels provides that there must be at least one Commissioner from each country but not more than two. With the proposed expansion to a Community of twelve the size of the college must alter and a number of possibilities are suggested in *Proposals for reform of the Commission of the European Communities* which is the report of the Independent Review Body chaired by Dirk Spierenburg. This is an important report which makes a number of recommendations about the structure of the Commission. The report was presented on 24 September 1979.

The report makes the proposals shown in Table 1 for the structure of the Commission in a Community of ten. (Greece will probably join on 1 January 1981.)

Council of Ministers

Although it is the responsibility of the Commission to initiate policy it is the Council of Ministers which makes decisions on Commission proposals (except that the Council may instruct the Commission to put forward proposals on a given subject). The appropriate member of the Commission should also attend meetings of the Council. Each country is represented by one minister according to the topic under discussion. In many cases a country will be represented by its foreign minister but if agriculture is being discussed then agriculture ministers attend. The Presidency of the Council rotates every six months; the order can be found in the *Guide to the Council of the European Communities*.

The nine heads of state or of government now meet regularly and these summit meetings are called 'European Councils'. Although these meetings are not required by the Treaties they are of obvious significance in the development of Community policy; moreover, it has become customary for the President of the Commission to be invited to these meetings.

4. Competition and Transport	Customs Union Service DG XIII B (Information Management)	DG Industrial Affairs
	DG IV (Competition) DG XV B (Taxation)	DG Competition
	DG VII (Transport)	DG Transport
5. Social and Regional Affairs	DG V (Employment and Social Affairs) DG XII A (Education, Training and Culture)	DG Social Affairs
	Environment and Consumer Protection Service DG XVI (Regional Policy)	DG Regional Policy
6. Agriculture and Fisheries	DG VI (Agriculture) DG XIV (Fisheries)	DG Agriculture and Fisheries
7. Energy and Research	DG XVII (Energy)	DG Energy
	Euratom Supply Agency DG XII (Research, Science and Education) except Directorate A DG XIII (Scientific and Technical Information and Information Management) except Directorate B Joint Research Centre	DG Research
8. Development	DG VIII (Development)	DG Development

TABLE 1[3] *Proposed structure of the Commission and its Services in January 1981*

Portfolios	Existing administrative units composing the portfolios	New administrative units
Presidency: representation of the Commission	Secretariat-General Legal Service DG X (Information/Spokesman's Group)	Secretariat-General Legal Service Information/Spokesman's Group
Vice-Presidency: work-planning, co-ordination, supervision of the organization including allocation of resources, permanent deputy of the President	DG IX (Personnel and Administration) DG XIX (Budgets) DG XX (Financial Control) Statistical Office Office for Official Publications Security Office —Co-ordination of Funds (Task Force)	Personnel and Administration Budgets Financial Control Statistical Office Office for Official Publications Security Office —Co-ordination of Funds (Task Force—attached to the Secretariat-General for administrative purposes)
1. External Relations	DG I (External Relations)	DG External Relations
2. Economic and Financial Affairs	DG II (Economic and Financial Affairs) DG XV A (Financial Institutions) DG XVIII (Credit and Investments)	DG Economic and Financial Affairs DG Credit and Investments
3. Industrial Affairs	DG III (Internal Market and Industrial Affairs)	DG Industrial Affairs

European Parliament

Much interest has centred on the fact that the European Parliament was directly elected for the first time in 1979. Formerly 198 members were chosen from the national parliaments; the directly elected Parliament is much larger, with 410 members.

The Parliament remains a consultative assembly rather than a legislature. It cannot enact legislation nor can it dismiss the Council. On the other hand it is consulted before the Council can legislate on a particular proposal from the Commission; this consultation invariably takes place even when not actually required by the Treaties. The Parliament can overturn the Community budget—a power which it has exercised; and it can compel the resignation of the Commission—a power which it has not yet exercised.

Court of Justice of the European Communities

The Court of Justice has the ultimate power to decide on all legal questions under the Treaties. There are nine judges, one from each country, who are assisted by four advocates-general. It is not in any sense a criminal court, its jurisdiction being concerned with international, constitutional, administrative and civil law.

Other bodies

The Commission, Council, Parliament and Court are the Institutions of the European Communities but there are other bodies which have an independent existence and should be noted.

The *Economic and Social Committee* is an advisory body which consists of 144 representatives who are said to represent the various categories of economic and social activity in the member countries. The ESC considers only Euratom and EEC business. There is a *Consultative Committee of the European Coal and Steel Community* which must not have fewer than sixty nor more than eighty-four members; they must be drawn in equal numbers from the three groups—producers, workers, and consumers and dealers.

The *European Investment Bank* was established by the Treaty of Rome (EEC)[4] in order 'to contribute, by having recourse to the capital market and utilizing its own resources, to the balanced and steady development of the common market in the interest of the Community'. It has a particular responsibility in the area of regional policy though its activities are not restricted to the member countries of the Community. The bank can operate in the associated states.

The *Court of Auditors* consists of nine members and is required to 'examine the accounts of all administrative expenditure and administrative revenue' of the European Communities.[5]

OFFICIAL PUBLICATIONS

The Official Publications Office was established in 1969 as an inter-institutional service attached to the Commission for administrative purposes. It is not a commercial publisher in the usual sense. It does not take the decision to publish in the first place nor does it accept any financial risk. The costs of publication are charged to the specific Institution and it is up to that Institution to reach its own decisions as to publications policy. In the Commission the Secretariat-General does this through its Comité consultatif des publications. The Official Publications Office is consulted as to whether a document will sell and what its price should be. For Commission publications price is usually three times the printing cost per item. Translation policy is also a matter for each individual Institution.

Rather than its publisher the Official Publications Office is more the official printer for the European Communities. But there were always certain exceptions even to this apparent monopoly:

—Publications of the European Investment Bank
—Publications of the Information Offices of the Commission other than in Belgium and Luxembourg
—Internal documents produced in the print shops of the individual Institutions
—Small print runs of documents distributed by mailing list to known individuals

However, the *Official journal* of 5 April 1979 (C89, p. 5) states that:

> The Commission has decided that its departments should make use, whenever appropriate, of the services of private publishers for their publishing requirements.
>
> A number of publications, mostly on scientific or technical subjects, are already being produced by private publishers.
>
> The agreements concluded with publishers are drafted to meet each individual case. However, as a general rule, the publisher undertakes publication under his own imprint and therefore takes responsibility for all production and marketing costs.

In fact DG XIII had been using commercial publishers for a number of years. The basis of this policy lies in the belief that it is more efficient to rely on existing expertise in the dissemination of specialized information than to use blanket free distribution or for the Commission to make its own arrangements for the marketing of information. Where the publication of a work is undertaken by a commercial publisher there will be no blanket free distribution to European Documentation Centres which never received very much scientific material anyway. Presumably one will now need to make more use of general bibliographic sources as well as of the official catalogues in order to trace these works.

The Official Publications Office arranges for free publications to be printed but it is then up to the individual Institution to handle the free distribution. (A list of addresses from which free publications may be obtained is given in Appendix I.) Limited distribution documents, usually mimeographed, are produced and distributed by the originating Institution. Limited distribution means that their free distribution is limited. Although such documents are not generally available to the public, many are held by libraries or can be obtained by direct application to the originating Institution. Priced publications, but no others, are dealt with by HMSO in the UK. (A list of sales offices is given in Appendix I.)

Much of the material available to the public is serial in form, either periodical or part of a series. There are comparatively few monographs. Changes of title and format are more than usually abundant. A valuable list is *Serial publications of the European*

Communities and its institutions held by the British Library Lending Division, 3rd ed., 1979, edited by G. P. Cornish.
Problems over title changes are compounded by linguistic difficulties. On the whole one does not wish to cavil over the distortion of meaning through translation. Translators have coped remarkably well with the multiplicity of languages in use. F. N. FitzGerald comments:

It appears that over the twenty years of using the first four languages certain standards have been achieved and the translations run fairly true, but this unfortunately is not the case for the new languages, Danish and English. A year ago in a seminar with some twenty Danish librarians, the point was strongly made that many of the Danish texts, including legal texts, were vague to the point of being meaningless. I can judge the English translations myself and can confirm this statement. It is, I presume, a question of 'running in' the translation motor for these two new Community languages.[6]

There have been various projects to produce multilingual glossaries both in hard copy and in machine-readable form. SYSTRAN has been developed to carry out automatic translation by computer.[7]
A large part of the information which can be obtained from official publications is statistical, and there is an emphasis on economic and social statistics. Management information in relation to common policies of the European Communities also occupies a substantial part of the literature.
Some two thousand staff are employed in the four Euratom research establishments (at Ispra in Italy, Geel in Belgium, Karlsruhe in Germany and Petten in the Netherlands) so that it can be seen that the Community is making its own contribution to the production of scientific information. The development of EURONET also demonstrates the concern with the free flow of information.
The Commission has a Treaty obligation to inform the public,[8] and there is an increasing body of literature which is intended to inform the public about the activities of the Communities. From time to time there are problems of confidentiality and it is inevitable that there will be some categories of documents to

which access is restricted. In the case of documentation on nuclear energy, for example, applications for confidential 'communications' have to be made through the United Kingdom Atomic Energy Authority in the first instance for UK users, and the applications are then vetted again by the Commission.

EUROPEAN DOCUMENTATION CENTRES

Throughout the world some 296 university libraries and 46 public libraries have been given the status of 'European Documentation Centre' or 'Depository Library'. These libraries are supposed to receive one free copy of every published work of the European Community Institutions in the official language of their choice. The scheme was introduced in 1963 so that it is unlikely that any one library has a complete collection though in the UK the collections in the Official Publications Library, British Library Reference Division, and the British Library Lending Division are particularly worthy of note.

The novel feature of the European Documentation Centre scheme was that it was designed to promote the study of European integration. EDCs are located in academic institutions which have established teaching and research in European integration. In practice EDCs are to be found in the libraries of the institutions concerned, although the manifest policy of the Commission was that they should be established in academic departments under the direction of the teaching staff. I have argued already that this policy was both impractical and unrealistic and those institutions which have decided to suit themselves do not appear to have been penalized by the Commission.[9]

The obligations of EDCs are directed exclusively towards teaching and research in particular institutions. Depository Libraries are rather different. In the immortal words of the anonymous compiler of *Addresses of the European Documentation Centres— EDC and the Depositary [sic] Librairies [sic]—DEP* they are libraries 'which are equipped to ensure and repercute information'. Apparently, Depository Libraries should be regional collections of official publications, fully catalogued, and available to members of the public without further formality. It is probable that Depository Libraries receive more favourable treatment than EDCs. The latter are more likely to be representative collections of official publications than complete collections. Depository Libraries receive more limited distribution documents, and the scientific literature which is not available to EDCs.

There are forty-six EDCs and four Depository Libraries in the UK. (A world list of EDCs and Depository Libraries is given in Appendix II.)

A large collection of Community publications is available for consultation at the London office of the Commission, 20 Kensington Palace Gardens, and at other Information Offices of the Commission throughout the world. (The Information Offices are listed in Appendix I.) The best collection of the official publications of the European Communities is to be found at the Central Library of the Commission in Brussels.

Notes

1. See Article 148 of the Treaty of Rome (EEC).

2. Noël, Emile, *Working together: the Institutions of the European Community*. Commission of the European Communities, 1979, p. 9.

3. Taken from the Spierenburg Report.

4. See 'Protocol on the Statute of the European Investment Bank', in *Treaties establishing the European Communities, Treaties amending these Treaties, Documents concerning the Accession*, 1978, pp. 459–80.

5. See 'Treaty amending certain financial provisions of the Treaties establishing the European Communities and of the Treaty establishing a single Council and a single Commission of the European Communities', op. cit., pp. 910–11.

6. 'Publications policy and activities of the Official Publications Office of the European Communities', *International journal of law libraries* 5(1), 1977, pp. 64–75.

7. See *Euronet Diane news*, No. 17, 1979, p. 7.

8. See Article 55 of the Treaty of Paris; Article 2 of the Treaty of Rome (Euratom).

9. 'European Documentation Centres in the United Kingdom', *Government publications review*, 4(2), 1977, pp. 127–9.

CHAPTER 2

Publications of the European Communities

Most official documents can be traced back to the Institution, Institutions or section from which they originated. The piece of information which discloses this may be rather cryptic in form, but in the case of a Commission document, for example, it is usually possible to get back as far as a Directorate-General and possibly a much smaller unit. This is an activity much favoured by those who compile the entries in the HMSO monthly catalogues. However, there are some documents of general scope and often of considerable legal significance which are published on behalf of all the Institutions and by the three Communities acting together. These are the Treaties and related documents and the *Official journal of the European Communities*. In the case of the *Official journal*, there is actually an office within the Commission (in the Secretariat-General) which is responsible for its publication, but in an official catalogue it would still be described as a publication of the European Communities because it appears under the authority of the three Communities and not one or more of the Institutions.

LANGUAGE

If a document is of legal significance then the status of the translation might turn out to be crucial. Official translations are available only in the official languages of the Communities. Up to 31 December 1972[1] these were French, German, Italian and Dutch. Since that date English, together with Danish, has become a Community language. There is no official translation into other languages which might be used in various Community countries, like Welsh and the Luxembourg language. English translations of some documents certainly already existed in 1972 but these were not official translations and were mainly published for information purposes. Whether or not they have any legal standing they may contain inaccuracies; in particular, one cannot advise the use of any version of the Treaties brought out prior to 1973, and this applies equally to the editions published by HMSO.[2]

LEGISLATION

The Treaties can be described as the primary legislation of the European Communities. They form, as it were, the written constitution under which the secondary legislation is made. The Treaties are by no means immutable and are subject to revision and extension though, of course, such alterations must be ratified by the member countries in the same way as a treaty.

Secondary legislation is not made by the European Parliament,[3] but by the Council and the Commission. The Commission may act on its own in certain administrative matters but its legislative function is more usually confined to submitting to the Council of Ministers the proposals which are voted upon there, after appropriate consultation has taken place. Secondary legislation has perhaps more in common with United Kingdom Statutory Instruments than with Public General Acts so far as scope and content are concerned. To the layman these acts may seem of bewilderingly little significance and in any event have more to do with administration than anything that is likely to have a profound effect on the law of individual countries. This is not to say that no local court ever has occasion to make reference to the Court of Justice of the European Communities for some elucidation of a point of European Community law: this does in fact happen frequently.[4]

Under the terms of the Rome Treaties, the Council and Commission can 'make regulations, issue directives, take decisions, make recommendations or deliver opinions' on EEC and Euratom matters. Article 189 of the Treaty establishing the European Economic Community goes on to give the following definitions:

A regulation shall have general application. It shall be binding
in its entirety and directly applicable in all Member States.

A directive shall be binding as to the result to be achieved, upon
each Member State to which it is addressed, but shall leave to
the national authorities the choice of form and methods.

A decision shall be binding in its entirety upon those to whom it
is addressed.

Recommendations shall have no binding force.[5]

Unfortunately, this terminology is different from that used in
the Treaty establishing the European Coal and Steel Community
where under Article 14 a decision is binding in its entirety, a
recommendation is binding as to the result to be achieved, and an
opinion is of no binding force.

THE TREATIES

The best edition of the Treaties was published by the Communities
in 1978: *Treaties establishing the European Communities, Treaties
amending these Treaties, Documents concerning the Accession.*
This version updates the one published in 1973, but see below, p.
19. It has been prepared on the basis of the official texts in force on
1 July 1978. It is interesting to note that a version has been
published in the Irish language.

Earlier versions of the Treaties and the texts as originally
ratified were available in official form in French as listed in
Catalogue des publications 1952–1971, Vol. 1, pp. 21–4. It should
also be remembered that the Treaties have been published else-
where on many occasions. Among the more important editions are
those published as Command papers by HMSO in the United
Kingdom Treaty Series; A. E. Kellerman et al. *eds, Guide to
EEC-Legislation;*[6] Sweet and Maxwell's *European Community
Treaties*, 3rd ed.; *Encyclopedia of European Community law*,[7]
Vol. B. Indeed, the volume of publications in the field of
European Community law must place the Treaties amongst the
most digested and reprinted documents of modern legal literature.

The Treaties are as follows:

Treaty establishing the European Coal and Steel Community

This Treaty was signed in Paris on 18 April 1951 by six countries—Belgium, France, Federal Republic of Germany, Italy, Luxembourg and the Netherlands. It was ratified in July 1952 and came into force on 23 July 1952.

Treaty establishing the European Economic Community

The six members of the ECSC signed this Treaty in Rome on 25 March 1957. It was ratified in the same year and came into force on 1 January 1958.

Treaty establishing the European Atomic Energy Community

The Euratom Treaty, also the work of the original six countries, went through the legal formalities at the same time as the EEC Treaty.

Treaty establishing a Single Council and a Single Commission of the European Communities

The six signed the so-called 'merger' Treaty in Brussels on 8 April 1965. It entered into force on 1 July 1967. The Assembly and the Court had been common Institutions of the three European Communities from the outset.

Treaty amending certain provisions of the Protocol on the Statute of the European Investment Bank

This Treaty was signed in Brussels on 10 July 1975. It came into force on 1 October 1977.

**Treaty amending certain financial provisions of the
Treaties establishing the European Communities and of
the Treaty establishing a Single Council and a Single
Commission of the European Communities**

This Treaty was signed in Brussels on 22 July 1975. It came into
force on 1 June 1977.

**Documents concerning the accession to the European
Communities of the Kingdom of Denmark, Ireland, the
Kingdom of Norway and the United Kingdom of Great
Britain and Northern Ireland**

Certain legal difficulties had to be overcome with the accession of
the new members to the European Coal and Steel Community.
The new members were Denmark, Ireland and the United
Kingdom; although Norway signed the Treaties, it failed to ratify.
Difficulties arose because of differences in the original Treaties
which had to be overcome by decisions of the Council of Ministers
in 1972. In effect, these decisions created a separate procedure for
accession to the ECSC.

These documents are part of the primary legislation of the
European Communities and can be found in: *Treaties establishing
the European Communities, Treaties amending these Treaties,
Documents concerning the Accession*, 1978.

It should be noted however that the 1978 edition omits some
material present in the 1973 edition. This consists of some of the
annexes to the Act concerning the Conditions of Accession and
the Adjustments to the Treaties. On p. 1127 of the 1978 edition
there is a note informing the reader that the text of Annex I was
published in the *Official journal*, No. L73, 27 March 1972.
Unfortunately, it has not been included in the *Special edition* of
the *Official journal*, and this means that there is no 'official'
English text. What is more curious is that it is Section XIV of
Annex I which defines the official languages. The effect of this
section is to amend Article 1 of Council Regulation No. 1 of 15
April 1958 (*Official journal*, No. 17/385 of 6 October 1958).
However, the version of the Act in the *Special edition* is as first
published, but translated into English and there is no mention of

the amendment in the volumes of corrigenda to the *Special edition*. It is greatly to be regretted that the investigation of points of European Community law should have been made so time-consuming and complex when using the original sources. A full English text of the 'Act concerning the Conditions of Accession and the Adjustments to the Treaties' can be found in United Kingdom Treaty Series No. 1 (1973) Cmnd 5179 I and II.

'Documents concerning the accession of the Hellenic Republic to the European Communities' are to be found in *Official journal*, L291 of 19 November 1979.

THE *OFFICIAL JOURNAL OF THE EUROPEAN COMMUNITIES*

The *Official journal* is the official gazette of the European Communities and is a very important vehicle for legal information and public notices. In particular, it gives the texts of secondary legislation, draft legislation and official announcements as well as information about the activities of Community Institutions. Unfortunately, information does not necessarily appear particularly promptly nor in a particularly digestible form. For example, notice of the coming into force of the Treaty signed on 10 July 1975 appears in *Official journal*, No. L91, 6 April 1978; that is to say a full six months after the event. Moreover, it is no small matter to retrieve this comparatively uncomplicated piece of information through the indexes.

Down the years there have been a number of changes of title and format as set out below. A complete collection of the *Official journal* can however be acquired in microfiche and 16mm or 35mm microfilm. This is of obvious benefit to those with a shortage of shelf space for, as the promotional literature points out, the *Official journal*, unbound, grows at the rate of a metre and a half a year.

Journal officiel de la Communauté européenne du charbon et de l'acier (1952–8)

The first issue appeared on 30 December 1952 and the last on 19

April 1958. The following issues were published:

1952	No. 1
1953	Nos. 1–14
1954	Nos. 1–22
1955	Nos. 1–23
1956	Nos. 1–30
1957	Nos. 1–38
1958	Nos. 1–13

After the Rome Treaties had come into force the *Journal officiel* extended its coverage to include EEC and Euratom matters and became:

Journal officiel des communautés européennes (1958–)

The first issue of the new journal appeared on 20 April 1958. From 1973 it has appeared in English as the *Official journal of the European Communities*.
From 1958 to 1967 the following issues were published:

1958	Nos. 1–33
1959	Nos. 1–67
1960	Nos. 1–84
1961	Nos. 1–86
1962	Nos. 1–142
1963	Nos. 1–191
1964	Nos. 1–220
1965	Nos. 1–226
1966	Nos. 1–246
1967	Nos. 1–322

In addition, for part of the period there was a supplement:

Supplément agricole au Journal officiel des Communautés européennes (1962–7)

This was a weekly concerned with the regulation of prices. Information of this kind has subsequently been carried in the

Official journal itself. The following issues of the *Supplément* were published:

1962	Nos. 1–20
1963	Nos. 1–49
1964	Nos. 1–50
1965	Nos. 1–50
1966	Nos. 1–50
1967	Nos. 1–47

In 1968 the *Journal officiel* was divided into two separately numbered parts: these were called *Législation* and *Communications et informations*. In English this is *Legislation* and *Information and notices*.

Legislation

Each issue is in two sections. The first part consists of Community Acts whose publication in the *Official journal* is obligatory under the terms of the Treaties. The greater part of this legislation comprises Commission regulations most usually concerned with the administration of the Customs Union and the Common Agricultural Policy. On the title page the entries for these more ephemeral Acts are printed in lighter type to distinguish them from more important Acts which appear in heavy type with an asterisk against them. This latter kind of legislation is the sort usually enacted by the Council of Ministers following proposals from the Commission and after consultation with other bodies and Institutions.

The second part consists of Acts whose publication is not obligatory under the Treaties. These are usually decisions made under the Rome Treaties which are binding upon those to whom they are addressed rather than regulations which are of wider applicability. (For a definition of these terms see above, p. 17.)

The following issues have been published:

1968	Nos. L1–315
1969	Nos. L1–329
1970	Nos. L1–285
1971	Nos. L1–289

1972	Nos. L1–307
1973	Nos. L1–368
1974	Nos. L1–359
1975	Nos. L1–338
1976	Nos. L1–368
1977	Nos. L1–361
1978	Nos. L1–379
1979	Nos. L1–350

All this represents a very considerable volume of legislation. For example, in 1977 Acts whose publication is obligatory were numbered to 3026/77 and other Acts were numbered to 77/809. (Note the different way in which the two kinds of Act are numbered and cited. An example of the former would be (EEC) 3026/77, and of the latter 77/809 EEC.) Few would deny that an output of close on four thousand legislative acts in a year is a formidable one.

Information and notices

The type of information contained in these issues is more diverse. An issue may be divided into one, two or three sections. The first is entitled 'Information' and documents some of the current activities of the Institutions. Usually found together are the minutes of proceedings, the opinions and resolutions of, and oral questions in the European Parliament. Usually appearing separately from the records of other business are written questions with answers and written questions without answers. It is a rule of procedure that questions from members of the European Parliament to which no answer has been given by the Commission within one month, or two months in the case of the Council, should be published in the *Official journal* anyway. This section notes actions pending, requests for preliminary rulings and judgments in the Court of Justice. It also gives brief information about some of the public business of the Commission, Council and some of their committees. Appearing regularly is the currency amount for the European Unit of Account in nineteen major currencies. A more unusual item is the Common catalogue of varieties of vegetable species (e.g. fifth complete edition, *Official journal* No. C54, 28

February 1979); and the Common catalogue of varieties of agricultural plant species (e.g. fifth complete edition, *Official journal*, No. C12, 15 January 1979).

The second section, entitled 'Preparatory Acts', is devoted to draft legislation. Here are to be found Commission proposals to the Council for new legislation, generally published soon after their formal submission. The opinions of the Economic and Social Committee appear in this section, as do the opinions of the Court of Auditors which are given on financial matters. The publication of draft legislation at this stage is important because it is the time a proposal enters the public domain in the formal sense. It is quite likely of course that the Commission will have consulted with interested parties already but now starts the open examination of new proposals.

The third section is entitled 'Notices' and is used to invite tenders especially for agricultural surpluses and to announce competitions for staff recruitment and the like. Since January 1978 much of the information previously carried in this section has been transferred to a *Supplement* (see below).

The following issues have been published:

1968	Nos. C1–141
1969	Nos. C1–163
1970	Nos. C1–152
1971	Nos. C1–127
1972	Nos. C1–142
1973	Nos. C1–117
1974	Nos. C1–161
1975	Nos. C1–299
1976	Nos. C1–309
1977	Nos. C1–316
1978	Nos. C1–313
1979	Nos. C1–330

Supplement

There is plenty of room for confusion of the various kinds of 'supplement' to the *Official journal*. Apart from the *Supplément agricole*, until the end of 1977 the index was known as the

Supplement to the Official journal of the European Communities, and in addition there was the possibility of a particular issue of the *Official journal* having a supplement as in the case of No. C12, 24 March 1973. The problem was made worse because of a lack of differentiation even in type face. Since January 1978 the index has been called *Index* and there is a third part of the *Official journal* called *Supplement*. It is particularly concerned with public contracts and business arising in connection with the European Development Fund, both tenders and the approval of projects financed. No. S246, 1979 gives the balance sheets and accounts for the European Development Fund in the financial year 1977.

The following issues have been published:

1978 Nos. S1–245
1979 Nos. S1–246

Annex. Debates of the European Parliament (1968–)

Although, as mentioned earlier, the minutes of proceedings of the European Parliament appear in *Information and notices*, from the session 1968–9 the full texts of the debates have been published in this Annex. Before 1968 the debates were issued only by the European Parliament itself (see p. 204). An English text has been available from No. 157.

The following issues have been published:

1968–9 Nos. 101–12
1969–70 Nos. 113–22
1970–1 Nos. 123–34
1971–2 Nos. 135–47
1972–3 Nos. 148–59
1973–4 Nos. 160–72
1974–5 Nos. 173–87
1975–6 Nos. 188–200
1976–7 Nos. 201–13
1977–8 Nos. 214–27
1978–9 Nos. 228–40
1979–80 Nos. 241–9

There are separate indexes or 'tables' for the *Annex*, one

volume for each session. The first to appear covered the session 1968–9, the first in English covering 1973–4. Each volume is in three sections:

I Index of names
II Index of subjects
III List of working documents

Special edition of the Official journal of the European Communities

This publication was required by Council Regulation (Euratom, ECSC, EEC) 857/72 of 24 April 1972. It appeared in 1972 and gives the official translation of the secondary legislation enacted between 1952 and 1972 which was still in force at the time of the accession of the United Kingdom, Denmark and Ireland. It is available in English and Danish only. It is arranged in chronological order and although there is a contents list in each of the separate parts as published there is no index. In the period covered by the *Special edition* somewhere in the region of twenty thousand Acts had been published in the *Official journal* but in fact only about ten per cent were still in force on 1 January 1973. It is also interesting to note that most of those Acts still in force had been amended at least once during their lifetime. It should be remembered that a lot of Acts may be in force for only a few hours, especially in the case of those relating to the Customs Union.

The *Special edition* includes 'binding acts of general application throughout the Community'; which means that they are in that category for which publication in the *Official journal* is obligatory. The conditions under which they actually applied in the United Kingdom, Denmark and Ireland were determined by the Act of Accession.

The following issues were published:

1952–8
1959–62
1963–5
1965–6
1967
1968   (I)

```
1968   (II)
1969   (I)
1969   (II)
1970   (I)
1970   (II)
1970   (III)
1971   (I)
1971   (II)
1971   (III)
1972   (I)
1972   (II)
1972   (III)
1972   10–31 October
1972   November
1972   1–8 December
1972   9–28 December
1972   28–30 December
1972   30–31 December
1972   31 December (L296)
1972   31 December (L300)
1972   31 December (L301)
1972   31 December (L302)
1972   31 December (L303–6)
1972   31 December (L307)
```
Supplement. Corrigenda 1952–72
Supplement. 1959–1962
Supplement. 1966–1972
Supplement. Consolidated edition of corrigenda
Supplement. 1965–1972. Omissions from the First and Second
series of the Special editions, 1952–1972

Special edition of the Official journal of the European
Communities. Second series

The second series contains English and Danish translations of Acts
still in force whose publication in the *Official journal* would not
have been obligatory. Although they were in force on 1 January
1973 the conditions under which they actually applied in the

United Kingdom, Denmark and Ireland were determined by the Act of Accession.

The following issues were published:

I	External Relations (1)
I	External Relations (2)
II	Agriculture and Food Aid
III	European Agricultural Guidance and Guarantee Fund
IV	Transport
V	Euratom
VI	Competition (a) and (b)
VII	Institutional questions
VIII	European Coal and Steel Community
IX	Resolutions of the Council and of the Representatives of the Member States
X	Miscellaneous

Indexes to the Official journal

JOURNAL OFFICIEL DE LA COMMUNAUTÉ EUROPÉENNE DU CHARBON ET DE L'ACIER. SUPPLÉMENT
The following were published:

Table 1952–5
Table annuelle 1956–8

JOURNAL OFFICIEL DES COMMUNAUTÉS EUROPÉENNES (1958–72). *SUPPLÉMENT*
The following were published:

Table annuelle 1958–62
Tables trimestrielles and Table annuelle 1963–4
Tables trimestrielles and Table annuelle (alphabétique et chronologique, analytique et méthodologique) 1965–7
Table annuelle (analytique et méthodologique) 1968–72

OFFICIAL JOURNAL OF THE EUROPEAN COMMUNITIES (1973–77). *SUPPLEMENT*
The index has appeared annually and each volume is in two sections—an alphabetical index and a methodological table.

INDEX TO THE OFFICIAL JOURNAL OF THE EUROPEAN COMMUNITIES (1978–)

Monthly indexes are used until the annual volume is available. Neither the monthly nor the annual indexes are usually too far in arrears.

Although the indexing of the *Official journal* is extremely detailed it is often detail of the kind that you can only find what you want when you know what it is you are looking for. The introduction to the Index gives the following explanation:

> The alphabetical part of this index has been drawn up in accordance with an outline plan that facilitates the retrieval of the required information. The outline plan, or classification of the alphabetical index, conforms generally to the structure of the Treaties and the organization of Community institutions.

To take a specific case, in *Official journal*, No. C5, 8 January 1979, there is a written question from Mr Kaspereit on the subject of Japanese car exports. There are two entries in the Index:

EUROPEAN PARLIAMENT—WRITTEN QUESTIONS
   Kaspereit, MEP
      Japanese car exports.

FOREIGN TRADE
   written questions
      Japanese car exports.

Provided that you already know that there is a written question by Mr Kaspereit on Japanese car exports you have a fair chance of getting there. You have a slightly more time-consuming task if you know that there is a relevant written answer and either look through them all, or through the ones under the foreign trade heading. If you did not know that there was a relevant written answer and just knew that there was some information on the Japanese car export trade then it would be necessary to look at each entry under the foreign trade heading in turn. In any event, the index does not bring related material together by subject. Material elsewhere in the *Official journal* on Japan or on car imports and exports or on the motor industry would have to be searched for separately. In this particular case there is a further weakness that the question related equally to American car exports which aspect has not been picked up by the indexing at all.

The onus is very much on the user of the index to develop a satisfactory search strategy of his own but some help is provided by a list of headings and sub-headings used, and there is also a list of key words which assist in directing the user to the most appropriate headings and sub-headings.

RECUEIL D'ACTES

Up to 1972 the secondary legislation of the European Communities was reprinted in 108 loose-leaf volumes, in the official languages. *Recueil d'actes* was mainly intended for the use of the governments of the Community countries and the Community Institutions. It included all legislation enacted, not merely that which was in force, except that certain material—budgetary and personnel matters—was automatically excluded because of its character. The volumes were arranged in ten groups, as follows:

	Number of volumes
Généralités	1
Agriculture	64
Énergie nucléaire	1
Finances	4
Problèmes institutionnels	5
Marché intérieur	18
Pays et territoires d'outre-mer, départements français d'outre-mer	1
Relations extérieures	2
Transports	3
Problèmes sociaux	6

There was also an index volume and a two-volume list of regulations.

There are no plans for any document to replace *Recueil d'actes*. It is possible that in future a list of all Community legislation may be issued.

COLLECTION OF THE AGREEMENTS CONCLUDED BY THE EUROPEAN COMMUNITIES

The purpose of this work is to collect together the texts of agreements concluded between the European Communities and 'non-member States or with other bodies governed by international law, particularly international organizations'. The volumes as published contain the texts in force on 31 December 1975. It is intended that there will be an annual supplement to each volume which will give details of those agreements which have expired and those which have been extended. We are also told that there will be a subject index to the set.

The five volumes published so far are as follows:

1 Bilateral agreements EEC–Europe 1958–1975
2 Bilateral agreements EEC–Europe 1958–1975
3 Bilateral agreements EEC–Europe 1958–1975
4 Bilateral agreements EEC–Asia, EEC–Africa, EEC–Amercia 1958–1975
5 Bilateral agreements EAEC, ECSC, Multilateral agreements EEC, EAEC, ECSC 1952–1975

Volume 6, which covers 1976, was published in 1979.

The loose-leaf volumes of *Collected Acts* which relate to association agreements are issued by the Council of Ministers. This publication is described on p. 200.

OTHER SOURCES OF SECONDARY LEGISLATION

This chapter has described the official publications of the European Communities but it would not be complete without some mention of a number of other sources which have appeared in an attempt to overcome the rather inaccessible nature of the secondary legislation. Firstly, there is the response from HMSO in the United Kingdom. In 1970, under the auspices of the Foreign and Commonwealth Office, HMSO published an unauthenticated translation of European Community regulations. When the

Special edition appeared it was felt that there was a need for a publication which arranged the legislation by subject and which had an index. The Foreign and Commonwealth Office produced a consolidated series of translations in 1972 arranged by subject in forty-two volumes with an index, but this has been entirely replaced by a facsimile of the *Special edition*. This work was issued through HMSO by the Statutory Publications Office and is entitled: *Secondary legislation of the European Communities*. The Department of Industry and the Ministry of Agriculture, Fisheries and Food took the official texts and arranged them in forty-two volumes in the same way as the Foreign and Commonwealth Office version. This subject edition improves further on the *Special edition* by noting Acts which had been amended before 31 December 1972 and by adding the alterations in Annex 1 of the Act concerning the Conditions of Accession and the Adjustments to the Treaties (see above, p. 19). The *Secondary legislation of the European Communities* appeared between 1973 and 1974. It has been kept up to date by the *Subject lists and table of effects*, prepared in the Department of Industry for the Statutory Publications Office and published by HMSO, to the end of 1979.

British business published by HMSO carries a weekly subject listing of new secondary legislation appearing in the *Official journal* which is a valuable current awareness service especially for those who would not usually have the opportunity to scan the *Official journal* itself.

Secondly, a number of commercial publishers have made their mark on the secondary legislation, usually with the needs of legal practitioners in mind. Volume 42A of the third edition of *Halsbury's Statutes of England* published by Butterworths in 1975 digests the secondary legislation in force at the end of 1972 under the headings used in the main part of the work. The volume can be bought separately and there is a supplement covering 1973–6. The single volume is issued under the title *European legislation 1952–1972*.

Sweet and Maxwell responded with a multi-volume loose-leaf *Encyclopedia of European Community law*. Volume *A* consists of United Kingdom sources; Volume *B* contains the Treaties; Volume *C* contains annotated texts of the secondary legislation.

North-Holland Publishing Company have published what they describe as a 'total information package'. The basic work is the two-volume *Guide to EEC-legislation*, edited by A. E. Kellerman et al. This work is intended to provide a subject key to current and lapsed secondary legislation. The work is kept up to date by annual cumulative supplements in hard copy and also microfiche updates. In addition, there is an optional Telex service for very recent information.

Common Market reports is a loose-leaf service which contains both regulations and decisions with a legal commentary. It is published by Commerce Clearing House in the United States.

There is no doubt that the law of the European Communities has become a major subject in legal publishing and we shall see a growth in the literature which digests and explains the law as has long been the case with British statute law.

Notes

1. The accession of the United Kingdom took place on 1 January 1973.

2. E.g. *Treaty setting up the European Economic Community*, HMSO, 1967.

3. The European Parliament is a consultative body and not a legislature. Moreover, the Treaties refer to an Assembly and not a Parliament.

4. Article 177 of the EEC Treaty.

5. The text of Article 161 of the Euratom Treaty is identical.

6. See below, p. 32.

7. See below, p. 33.

CHAPTER 3

Commission—General publications

BULLETIN OF THE EUROPEAN COMMUNITIES

Prior to 1967 the European Coal and Steel Community and the European Economic Community published separate monthly bulletins; there was no comparable periodical from Euratom. The ECSC titles were:

> *Bulletin mensuel d'information* (1956–9)
> *Bulletin de la Communauté du charbon et de l'acier* (1960–7)

The EEC title was:

> *Bulletin of the European Economic Community* (1958–67)

After the fusion of the executives there has been only one title which carries information on all three Communities:

> *Bulletin of the European Communities* (1968–   )

The ECSC bulletin

The *Bulletin mensuel d'information* was published quarterly in the official languages from 1956 to 1959. In 1960 the title was changed to *Bulletin de la Communauté du charbon et de l'acier*. From 1956 to 1962 these bulletins were numbered within the year and issued free of charge. In 1963 it became a priced publication and the numbering system was changed to consecutive rather than annual numbering. This was made retrospective so that No. 1, 1963 became No. 40. In all there were seventy-one issues. Regular features were quarterly reports on the activities of the ECSC; annually a résumé of the General report on the activities of the Community; and an annual review of the long-term energy outlook for the ECSC. Although publication was in the official languages, some issues (e.g. No. 60, 1965, on 'High Authority policy concerning research on industrial health, medicine and safety') were translated into English.

Bulletin of the European Economic Community (1958–67)

There was only one issue in 1958, five in 1959 and ten in 1960. From 1961 to 1967 it appeared monthly. The first issue to be printed was No. 2, 1960; before that it had been mimeographed. There were two regular sections from 1959 to No. 9/10, 1964. The first was a report of the activities of the EEC and the other was on the work of the individual Institutions. It also carried articles on topics of immediate interest. From No. 11, 1964, until 1967 the section on EEC activities was divided into internal and external affairs with a new section added on relations between the EEC and the Associated States.

It was published in the official languages and English and Spanish. There were annual indexes for the years 1964 to 1967.

Supplements to the *Bulletin of the European Economic Community*

The EEC Commission began the practice of publishing many of its more important documents as supplements to the bulletin. Up to 1966 major Commission proposals to the Council were made available to the public in this format but this role was subsequently transferred to the *Official journal*.[1] From 1961 to 1967 forty-nine supplements were published. The contents are listed on pp. 253–63 of the *Catalogue des publications 1952–1971*, Vol. 1.

All the supplements were available in English.

Bulletin of the European Communities (1968–   )

The *Bulletin of the European Communities* reports monthly on the activities of the Commission and the other Institutions of the European Communities. It is edited by the Secretariat-General of the Commission. From 1968 to 1972 it was published in the official languages and English and Spanish. From 1973 it has appeared in the six official languages and Spanish.

The issues for 1968 were arranged in a similar fashion to the later issues of the *Bulletin of the European Economic Community*. In 1969 there were regular sections on the establishment and operation of the single market; towards economic union; the Communities and the Associated States; the Communities, non-member countries and international organizations; and the institutions and organs of the Communities. In 1970 the contents were arranged in three sections which have remained broadly similar in scope through the successive volumes, even though the actual wording of the heading may have changed. In No. 1, 1979, they are: 'Part one Special features'; 'Part two activities in . . .'; 'Part three documentation'. Part one consists of articles on matters of current interest. No. 2, 1979 contains the address by the President of the Commission to the European Parliament on the Commission's programme for 1979. No. 3, 1979 contains a Commission memorandum on the European Communities and the European Convention on Human Rights.

Part two forms the largest part of each issue and is used to summarize developments in each main policy area in the month in question.

Material is grouped by topic in three categories headed:

1. Building the Community
2. Enlargement and external relations
3. Institutional and political matters

This makes the *Bulletin* a very comprehensive monthly overview of what is happening in the European Communities and a useful starting point for enquiries about recent business; though perhaps most useful for signposting material elsewhere—like *Official journal* references.

Certain pieces of official information are recorded in Part three.

Sub-headings which appear regularly are:

Units of account
Additional references in the *Official journal*
Infringement procedures

The 'additional references in the *Official journal*' relate to matters dealt with in previous issues of the *Bulletin*. This is a useful means of referring forward from a given piece in the *Bulletin*. 'Eurobarometers' also appear in this section. No. 1, 1979, contains the initial results of a public opinion poll in the nine Community countries on direct elections to the European Parliament. These public opinion polls have been conducted every spring and autumn since 1973 (see below p. 132).

At one time the contents of the *Official journal* were summarized in the section on documentation, but this was discontinued after No. 2, 1975. This was actually a useful English-language approach to the *Official journal* from 1968 to 1972 which had carried on from the service offered in the *Bulletin of the European Economic Community* from 1962 to 1967. At the end of each *Bulletin* there is a separately paginated section entitled 'Publications of the European Communities' which is also available as an offprint (see below, p. 232).

Supplements to the *Bulletin of the European Communities*

Important Commission documents, including some of the more significant proposals for legislation appear as separately published supplements to the *Bulletin of the European Communities*. The format is rather more readable than the *Official journal* and presumably publication in a supplement is intended to make a document more widely circulated. Supplement No. 8/75 is actually described as a 'green paper' thus adopting the United Kingdom government term for a consultative document.

From 1968 to 1971 forty-nine supplements were published, the contents of which are listed on pp. 264–6 of the *Catalogue des publications 1952–1971*, Vol. 1. The titles of the later supplements are:

Year/No.   *Title*

1972

1   The enlarged Community: outcome of the nego-
             tiations with the applicant states
2   Memorandum from the Commission on a Com-
             munity policy on development co-operation:
             programme for initial actions
3   Proposals for harmonizing consumer taxes other
             than VAT
4   Report by the *ad hoc* committee studying the
             problem of expanding the authority of the
             European Parliament (Vedel report)
5   A Community programme concerning the en-
             vironment
6   Objectives and instruments of a common policy
             . for scientific research and technological de-
             velopment
7   Exemption from taxes granted to imports made
             by travellers
8   Proposed Directive and draft Council Recom-
             mendation on a prospectus to be published
             when securities are admitted to official stock
             exchange quotation
9   Community measures for the alignment of legisla-
             tion (1958–71)
10   Proposal for a fifth Directive on the structure of
             sociétés anonymes
11   Necessary progress in Community energy policy
12   Report on the Convention of Jurisdiction and the
             enforcement of judgments in civil and commer-
             cial matters

1973

1   Renewal and enlargement of the association with
             the AASM and certain Commonwealth de-
             veloping countries
2   Development of an overall approach to trade in

7   Community's economic and financial situation since enlargement: inventory and survey of future developments
8   Development aid: fresco of Community action tomorrow

1975

Special supplements: Directory of the Commission of the European Communities. April and September 1975
1   The Community's supplies of raw materials
2   Stocktaking of the Common Agricultural Policy
3   Community measures for the approximation of laws (1972–)
4   Statute for the European Company (amended proposal for a Regulation)
5   Report on European Union
6   Development and raw materials: problems of the moment
7   Towards European citizenship
8   Employee participation and company structure in the European Community
9   Reports on European Union (European Parliament, Court of Justice, Economic and Social Committee)
10   Harmonization of systems of company taxation
11   Action programme for the European aeronautical sector

1976

1   European Union: Report by Mr Leo Tindemans to the European Council
2   Opinion on Greek application for membership
3   Action programme in favour of migrant workers and their families
4   Common research and development policy: objectives, priorities and resources
5   Protection of fundamental rights within the European Community

Bulletin of the European Communities. Index/contents

Five annual indexes to the *Bulletin* were published for the years
1968 to 1972. For the years 1973 and 1974 the scope was expanded
to include entries for the . . . *general report on the activities of the
European Communities*. For 1975 onwards there has been a
contents list, produced annually, for that year's *Bulletin* only. The
entries for 1975 are to be found in *Bulletin of the European
Communities*, No. 1, 1976, pp. 71–4; for 1976 in No. 1, 1977, pp.
I–XIII. The contents lists for the years 1977 onwards have been
issued separately.

It is difficult to understand why a contents list has been persisted
with when an alphabetical subject index would have obvious
advantages to the user. The structure chosen also makes cumulation virtually impossible. Headings are often vague and general. In
1978 there was an article on an EEC–China trade agreement
listed under:

—Principal chapters and supplements
  External relations
    Other countries.

Moreover, the entries themselves may puzzle the uninitiated: 1/1.2.1 to 1.2.3. turns out to mean *Bulletin* No. 1 of the year in question, 'points' 2.1 to 2.3 in Part one. There may even be circumstances when the user may find it more profitable to scan each individual issue of the *Bulletin*.

GENERAL REPORTS ON THE ACTIVITIES OF THE COMMUNITIES

The best overview of what has happened in the Communities in a given period is provided by the *General report* which is published annually after having been presented to the European Parliament—a Treaty requirement. All these reports were published in the official languages and, up to 1972, they were translated into English.

European Coal and Steel Community

Article 17 of the Treaty of Paris required that the High Authority of the ECSC should present a report on the activities of the ECSC to the Assembly. From 1953 to 1967 fifteen such reports were published. The reports all cover the same kind of ground, so that they can readily be used to trace the development of Community policy. Inevitably, though, as the Community became more complex so the nature of the remarks became more general. The following were published:

Number	Period covered
First	10.8.52–12.4.53
Second	13.4.53–11.4.54
Third	12.4.54–10.4.55
Fourth	11.4.55–8.4.56
Fifth	9.4.56–13.4.57
Sixth	14.4.57–13.4.58

Seventh	14.4.58–1.2.59
Eighth	1.2.59–31.1.60
Ninth	1.2.60–31.1.61
Tenth	1.2.61–31.1.62
Eleventh	1.2.62–31.1.63
Twelfth	1.2.63–31.1.64
Thirteenth	1.2.64–31.1.65
Fourteenth	1.2.65–31.1.66
Fifteenth	1.2.66–31.1.67

European Economic Community

Article 156 of the Treaty of Rome (EEC) required that the Commission of the EEC should present an annual report to the Assembly in the same way that the ECSC High Authority was required to do. From 1958 to 1967 ten reports were published:

Number	Period covered
First	1.1.58–17.9.58
Second	18.9.58–20.3.59
Third	21.3.59–15.5.60
Fourth	16.5.60–30.4.61
Fifth	1.5.61–30.4.62
Sixth	1.5.62–31.3.63
Seventh	1.4.63–31.3.64
Eighth	1.4.64–31.3.65
Ninth	1.4.65–31.3.66
Tenth	1.4.66–31.3.67

The tenth and last of these reports contains chapters on the establishment of the Common Market; progress towards common policies; Association agreements in force; external relations; and the activities of the Institutions; as well as a general introductory survey.

Euratom

Article 125 of the Treaty of Rome (Euratom) required the

presentation of an annual report by the Commission to the Assembly. From 1958 to 1967 ten reports were published:

Number	Period covered
First	January–September 1958
Second	September 1958–March 1959
Third	March 1959–April 1960
Fourth	April 1960–March 1961
Fifth	April 1961–March 1962
Sixth	March 1962–February 1963
Seventh	March 1963–February 1964
Eighth	March 1964–February 1965
Ninth	March 1965–February 1966
Tenth	March 1966–February 1967

The last four reports were each in two volumes. The first volume was, according to the *Seventh* report:

a concise and comprehensive six-chapter survey of Euratom's activities, dealing in turn with the energy situation, the broad outline of the research programme, and going on to discuss the organization's work in sponsoring the industrial use of nuclear energy, health protection and biology, ways and means of achieving Euratom's various objectives and finally external relations.

The second volume was entitled *Documentation attached to . . . general report on the activities of the Community*, and gave more detailed information on the topics surveyed in the first.

The last six reports all included comprehensive lists of the Euratom technical reports published in a given period (see p. 246).

European Communities

Article 18 of the Treaty of Brussels (1967) states: 'The Commission shall publish annually, not later than one month before the opening of the session of the Assembly, a general report on the activities of the Communities.' So, from 1968 onwards there is one annual report which covers the activities of all three Communities.

The Assembly referred to above is of course the European

Parliament which receives the report at its first meeting in February each year. The President of the Commission, or in his absence one of the Vice-Presidents, gives an address to the Parliament with the formal presentation of the report which is an opportunity to review the events of the past year and outline Commission policy for the current year. The address is printed at the beginning of the final version of the report which is then made generally available. This address is also published separately. A provisional edition of the report, without the address, is printed some time before the definitive version is made available, but is intended for official use.[2]

There is no alphabetical index to the contents of the report which is a pity to say the least, but there is a fairly detailed summary. For the years 1973 and 1974 there were entries for the report in the *Index* to the *Bulletin of the European Communities*, but this has not been continued. The failure to produce adequate indexes is a recurrent problem with the official publications of the European Communities.

The *First general report on the activities of the Communities* covered the year 1967. From the seventh report covering 1973 the title has been changed slightly to . . . *general report on the activities of the European Communities*.

Three separate volumes are published in conjunction with the *General report*; these relate to agriculture, competition policy and social affairs. The chapter on community law is also published as a separate item—see below, p. 66. The chapter on agricultural policy is not published separately but should be read alongside the fuller report.

The agricultural situation in the Community

This annual was first published for the year 1975 and was an abridged version of *COM* (75) 601 final of 10 December 1975, which was a communication from the Commission to the Council of Ministers. The 1978 edition lists eight reports of major significance, mostly *COM* documents, to which attention is drawn in the foreword. It seems then that this report is an attempt to close the information gap between a fairly general summary in the . . . *general report on the activities of the European Communities* and largely technical documents on what is after all an extremely complicated area of Community activity. Notice also that the *General report* is directed at the European Parliament but that *The agricultural situation in the Community* arises from documentation aimed at the Council of Ministers, and was in the first place appended to the Commission's proposals on prices. The text, excluding much of the statistical data, was also made available, up to 1977, as a special issue of the *Newsletter on the Common Agricultural Policy*—see below, p. 134. What we have here then is plainly the Commission's main public statement on the way in which it sees agricultural policy developing.

. . . report on competition policy

On 7 June 1971 the European Parliament passed a 'Resolution concerning the Rules on Competition and the position of European Enterprises within the Common Market and in the World Economy', in which it asked the Commission to make an annual report on the development of competition policy. This document is published as an annex to the . . . *general report on the activities of the Communities*. The *First report on competition policy* was annexed to the *Fifth general report on the activities of the Communities*, and covered the period up to the end of 1971. The *Eighth report on competition policy* which covers the year 1978 has three main sections:

Competition policy towards enterprises
Competition policy and government assistance to enterprises
The developments of concentration in the Community

Report on the development of the social situation in the Communities in . . .

Article 122 of the Treaty of Rome (EEC) states: 'The Commission shall include a separate chapter on social developments within the Community in its annual report to the Assembly.' In fact, this provision has been interpreted more broadly and as well as a 'chapter' on social policy there has been a more detailed document presented as an annex to the main report. From 1958 to 1967 it was published as an addendum to the . . . *general report on the activities of the Community* (EEC). It is now published in conjunction with the . . . *general report on the activities of the European Communities*, and although the Article quoted above applies to the EEC, the report relates to all three communities. The *Report on the development of the social situation in the Communities in 1978* has three main sections:

General and political introduction
Outline of activities by the Institutions of the European Communities in the social field in 1977
Development of the social situation in 1977

COM AND *SEC* DOCUMENTS

COM and *SEC* documents form the greater part of the official working documentation of the Commission which is generally available to the public. Strictly, these documents are not really public property at all, and are not sales publications. They are produced and distributed in large numbers and are usually available on request, but they do belong essentially to the limited distribution category even though they do circulate widely. *COM* and *SEC* documents are mimeographed, not printed, and have a paper cover.

Each document originates in one of the Directorates-General of the Commission, or possibly through several of them acting in concert. Officially, a Directorate-General does not originate policy, it only acts as instructed, and in this respect it might be said to have a role which is closely analogous to that of a UK department of state or ministry. It is a moot point how responsibility for the formulation of policy is apportioned. All documents are submitted to the Secretariat-General of the Commission before they can be placed on the agenda for a meeting of the Commission proper. The Commission, as the legal initiator of Community policy, approves the final draft of a document before it is made public.

COM is a contraction of 'Commission' and *SEC* of 'Secretary-General'. *SEC* documents are less formal, consisting of interim reports, draft resolutions, discussion documents and so on. *COM* documents are produced for the information of, or for action by, the Council of Ministers. Draft Regulations, for example, are sent from the Commission to the Council in the form of *COM* documents. The complete range of Commission business is represented by *COM* and *SEC* documents in the initiation of new policies, and by 'Communications' and reports in the administration of existing policies.

Matters which require a decision by the Council of Ministers may be referred to the European Parliament. EEC and Euratom business may also be referred to the Economic and Social Committee. As a result, *COM* documents then become part of the working documentation of these bodies: for example, Commission reports and proposals under consideration by the European Parliament appear in the series *Working documents* of the European Parliament, but they are not printed separately. They are distributed with only a title page and a copy of the formal letter from the Council of Ministers to the President of the European Parliament.

There is little attempt at bibliographic control of *COM* and *SEC* documents. This is not necessarily a problem when their lives are intended to be limited—either because they become enshrined in legislation or are published in some other form. Legislative proposals—'preparatory acts'—are published in the *Information and notices* section of the *Official journal*; some documents of major importance appear as *Supplements* to the *Bulletin of the European Communities*. Unfortunately, some Commission proposals have an undesirable longevity because of the nature of the decision-making process. In 1977 alone the Commission submitted no fewer than 609 proposals to the Council of Ministers. But, as Commissioner Tugendhat once complained:

> Although the Commission has recently achieved some striking successes, it cannot be denied that the number of Commission proposals which the Council rejects or shelves indefinitely is currently very high, and this can make a commissioner's job, at times, a very frustrating one.[3]

Moreover, this is by no means a recent phenomenon for in the summer of 1972 there were before the Council of Ministers roughly 150 draft regulations and directives, some of which had been there for five years or more.[4] In a speech to the European Parliament on 15 February 1979 the President of the Commission, Roy Jenkins, said that the Council of Ministers had adopted 645 out of 747 Commission proposals in 1977 and 592 out of 746 in 1978, but added that 'some of the more important proposals lie in the minority which have not been adopted'. It was pointed out subsequently that there were still 278 proposals pending some of which went back to 1968.

The only regular source for tracing *COM* documents is the *Bulletin on documentation* which lists them by subject along with other documents and publications. The Commission has been developing its own system for controlling internal documentation since 1971. This project is now known as ECO1 having previously been called ECDOC. The object is to create a file in machine-readable form of all the documents which have appeared on the agenda of meetings of the Commission as well as other official documents. In its third year of operation there were already 40,000 documents in the system.[5] Interesting as this project may be to outside users of Community documents, its use is still restricted to the Commission which is not surprising because of problems of confidentiality with many of the documents. ECO1 is one of the CIRCE files (see below, p. 241).

For UK users there is a useful weekly list of *COM* documents which have been deposited in the House of Commons Library, given in *British business/Trade and industry* published by HMSO. The list includes consultative documents, draft legislation and explanatory statements on draft legislation. There are many *COM* documents, of course, which do not fall into these categories. The chief importance of this listing is that it includes not only the *COM* document number but the number assigned to each document by the Council of Ministers. It is usual for the Council of Ministers numbering to be used in Parliamentary debates as reported in *Hansard*, and this can be a cause of some confusion.

COM and *SEC* documents are identified and cited by a document number which consists of the prefix *COM* or *SEC*, a date code and running number. The document number is followed by the word 'final' which indicates that it is a final draft so far as the Commission is concerned. For example, 'Proposal for a Council Decision adopting a first three year plan of action in the field of information and documentation in science and technology', 18 September 1974, is cited as '*COM* (74) 1423 final'.

COM documents are probably the single most important source of detailed current information on Commission thinking and draft legislation. This series also contains a wealth of data on matters relating to the European Communities. Though they may seem inaccessible they are comparatively easy to obtain through the Information Offices of the Commission and they have been made available to European Documentation Centres since 1974. It is a pity that many of these documents are not published in more conventional publishing formats.

It should be remembered that probably less than one-third of *COM* documents are subsequently published in the *Official journal*.

The following list includes some of the more interesting *COM* documents published in 1979:

8 Multinational programme for the attainment of the customs union

10 Commission proposals on the fixing of prices for certain agricultural products and on certain related measures

11 Economic effects of the agri-monetary system (updated version 1979)

22 Negotiations for the accession of Greece. Communication from the Commission to the Council concerning the preparation of Greek-language versions of Community legal acts

23 Aspects of external measures by the Community in the energy sector

49 Balance sheets and accounts of the European Development Funds for the 1977 financial year

50 The situation of the agricultural markets. 1978 report

59 First Commission report to the Council on the functioning of the Committee for Proprietary Medicinal Products and its impact on the development of intra-Community trade

64 Information programme for 1979

73 Communication from the Commission to the Council on the development of the common fisheries policy

83 Proposal for a Council Directive on the protection of workers from harmful exposure to chemical, physical and biological agents at work

85 Global appraisal of the budgetary problems of the Community

727 Participation of Euratom in the International Convention on the Physical Protection of Nuclear Material

731 Comparative costs of feed grains in Italy and in the other regions of the Community

735 Commission communication to the Council on food aid in the form of butter oil

739 Proposal for a Council regulation (EEC) concluding the cooperation agreement between the European Economic Community and Indonesia, Malaysia, the Philippines, Singapore and Thailand—member countries of the Association of the South-East Asian Nations

742 1980 programme for the attainment of the Customs Union

768 Proposal for a Council decision on the revision of the Paris Convention for the Protection of Industrial Property

771 Communication from the Commission to the Council concerning the creation of a 'Consultative Committee of the Fusion Programme'

781 Two proposals for Council directives on the approximation of the laws of the member states relating to the fuel consumption of motor vehicles and to the engine power of motor vehicles respectively

790 Commission report to the Council on the location of Community departments

793 Proposal for a multiannual Community programme of research and development in biomolecular engineering (indirect action 1981–1985)

Notes

1. *Bulletin of the European Economic Community*, April 1966, p. 3.

2. The report also appears in the *Working documents* of the European Parliament.

3. Quoted in Drew, J., *Doing business in the European Community*. Butterworths, 1979.

4. Prag, D. and Nicholson, E. D., *Businessman's guide to the Common Market*. Pall Mall, 1973, p. 102.

5. Chillag, J. P. *in* Palmer, D. M., *Sources of information on the European Communities*. Mansell, 1979, p. 95.

CHAPTER 4

Commission—Non-statistical Publications

This chapter attempts to summarize the range of Commission publications, other than those of Eurostat and those of a general character described in the previous chapter. If the range of publications on a particular topic appears limited this should not be taken to indicate an area in which the Commission shows little interest; the *Official journal*, the supplements to the *Bulletin of the European Communities* and *COM* documents are all sources of information on a broad spectrum of Commission activities and cannot be ignored. For some subjects nearly all the relevant information can be found in the general sources. On the other hand there are a large number of one-off publications, periodical titles and series which it is convenient to consider separately. They are arranged in this chapter as nearly as possible in conformity with the headings chosen in the official catalogues which is probably more helpful than trying to attribute them to specific Directorates-General.

There are very many internal documents generated within the Commission's own offices the majority of which are not expected to circulate freely. In many cases these are early drafts of works which will subsequently appear as *COM* documents. The existence of these documents is the *raison d'être* for the ECO1 project, and they are not surprisingly beyond the scope of this work. Many reports and other documents are described, especially the work of outside experts commissioned by the Commission.

In recent years there has been a tendency for the Commission to rely more on sales publication than on limited distribution as can be seen clearly in the case of the studies of concentration in particular industries. Many *Eur* documents can be traced through the sales catalogues even when they are available in microfiche only and then often in only one language. Unfortunately, many important documents still remain in the relative obscurity of the limited distribution category—the Spierenburg Report being a notable example.

It should also be remembered that there are an increasing number of publications handled by commercial publishers on behalf of the Commission.

EXTERNAL RELATIONS AND FOREIGN TRADE

DG I External relations has been responsible for few publications in its own right. It does publish a regularly updated foreign diplomatic list for the European Communities entitled *Corps diplomatique accrédité auprès des Communautés européennes*. The Washington office of the Commission has produced a short pamphlet entitled *Myth and reality: a reference manual on US–European Community relations*. There are a number of documents in the series *Information* which are also of interest. A number of documents of only historic importance are listed in *Catalogue des publications 1952–71*, Vol. 1, pp. 80–2.

Apart from statistical publications there are a number of works concerned with foreign trade. There is a loose-leaf *List of customs offices authorised to deal with Community transit operations*, and another on *Customs valuation*. The *Practical guide to the use of the European Communities' scheme of generalised tariff preferences* has been published in three editions of which the latest is dated 1979. *The customs union: today and tomorrow* is the report of a conference held in Brussels, 6–8 December 1977. Two other publications are *Exporting to the European Community: information for foreign exporters*, 1977, and *Relief from taxes granted to imports made by private persons*, 1979. The Common Customs Tariff is revised annually and published in the *Official journal*, L342 of 31 December 1979 being the most recent. The Commission publishes a loose-leaf volume entitled *Explanatory notes to the Customs Tariff of the European Communities* for which there are regular updating supplements.

DG I is an example of one of the more important Commission portfolios but one which does not produce many publications, especially so far as the formation of foreign policy is concerned.

DEVELOPMENT AND CO-OPERATION

There are a great many trade and co-operation agreements with third world countries in Asia, North Africa and Latin America.

Association agreements have had more wide-ranging effects. The Treaty of Rome (EEC) made arrangements for a five-year association between the Community and the overseas dependencies of the Community countries. The terms were renegotiated when these territories became independent. Four successive agreements have been made:

First Yaoundé Convention, signed 20 July 1963
Second Yaoundé Convention, signed 29 July 1969
First Lomé Convention, signed 28 February 1975
Second Lomé Convention, signed 31 October 1979.

The ACP states are:

Bahamas	Grenada
Barbados	Guinea
Benin	Guinea Bissau
Botswana	Equatorial Guinea
Burundi	Guyana
Cameroon	Upper Volta
Cape Verde	Jamaica
Central African Republic	Kenya
Comoros	Kiribati
Congo	Lesotho
Ivory Coast	Liberia
Djibouti	Madagascar
Dominica	Malawi
Ethiopia	Mali
Fiji	Mauritius
Gabon	Mauritania
Gambia	Niger
Ghana	Nigeria

Papua New Guinea
Rwanda
St. Lucia
Western Samoa
São Tomé and Principe
Senegal
Seychelles
Sierra Leone
Solomon Islands
Somali Democratic
  Republic

Sudan
Surinam
Swaziland
Tanzania
Chad
Togo
Tonga
Trinidad and Tobago
Tuvalu
Uganda
Zaire
Zambia

The text of the First Lomé Convention was published in *The Courier: European Community–Africa–Caribbean–Pacific*, No. 31, March 1975; the Second in No. 58, November 1979.

Aid takes various forms, an unusual feature being 'Stabex' which is a mechanism for the stabilization of export earnings in the ACP countries. Some financial aid is available from the European Investment Bank but the greater part comes from the European Development Fund.

European Development Fund

Individual Community countries may give foreign aid independently but there have been four European Development Funds administered by the European Communities. The next EDF is due to take effect in 1980 (see 'Draft internal agreement on the financing and administration of Community aid', *COM* (79) 524 final).

The First EDF was set up by the Treaty of Rome (EEC), implementing the Convention on the Association of the Overseas Countries and Territories with the Community. An analysis of the projects undertaken is provided by a limited distribution publication of DG VIII which appeared first in 1960 as a semi-annual but more recently as an annual, each issue replacing those published previously. The most recent is *Fonds Européen de Développement, 1er FED, situation annuelle des projets en exécution, date de mise à jour: 31 décembre 1974.*

The Second EDF was established in pursuance of the first Yaoundé Convention. An analysis of the projects undertaken is provided in another limited distribution publication of DG VIII which in this case was quarterly until the first issue of 1971 when it became semi-annual. The most recent is *Fonds Européen Développement, situation semestrielle des projets du 2ème FED, en exécution, date de mise à jour: 30 Juin 1975.*

The Third EDF was established in pursuance of the second Yaoundé Convention. An analysis of the projects undertaken is provided in another limited distribution publication of DG VIII which has appeared as a semi-annual since 1971. The most recent is *Fonds Européen de Développement, situation semestrielle des projets du 3ème FED en exécution, date de mise à jour: 31 Décembre 1975.*

Further information on the First and Second EDFs and on some other aspects of development and co-operation can be found in the Commission document entitled *Memorandum on a Community policy on development cooperation: synoptic and programme for initial actions (Communications of the Commission to the Council of 27 July 1971 and 2 February 1972)*, 1972.

There is a summary of operations from 1959 to the end of 1976 in *Official journal* C112 of 9 May 1977. Information about tenders can also be found in the pages of the *Official journal*. The most recent summary of aid under the Fourth EDF can be found in 'Commission report to the ACP–EEC Council of Ministers on the administration of financial and technical co-operation in 1978, under the Lomé Convention', *COM* (79) 395 final. The balance sheets and accounts in the financial year 1977 can be found in the *Official journal*, S246 of 31 December 1979.

Investment laws of ACP countries

This is a two-volume work which aims to reproduce the texts of investment legislation of the signatories of the Lomé Convention. It is the fourth edition, previous editions having appeared in 1966, 1971 and 1974. Vol. 1 was published in 1978 and covers the French-speaking countries. Vol. 2 was published in 1979 and covers the English-speaking countries. This work is available in the official languages.

Other publications

In 1979 the Commission published an *Annual report on the development cooperation policies of the Community and its Member States, 1977–1978*, which is the first such report. The position before this report is summarized in a publication of 1977 entitled *The development cooperation policies of the European Community from 1971 to 1976*. The management of financial and technical co-operation between the EEC and the AASM in 1973 is described in detail in *European Development Fund, 1974*. Current information is provided by *The Courier: European Community–Africa–Caribbean–Pacific* (No. 30, 1975–) which was formerly known as *Association news* (Nos. 17–29) and *Courrier de l'Association* (Nos. 1–16). The first issue appeared in 1963.

On the specific questions of establishing industries or trade relations with associated countries DG VIII issued a nineteen-volume series in 1974 entitled *Conditions for the setting-up of industrial undertakings in the associated African states and Madagascar. General information on EDF invitation to tender*. In this series which was published in English and French only there is a volume devoted to each of the AASM countries. The first edition which was published in 1972 was limited distribution. The second edition was available gratis.

There were five volumes in the series *Studies—Overseas Development Series (Études—Série: Développement de l'Outre-mer)*. They were published between 1963 and 1967 and Nos. 2, 3 and 4 were translated into English. They are listed in *Catalogue des publications 1952–1971*, Vol. 1, pp. 85–6.

There were four volumes in the series *Studies—Development Aid Series (Études—Série: Aide du Développement)*. They were published between 1967 and 1972. Only No. 4 was translated into English. The titles in this series are listed in *Catalogue des publications 1952–1971*, Vol. 1, p. 86.

There is a new series *Studies—Development Series* of which only No. 1 has appeared so far, entitled 'Integrated rural development projects carried out in Black Africa with EDF aid. Evaluation and outlook for the future', 1979.

No. 2 of a new series entitled *Dossiers: Development Series* was published in 1979 on 'Europe and the third world: a study on interdependence'.

Some older material is listed in *Catalogue des publications 1952–1971*, Vol. 1, pp. 87–9, under the heading, 'Études et documents d'information interne'. These were limited distribution documents intended for the use of the Institutions of the European Communities and the associated countries.

COMMUNITY LAW

The Legal Service of the Commission prepares *National decisions concerning Community law: selective list of references to published cases (Décisions nationales relatives au droit communautaire: liste sélective de références aux décisions publiées)*. Twenty-three issues have been published between 1966 and 1979. From No. 16, 1974, its coverage has included the three new countries. Most of the entries for UK law have been digested from *Common Market law reports*. Entries are in the official languages.

There have been two volumes in *Studies: Labour Law Series*:

Number	Title
1	The contract of employment in the law of Member States of the European Communities; synoptic report: Denmark, the United Kingdom, Ireland, 1978
2	Comparative study of employees' inventions law in the Member States of the European Communities, 1978

In 1971 the Commission published a four-volume limited distribution work in French only entitled *Répertoire des actes juridiques en vigueur de droit communautaire dérivé et conventionnel connexe*.

The European Community, international organisations and multilateral agreements which was published in English and French only in 1977 is an attempt to examine the relationship between Community law and traditional national and international law.

The annual publication entitled *Community law* is an extract from the *General report on the activities of the Communities*.

COMPETITION AND INTERNAL MARKET

There are various provisions in the Treaty of Rome (EEC) which authorize the Commission to take action to counteract agreements or concerted practices between private or public undertakings which restrict the normal operation of competition and affect trade between the countries of the European Communities. The Commission aims to prevent the abuse of economic power and also to encourage companies to rationalize production and distribution and to keep abreast of scientific and technical progress.

There has been a substantial body of research into conditions in various industries in the Community countries much of it carried out by experts from outside the Commission. The older studies were always limited distribution documents but in recent years they have been sales publications. There follows a list arranged by country of the older studies, followed by a list of the more recent volumes in the series *Evolution of Concentration and Competition Series*.

Belgium

Étude sur l'évolution de la concentration dans quelques sous-secteurs de l'industrie du textile en Belgique, 1973

Étude sur l'évolution de la concentration dans l'industrie de la construction électrique en Belgique, 1973

Étude sur l'évolution de la concentration dans quelques sous-secteurs de l'industrie chimique en Belgique, 1973

Étude sur l'évolution de la concentration dans l'industrie alimentaire en Belgique, 1975

Étude sur l'évolution de la concentration dans l'industrie pharmaceutique en Belgique, 1975

L'évolution de la concentration dans l'industrie de la brasserie et des boissons en Belgique, 1976

Étude sur l'évolution de la concentration dans quelques sous-secteurs de l'industrie du textile en Belgique, 1975

The first three of these studies were limited distribution documents, the remainder sales publications.

Denmark

A study of the evolution of concentration in the Danish pharmaceutical industry, 1974
A study of the evolution of concentration in the Danish electrical appliances industry, 1974
A study of the evolution of concentration in the Danish food distribution industry, 1976
A study of the evolution of concentration in the Danish food processing industry, 1976

The first two of these studies were limited distribution documents, the remainder sales publications.

France

Étude sur l'évolution de la concentration dans quelques sous-secteurs de l'industrie du textile en France, 1973
Étude sur l'évolution de la concentration dans quelques sous-secteurs de l'industrie du papier en France, 1973
Étude sur l'évolution de la concentration dans quelques sous-secteurs de l'industrie chimique en France, 1973
Étude sur l'évolution de la concentration dans quelques sous-secteurs de l'industrie de la construction de machines non électriques en France, 1973
Étude sur l'évolution de la concentration dans un sous-secteur de l'industrie de la construction de matériel de transport en France, 1973
Étude sur l'évolution de la concentration de la construction électrique en France, 1974
Étude sur l'évolution de la concentration dans l'industrie alimentaire en France, 1975
L'évolution de la concentration dans l'industrie de la brasserie en France, 1975
Étude sur l'évolution de la concentration dans l'industrie alimentaire en France—tableaux de concentration, 1975
Étude sur l'évolution de la concentration dans l'industrie du textile en France, 1975
Étude sur l'évolution de la concentration dans l'industrie pharmaceutique en France, 1975

Étude sur l'évolution de la concentration dans l'industrie des spiriteux en France, 1976

L'évolution de la concentration dans l'industrie des champagnes et mousseux en France, 1976

Étude sur l'évolution de la concentration dans la distribution des produits alimentaires en France, 1976

Étude sur l'évolution de la concentration dans les industries des boissons et des boissons non alcoolisées en France, 1976

Étude sur l'évolution de la concentration dans l'industrie des pneumatiques en France, 1977

Étude sur l'évolution de la concentration dans l'industrie des pâtes, papiers et cartons en France, 1977

The first six of these studies were limited distribution documents, the remainder sales publications.

Germany

Untersuchung zur Konzentrationsentwicklung in verschiedenen Untersektoren der Maschinenbauindustrie in Deutschland, 1973

Untersuchung zur Konzentrationsentwicklung in verschiedenen Untersektoren der elektrotechnischen Industrie in Deutschland, 1973

Untersuchung zur Konzentrationsentwicklung in verschiedenen Untersektoren der Papier- und Pappeindustrie in Deutschland, 1973

Untersuchung zur Konzentrationsentwicklung in verschiedenen Untersektoren der Textilindustrie in Deutschland, 1973

Untersuchung zur Konzentrationsentwicklung in einem Untersektor des Fahrzeugbaues in Deutschland, 1973

Untersuchung der Konzentrationsentwicklung in verschiedenen Untersektoren der chemischen Industrie in Deutschland, 1973

Untersuchung zur Konzentrationsentwicklung in der Ernährungsindustrie in Deutschland, 1973

Untersuchung zur Konzentrationsentwicklung in verschiedenen Untersektoren der Maschinenbauindustrie in Deutschland, 1975

Untersuchung zur Konzentrationsentwicklung in verschiedenen Untersektoren der elektrotechnischen Industrie in Deutschland, 1975

Untersuchung zur Konzentrationsentwicklung in einem Unter-sektor des Fahrzeugbaues in Deutschland, 1975
Untersuchung zur Konzentrationsentwicklung in verschiedenen Untersektoren der Papier- und Pappeindustrie in Deutschland, 1976
Untersuchung der Konzentrationsentwicklung in der Reifenin-dustrie sowie ein Branchenbild der Kraftfahrzeug-Elektrikindustrie in Deutschland, 1976
Untersuchung zur Konzentrationsentwicklung in ausgewählten Branchen und Produktgruppen der Ernährungsindustrie in Deuts-chland, 1976
Untersuchung zur Konzentrationsentwicklung in der Nahrungs-mitteldistribution in Deutschland, 1976
Untersuchung zur Konzentrationsentwicklung in der Getränkein-dustrie in Deutschland, 1976
Die Distribution von alkoholischen und nichtalkoholischen Getränken in der Bundesrepublik Deutschland—unter beson-derer Berücksichtigung konzentrativer Entwicklungstendenzen, 1977

The first seven of these studies were limited distribution docu-ments, the remainder sales publications.

Ireland

A study of the evolution of concentration in the Irish food industry 1968–1973, 1975

This was a sales publication.

Italy

Evoluzione della concentrazione dal 1962 al 1969 in alcuni settori dell'industria Italiana, 1973
Analisi generale della concentrazione industriale in Italia dalla costituzione del mercato comune (1959–1968), 1973
Studio sull'evoluzione della concentrazione in alcuni settori dell'industria tessile in Italia, 1973

Studio sull'evoluzione della concentrazione nell'industria di cicli, motocicli e ciclomotori in Italia, 1973

Studio sull'evoluzione della concentrazione in Italia dell'industria della carta e della sua trasformazione, 1973

Studio sull'evoluzione della concentrazione in alcuni settori dell'industria chimica in Italia, 1973

Studio sull'evoluzione della concentrazione nell'industria della costruzione elettrica in Italia, 1974

Studio sull'evoluzione della concentrazione nell'industria della costruzione di macchine non elettriche in Italia, 1974

Studio sull'evoluzione della concentrazione nell'industria alimentare in Italia, 1974

Studio sull'evoluzione della concentrazione dell'industria farmaceutica in Italia, 1975

Studio sull'evoluzione della concentrazione nell'industria di cicli, motocicli e ciclomotori in Italia 1970–1972, 1975

Studio sull'evoluzione della concentrazione nell'industria della costruzione elettrica in Italia (1970–1974), 1975

Studio sull'evoluzione della concentrazione nell'industria cotoniera Italiana (NICE 233) 1975

Studio sull'evoluzione della concentrazione industriale in Italia (1968–1974), 1976

Studio sull-evoluzione della concentrazione nel settore della costruzione di macchine per ufficio in Italia, 1976

Studio sull'evoluzione della concentrazione nel settore della costruzione di macchine per l'industria tessile in Italia, 1976

Studio sull'evoluzione della concentrazione dell'industria cartaria in Italia, 1976

Studio sull'evoluzione della concentrazione nell'industria della costruzione di macchine non elettriche in Italia, 1976

Studio sull'evoluzione della concentrazione nella distribuzione dei prodotti alimentari in Italia, 1976

Studio sull'evoluzione della concentrazione nell'industria delle bevande in Italia, 1976

Studio sull'evoluzione della concentrazione nel settore dei detersivi per uso domestico in Italia dal 1968 al 1975, 1977

Studio sull'evoluzione della concentrazione nei settori dell'edizione e della stampa in Italia (1968–1975), 1978

The first ten of these studies were limited distribution documents, the remainder sales publications.

Netherlands

Studie betreffende de ontwikkeling van de concentratie in enkele bedrijfstakken in de chemische industrie in Nederland, 1973

Studie betreffende de ontwikkeling van de concentratie in de rijwiel- en bromfietsenindustrie in Nederland, 1973

Studie betreffende de ontwikkeling van de concentratie in enkele bedrijfstakken in de papier- en papierwarenindustrie in Nederland, 1974

A study of the evolution of concentration in the food industry in the Netherlands, 1974

A study of the evolution of concentration in the pharmaceutical industry in the Netherlands, 1975.

A study of the evolution of concentration in the Dutch paper products industry, 1976

A study of the evolution of concentration in the Dutch beverages industry, 1976

The first four of these studies were limited distribution documents, the remainder sales publications.

United Kingdom

A study of the evolution of concentration in the food industry for the United Kingdom, 1975

A study of concentration in the United Kingdom paper industry, 1975

A study of the evolution of concentration in the food industry for the United Kingdom, 2 vols., 1975

A study of the evolution of concentration in the mechanical engineering sector for the United Kingdom, 1975

A study of the evolution of concentration in the United Kingdom mechanical engineering industry—concentration tables, 1975

A study of the evolution of concentration in the pharmaceutical industry for the United Kingdom, 1975

A study of the evolution of concentration in the United Kingdom textile industry, 1975

A study of the evolution of concentration in the beverages industry for the United Kingdom, 1977

A study of the evolution of concentration in the electrical appliances industry for the United Kingdom, 1977
A study of the evolution of concentration in the manufacture and supply of tyres, sparking plugs, and motor-vehicle accumulators for the United Kingdom, 1977
A study of the evolution of concentration in the food distribution industry for the United Kingdom, 2 vols., 1977
A study of the evolution of concentration in the press and general publishing industry in the United Kingdom, 1977

The first two of these studies were limited distribution documents, the remainder sales publications.

Evolution of Concentration and Competition Series

Number	Title
1	Étude de l'évolution de la concentration dans le secteur de la pâte, du papier et du carton en Belgique, 1978
2	Étude sur la construction électrique grand public et sa distribution en France, Vol. 1, 1978
4	Étude de l'évolution de la concentration dans l'industrie du machinisme agricole en France, 1978
5	Untersuchung zur Konzentrationsentwicklung in der Nahrungsmitteldistribution in Deutschland, 1978
6	A study of the evolution of concentration in the sector of hoists, lifts and conveyers and in the sector of office machinery for Belgium, 1978
7	Évolution de la concentration dans l'industrie de la presse en France, 1978
8	Étude sur la concentration, les prix et les marges dans la distribution de produits alimentaires, Vol. 1, 1968
B8	Étude sur la concentration, les prix et les marges dans la distribution de produits alimentaires, Vol. 2, 1978
9	Evolution of concentration in the soap and detergents industry for the United Kingdom, 1978

A39   Die Distribution von Schallplatten klassischer Musik
           in der Bundesrepublik Deutschland, 1979

Studies—Competition: Approximation of Legislation
Series (Études—Série Concurrence: Rapprochement des
Législations)

Eighteen volumes were issued in this series between 1966 and 1971
and they are listed in *Catalogue des publications 1952–1971*, Vol.
1, pp. 95–7. Nos. 1–8 appeared under the earlier series title:
Études—Série Concurrence. Nos. 9, 14 and 15 were translated into
English. The following have since been published:

Number	Title
19	Éffets du prix et du revenu sur la consommation des boissons dans les États membres des Communautés, 1972
20	Le droit économique des États membres des Communautés européennes dans le cadre d'une Union économique et monétaire: rapport intérimaire [etc], 1973
20	—Volume 1: Rapport sur le droit économique en république fédérale d'Allemagne, 1973 —Volume 2: Rapport sur le droit économique français, 1973 —Volume 3: Rapport sur le droit économique italien, 1973 —Volume 4: Rapport sur le droit économique néerlandais, 1973
21	Rapport sur l'application de la TVA aux opérations immobilières au sein de la Communauté, 1971
22	Les opérations financières et bancaires et la taxe sur la valeur ajoutée, 1973
23	Étude sur l'application de la taxe sur la valeur ajoutée aux petites entreprises dans les six anciens États membres de la Communauté, 1973
24	Étude des problèmes particuliers posés par l'application de la taxe sur la valeur ajoutée au secteur

	agricole des pays de la Communauté européenne, 1973
25	Participation by banks in other branches of the economy, 1975
26	Report by the Commission on the behaviour of the oil companies in the Community during the period October 1973 to March 1974, 1976
27	The law of property in the European Community, 1976
28	The law of suretyship and indemnity in the United Kingdom of Great Britain and Northern Ireland and Ireland, 1976
29	Spatial pricing and competition, 1976
30	Advantages and disadvantages of an integrated market compared with a fragmented market, 1977
31	Control of securities markets in the European Economic Community, 1978

Studies—Commerce and Distribution Series

The following volumes have been published:

Number	Title
1	Market structures and conditions of competition in the wholesale trade in the countries of the EEC, 1976
2	Synoptic tables of the specific measures taken by the Member States of the European Communities in the field of commerce, 1976
3	Synoptic tables of the specific measures taken by the Member States of the European Communities in the field of commerce, 1977
4	The aspects of establishment, planning and control of urban retail outlets in Europe, 1978
5	The cooperation between firms in the Community, franchising, 1978
6	Preliminary study on competition in the retail trade (developments, problems, measures), 1978

Miscellaneous publications

Apart from the main series of studies and reports mentioned above there are a number of other publications worthy of note:

> *Directives concerning the elimination of technical barriers to trade in industrial products adopted by the Council before 1 January 1973*, 1975
>
> *Market structures and conditions of competition in the wholesale trade in the countries of the EEC*, 1976
>
> *Methodology of concentration analysis applied to the study of industries and markets*, 1977
>
> *The rules governing medicaments in the European Community*, 1978
>
> *Élimination des entraves techniques aux échanges: véhicules à moteur, cyclomoteurs et motocycles, tracteurs et machines agricoles, bateaux et leurs équipements de bord*, 1978
>
> *Recapitulatory list of Directives and proposals for Directives relating to the elimination of technical barriers to trade for industrial products*, 1979

Many older documents on competition policy and right of establishment can be found in *Catalogue des publications*, Vol. 1, pp. 94–102 and in *Catalogue of the publications of the European Community Institutions 1972–1973*, pp. 139–61.

The annual *Report on competition policy* is annexed to the *General report on the activities of the Communities* (see above, p. 47).

ECONOMIC, MONETARY AND FINANCIAL AFFAIRS

This is an area of critical concern to the European Communities. In addition to a considerable amount of statistical data from Eurostat the Directorate-General for Economic and Financial Affairs (DG II) publishes a great deal of economic information.

From 1960 to 1977 there was a quarterly publication *The economic situation in the Community (La situation économique de la Communauté)* for which there was an English version available from 1962. It was intended to be a report on economic development and short-term trends in the individual countries and in the Community as a whole. In each year one issue was devoted to the Commission's proposal for the annual report on the economic situation in the Community before its adoption by the Council of Ministers. After the signing of the Treaty of Rome (EEC) there was an initial general survey which is still of interest entitled *Report on the economic situation in the countries of the Community*, 1958.

The quarterly, *The economic situation in the Community* was complemented by a monthly *Graphs and notes on the economic situation in the Community* (1959–77). From 1959 to 1974 this was published in three bilingual editions: German/Dutch, French/Italian and French/English. In 1975 the French/English version was replaced by one in English/Danish. The following features appeared monthly:

industrial production
rate of unemployment
consumer prices
balance of trade

The remainder appeared quarterly:

exports
trade between member countries
discount rate and call-money rate
money supply
effective exchange rates
imports
terms of trade
wholesale prices
retail sales
wages
output in the metal products industries
dwellings authorized
central government budget
share prices
long-term interest rates

In 1978 a new publication entitled *European economy* was brought out in place of the two periodicals described above.

European economy (1978–)

This appears three times a year, in March, July and November. The November issue contains the 'annual economic report' which is the Commission's proposal to the Council for establishing economic policy guidelines to be followed by the member countries; and the 'annual economic review' which is the background analysis to the annual report. The other two issues review the current economic situation in the Community and contain reports and studies on economic policy. Main economic indicators are also given in each issue in an annex; in No. 4, 1979 there are forty-two time series.

In 1979 there was a 'special issue' which contained the 'Report of the Group of Experts on Sectoral Analyses' entitled 'Changes in industrial structure in the European economies since the oil crisis, 1973–78: Europe—its capacity to change in question!'.

There are three regular supplements to *European economy*. *Series A* is called 'Recent economic trends' and appears eleven times a year. It gives the most recent trends in industrial production, consumer prices, unemployment, the balance of trade, exchange rates and other indicators.

Series B is called 'Economic prospects—business survey results'. It appears eleven times a year. It reports the main results of the opinion surveys among chief executives in Community industries.

Series C is called 'Economic prospects—consumer survey results'. It reports three times a year on the survey of consumer opinion on the economic outlook in the Community.

Results of the business survey carried out among managements in the Community

From 1962 to 1975 this was known as the *Report of the results of the business surveys carried out among the heads of enterprise in the Community*. Up to 1975 each issue, published in the four official languages and English, contained the reports of four of the monthly surveys. Data for the UK has been included since 1975 but Denmark does not yet fully utilize the Community questionnaire.

Since 1976 results have been reported monthly. Fourteen questions are addressed to manufacturing industry on the following matters:

production trends
order books
export order books
stocks of finished products
production expectations
selling price expectations
employment expectations
limits to production
production capacity
duration of assured production
new orders in recent past
export expectations for the months ahead
capacity utilization
stocks of raw materials

A further question is addressed to all industries, including manufacturing, extractive and food, on investment trends and prospects.

The questionnaires are administered on a national basis. In the UK the Confederation of British Industry carries out the manufacturing industry surveys and the Department of Industry the investment surveys.

A selection of recent results of these surveys appears also in *Series B* of *European economy*.

Studies—Economic and Financial Series

Eight volumes were issued in this series between 1962 and 1970. These are listed in *Catalogue des publications 1952–1971*, Vol. 1, pp. 103–4. Nos. 5 and 7 were translated into English. The following have since been published:

Number	Title
9	The United Kingdom economy, 1975
10	The Irish economy, 1975
11	The trend of public finance in the Member States of the Community from 1966 to 1970, 1976

12	The impact of rising prices on taxation and social security contributions in the European Community, 1976
A13	Report of the study group on the role of public finance in European integration, Vol. 1, General report, 1977
B13	Report of the study group on the role of public finance in European integration, Vol. II, Individual contributions and working papers, 1977
14	The Danish economy, 1979

Miscellaneous publications

There is a series, *Medium term economic policy*, which includes seven volumes of studies 'on the possible part played by certain primary non-employment incomes in the inflationary process in . . .'. These are:

Volume	Country
4	Belgium
5	Germany
6	United Kingdom
7	Netherlands
8	Italy
9	Ireland
10	Luxembourg

These volumes were published between 1976 and 1977.
Other recent publications include:

System of structural indicators, 1975
European economic integration and monetary unification, report by the Study Group on Economic and Monetary Union, 2 vols, 1975
Grants and loans from the European Community, 1976
Analysis of the financial management in respect of the revenue and expenditure account of the European Communities for the financial year 1975, 1977
Ecological and economic necessity of waste recycling, 1979

Older publications are listed in *Catalogue des publications 1952–1971*, Vol. 1, pp. 105–7.

TAXATION

The European Communities are interested in taxation from the point of view of preventing the distortion of competition and removing restrictions on the free movement of goods, services and capital. Activities centre around the harmonization of taxation.

The Directorate-General for Financial Institutions and Taxation has published nine editions of the *Inventory of taxes: levied by the State and the local authorities (Länder, départements, régions, districts, provinces, communes) in the Member States of the European Communities*, the latest edition was published in 1979.

There are two volumes in the series: *Studies—Taxation Series:*

Number	Title
1	Tax policy and investment in the European Community, 1975
2	Cigarette tax harmonization, 1975

REGIONAL POLICY

The objective of Community policy is to reduce the disparities between rich and poor areas in the Community countries. One of the chief instruments of regional policy is the European Regional Development Fund. The Fund has been set up to help finance two types of investment:

industrial or service sector investments which create new or guarantee existing jobs
public infrastructure works which contribute to the development of the region concerned

The annual report of the European Regional Development Fund for 1975 was supplement No. 7, 1976 to the *Bulletin of the European Communities*. The annual reports for 1976, 1977 and 1978 were published separately in the official languages. Each report appears first as a *COM* document; the annual report for 1978 is *COM* (79) 349 final.

The *Principal regulations and decisions of the Council of the European Communities on regional policy* was published in 1979. There is also a *Regional development atlas*, 1979.

Apart from the Eurostat series the only series of current interest is *Studies/Programmes—Regional Policy Series*.

Regional Policy Series

Some of the publications in this series are called *Studies* and some *Programmes* but it is in fact a single numbered series. It is difficult to establish what the policy is on translation; a few titles have been translated into all the official languages, some are in one language only and yet others in several languages. The following have been published:

Number	Title
1	The development of the Flemish economy in the international perspective: synthesis and options of policy, 1974
2	Regional development programme for Greenland 1977–1979, 1978
3	Non-production activities in UK manufacturing industry, 1977
4	Regional concentration in the countries of the European Community, 1977
5	Feasibility-Studie über den Stand und die Entwicklungsmöglichkeiten von vorausschauenden regionalen Arbeitsmarktbilanzen in der Europäischen Gemeinschaft, 1977
6	Regional development programme for the Mezzogiorno 1977–1980, 1978
7	Regional development programme Ireland 1977–1980, 1978
8	Regional development programmes Netherlands 1977–1980, 1978
9	Les travailleurs frontaliers en Europe (in preparation)

10	Regional development programme United Kingdom 1978–1980, 1978
11	Regional development programmes Grand Duchy of Luxemburg, 1978
12	Regional development programmes Denmark, 1978
13	Regional development programmes France 1976–1980, 1978
14	Regional development programmes Belgium 1978–1980, 1979
15	Regional incentives in the European Community: a comparative study, 1979
16	Programmes de développement régional République fédérale d'Allemagne, y compris Berlin (Ouest) 1979–1982, 1979
17	The regional development programmes, 1979

Collection d'économie et politique régionale

This was a series begun by the High Authority of the European Coal and Steel Community. None were translated into English and not all were available in the four official languages. There were two sub-series: *La conversion industrielle en Europe*, which consisted of eleven volumes published between 1961 and 1972; and *Programme de développement et de conversion* which consisted of ten volumes published between 1962 and 1968. All these titles are listed in *Catalogue des publications 1952–1971*, Vol. 1, pp. 111–13.

Cahiers de reconversion industrielle

Eighteen of these limited distribution pamphlets were published between 1964 and 1971. They are listed in *Catalogue des publications 1952–1971*, Vol. 1, pp. 114–15. Nos. 6 and 16 were translated into English. The following have been published subsequently:

Number	Title
18	La reconversion des charbonnages dans les bassins belges, 1972

19	La reconversion des charbonnages dans les bassins allemands—Ruhr, 1972
20	La reconversion des charbonnages dans les bassins de la République fédérale—Aix-la-Chapelle, 1972
21	La reconversion dans l'industrie charbonnière et sidérurgique en Italie, 1972
22	La reconversion des bassins houillers en France, 1972
23	La reconversion des charbonnages dans les bassins de la République fédérale—Sarre, 1972

Les régions dans l'Europe

Three issues of this limited distribution periodical were published in the official languages between 1969 and 1971, but none since then.

Miscellaneous publications

A number of older documents on regional policy are listed in *Catalogue des publications 1952–1971*, Vol. 1, p. 110.

Regional development in the Community: analytical survey was published in 1971; this updates a previous survey of 1969.

SOCIAL AFFAIRS

There are six main areas in which the Commission is interested: social policy, especially in relation to migrant workers; manpower and employment; education and training, especially vocational training; occupational health and safety; consumer affairs; the environment. These are not of course mutually exclusive categories and a publication might well relate to more than one of these areas although for convenience each document will only be listed once: in the official catalogues documents are often listed under more than one heading.

Social policy

STUDIES—SOCIAL POLICY SERIES
(ÉTUDES—SÉRIE POLITIQUE SOCIALE)
Twenty-one volumes were issued in this series between 1963 and 1970. The titles are listed in *Catalogue des publications 1952–1971*, Vol. 1, pp. 120–3. Nos. 15 and 21 were translated into English. The following have since been published:

Number	Title
22	L'information relative aux revenus et aux patrimoines dans les pays de la Communauté, 1972
23	The effects of the reduction in manpower in the mining industry on mining social security systems and pension systems in particular, 1972
24	The dynamics of unemployment and employment: Belgium, 1947–1973, 1976
25	Temporary-employment business: comparative study of provisions laid down by law and regulation in force in the Member States of the European Communities, 1976
26	Educational leave in Member States, 1976
27	L'apprentissage en Belgique, 1976
28	L'apprentissage en République fédérale d'Allemagne, 1976
29	Apprenticeships in France, 1976
30	Apprenticeships in the United Kingdom, 1976
31	Apprenticeships in the Grand Duchy of Luxembourg, 1977
32	Apprenticeships in Denmark, 1977
33	Apprenticeships in Ireland, 1977
34	L'apprentissage en Italie, 1977
35	Apprenticeships in the Netherlands, 1977
36	The organization, financing and cost of health care in the European Community, 1979
37	Analyse comparative des instruments de la politique de l'emploi dans certains pays membres, 1977
38	Pharmaceutical consumption: trends in expenditure; main measures taken and underlying objectives of

public intervention in this field, 1978
39   The cost of hospitalization: micro-economic
approach to the problems involved, 1979

Very few of these recent studies are available in more than two
of the official languages.

*COMPARATIVE TABLES OF THE SOCIAL
SECURITY SYSTEMS IN THE MEMBER
STATES OF THE EUROPEAN COMMUNITIES
(TABLEAUX COMPARATIFS DES RÉGIMES
DE SÉCURITÉ SOCIALE APPLICABLES DANS
LES ÉTATS MEMBRES DES COMMUNAUTÉS
EUROPÉENNES)*
In the past this has been available in three sections:

General system (Régime général)
Mining system (Régime minier)
Régime agricole

Only the *General system* appears to be current. There have been
ten editions in the official languages. The purpose of this publication is to enable one to compare the basic features of the different
social security systems throughout the European Communities.
Statistical data can be found in the *Report on the development of
the social situation in the Community* (see above, p. 47). *Comparative tables of the social security systems relating to employees in the
three new Member States of the European Communities: Denmark—Ireland—United Kingdom; situation on 1 July 1972*, was a
supplement to the seventh edition. The eighth edition was the first
to include data on the enlarged Community. The following have
been published:

Edition	Published	Situation at
1	1961	30.6.1961
2	1962	30.6.1962
3	1964	1.7.1964
4	1966	1.7.1966
5	1968	1.7.1968
6	1970	1.7.1970
7	1973	1.7.1972

8	1975	1.7.1974
9	1977	1.7.1976
10	1979	1.7.1978

The first five editions of *Mining system* were published in the official languages. The sixth was the only one to appear in English. The following were published:

Edition	Published	Situation at
1	1961	January 1961
2	1963	1.1.1963
3	1966	1.1.1965
4	1968	1.4.1967
5	1970	1.7.1969
6	1973	1.7.1972

There were only two editions of *Régime agricole*, both published in the official languages. The first describes the situation at 1.7.1965 and the second at 1.7.1966.

THE EUROPEAN SOCIAL BUDGET
1980–1975–1970
This study, which was published in 1979, is an attempt to assess the overall expenditure on social security in the individual countries and in the Community as a whole.

MIGRANT WORKERS
There are a number of important publications in this area which reflects the Commission's interest in encouraging freedom of movement of labour within the European Communities.

There is a valuable loose-leaf *Practical handbook of social security for employed persons and their families moving within the Community* which first appeared in the official languages in 1973 and has been kept up to date.

Social security for migrant workers is a series of booklets designed to assist the nationals of Community countries moving from one member country to another. All the booklets are available in each of the official languages. There is a 'Guide No. 1—general guide' for each of the nine member countries and four other titles as follows:

Number	Title
2	Temporary stay
3	Workers posted abroad or employed in more than one Member State
4	Pensioners
5	Members of the family

Rapport annuel sur la mise en oeuvre des règlements concernant la sécurité sociale des travailleurs migrants (1961–72) was a series of reports concerning regulations brought into effect in relation to social security for migrant workers. The following were published:

Report	Published	Covering the years
1	1961	1958–9
2	1963	1960
3	1963	1961
4	1965	1962
5	1966	1963
6 & 7	1967	1964–5
8 & 9	1969	1966–7
10 & 11	1972	1968–9

Some older publications, issued by the Commission administrative pour la sécurité des travailleurs migrants, are listed in *Catalogue des publications 1952–1971*, Vol. 1, pp. 129–33.

MISCELLANEOUS PUBLICATIONS

National health survey systems in the European Economic Community is a technical document published in English only in 1977 (Eur 5747).

Some older publications are listed in *Catalogue des publications 1952–1971*, Vol. 1, pp. 127–9.

Manpower and employment

There is a European Social Fund designed to improve employment opportunities for workers in the European Communities and raise living standards. The Fund was created under Articles 123–8 of the Treaty of Rome (EEC) and subsequently reformed by a Council decision of 1 February 1971. The relevant legislation was reprinted in *Le nouveau fonds social européen: textes officiels*, 1972. The annual reports of the European Social Fund appear first as *COM* documents although the *Second annual report* was a sales publication of 1975 (covering the financial year 1973). The fifth report is *COM* (77) 398 final; the sixth is *COM* (78) 476 final; the seventh is *COM* (79) 346 final.

There was an annual report on the state of the labour market in general entitled *Les problèmes de main-d'oeuvre dans la Communauté* (1964–71), published in the official languages. Machinery for clearing vacancies at a Community level was described in *Système européen de diffusion des offres et des demandes d'emploi enregistrées en compensation internationale [SEDOC]*, 1974. In 1975 a *Directory of occupational activities and occupations for international clearance* was published in the official languages.

The relevant legislation relating to freedom of movement is reprinted in *Freedom of movement for workers within the Community: official texts*, 1975.

Other recent publications on manpower and employment include:

Women and employment in the United Kingdom, Ireland and Denmark, 1975

Conference on work: organization, technical development and motivation of the individual, 1975

Outlook for employment in the European Community to 1980, 1976

The handicapped and their employment: a statistical study of the situation in the Member States of the European Communities, 1978

The attitude of the working population to retirement, 1979

Femmes et hommes d'Europe en 1978: attitudes comparées à l'égard de quelques problèmes de société, 1979

Some older publications are listed in *Catalogue des publications 1952–1971*, Vol. 1, pp. 119–27.

Education and training

STUDIES—EDUCATION SERIES
The following have been published:

Number	Title
1	The children of migrant workers, 1977
2	Guidance and orientation in secondary schools, 1977
3	Le développement européen de l'éducation permanente, 1977
4	Management education in the European Community, 1978
5	Pupil exchange in the European Community: Venice Colloquium, 24–28 October 1977, 1978
6	Nouveaux modèles d'enseignement supérieur et égalité des chances: prospectives internationales, 1978
7	Joint programmes of study: an instrument of European cooperation in higher education, 1979
8	In-service education and training of teachers in the European Community, 1979
9	Equality of education and training for girls (10–18 years), 1979
10	Academic recognition of diplomas in the European Community: present state and prospects, 1979

STUDIES—CULTURAL MATTERS SERIES
The following have been published:

Number	Title
1	The mobility of cultural workers within the Community, 1976
2	Le droit d'auteur dans la Communauté européenne, 1978

VOCATIONAL TRAINING (1974–)
From 1974 to 1976 this was published in collaboration with the British Association for Commercial and Industrial Education by the Commission. Since 1977 it has been published by the Euro-

pean Centre for the Development of Vocational Training. It is quarterly in the official languages. There were eight supplements published between 1977 and 1978 on the state of vocational training in the following countries:

Netherlands, 1977
United Kingdom, 1977
Ireland, 1977
Denmark, 1977
France, 1978
Belgium, 1978
Luxembourg, 1978
Germany, 1978

DOCUMENTATION PÉDAGOGIQUE: FORMATION PROFESSIONELLE (1969–72)

This was a quarterly in the official languages published in collaboration with L'Institut Européen pour la Formation Professionelle. It listed books, research reports and other important documents dealing with vocational training. It also included films and other teaching aids. This bibliography was continued as a feature of *Vocational training* from 1974 to 1977.

OTHER PUBLICATIONS ON VOCATIONAL TRAINING

Some of the more recent publications include:

Information-processing training in adult education, 1975
The evaluation of vocational training, 1976
Vocational guidance and training for women workers, 1978
Analysis of vocational preparation in the Member States of the European Community, 1979
Report on vocational guidance activities in the Community, 1977
Annual report 1978: CEDEFOP, European Centre for the Development of Vocational Training, 1979

Some older documents are listed in *Catalogue des publications 1952–1971*, Vol. 1, pp. 134–6.

UNIVERSITIES

There is an irregular series published in a bilingual English/French

edition entitled *University studies on European integration*. Nos.
1–8, 1963–74 were published by the European Community Institute for University Studies. No. 9, 1977 and No. 10, 1978 were
published in association with the Centre for European Studies at
the Catholic University of Louvain. It is usually a single volume
except for No. 4, 1967 which consists of two volumes. It is an
analytical bibliography of European studies research carried out in
universities in the member states of the European Communities.

There is a monthly entitled *European University news* (1965–   )
published in a bilingual English/French edition by the Association
pour la Communauté Européenne Universitaire. In 1979 there
was a special issue on 'summer courses on European integration';
and in 1978 there was a special issue on 'postgraduate degrees in
European integration'.

The second edition of *Higher education in the European Community: a handbook for students* was published in 1979.

The *Register of current university research into European integration* is published by the University Association for Contemporary European Studies, King's College, London.

MISCELLANEOUS PUBLICATIONS ON EDUCATION

Some of the more recent publications include:

> *School and professional education of the children of Italian
> workers in the Saar*, 1975
> *Schooling and professional training of children of Italian and
> Portuguese workers in the Moselle region*, 1975
> *Teaching aids on the European Community: Europe at school;
> Catalogue*, 1978
> *Environmental education in the age group 9–14 years in the
> European Communities: an account of trends within the
> Member states* (Eur 5930), 1978

Occupational health and safety

MINES SAFETY AND HEALTH COMMISSION

This was known formerly as the Mines Safety Commission. There
is a series of annual reports (1959–   ) of which not all the earlier
volumes were translated into English. Since the *14th report*

relating to 1976 this has been a sales publication in the official languages. These reports contain bibliographies of the work of the Commission.

Other publications are listed in *Catalogue des publications 1952–1971*, Vol. 1, pp. 147–8; and in *Catalogue of the publications of the European Community Institutions 1972–1973*, p. 295–303.

STEEL INDUSTRY SAFETY AND HEALTH COMMISSION

This was formerly known as the Commission on Safety and Health in the Iron and Steel Industry. There is an annual report (1970–   ) in the official languages. These reports contain bibliographies of the work of the Commission.

Older publications are listed in *Catalogue des publications 1952–1971*, Vol. 1, pp. 148–50; and in *Catalogue of the publications of the European Community Institutions 1972–1973*, pp. 295–303.

RADIOLOGICAL PROTECTION

There is a series of *Eur* publications relating to occupational health and safety in which the following titles have appeared recently:

Radioactive isotopes in occupational health (Eur 5524), 1976
Technical recommendations for the use of radiophotoluminescence dosimetry in individual monitoring (Eur 5655), 1977
A European neutron dosimetry intercomparison project (ENDIP): results and evaluation (Eur 6004), 1978
Programme: radiation protection; progress report 1977 (Eur 5972), 1978

INDUSTRIAL HEALTH AND SAFETY

Eur publications in this series include:

Training in industrial safety (Eur 5224), 1976
Guidance notes for safe diving: compiled by the European Diving Technology Committee (Eur 5695), 1977
A practical method of investigating accident factors: principles and experimental application (Eur 5500), 1977
Evaluation of the work load in hot environments (Eur 5556), 1977
Oxygen: precautions to be taken in the preparation of plant and equipment. Steel industry (Eur 5923), 1978

Accident prevention programme (Eur 5922), 1978

Trends in industrial safety at 'Cockerill-Liège' 1956–1974 (Eur 5927), 1978

Health in mines: synthesis report on research in the third programme 1971–1976 (Eur 5931), 1978

Blast furnace tapping (Eur 5896), 1978

First aid and rescue (Eur 5928), 1978

Oxygen enriched atmospheres (Eur 6047), 1979

Maintenance and repair work on gas lines and apparatus: water seals and drain seal pots (Eur 6048), 1979

Training of industrial safety advisers (Eur 6091), 1979

Integration into an industrial environment of unskilled production workers: the experience of the Forges de Basse-Indre (Eur 6205), 1979

OLDER PUBLICATIONS

There are several collections of documents listed in *Catalogue des publications 1952–1971*, Vol. 1, pp. 139–50. Among these are:

Collection d'hygiène et de médecine du travail

Collection de traumatologie et de réadaption

Collection 'Physiologie et psychologie du travail'

Consumer affairs

REPORTS OF THE SCIENTIFIC COMMITTEE FOR FOOD

The following have been published in the official languages:

First series, 1975
Second series, 1976
Third series, 1977
Fourth series, 1977
Fifth series, 1978
Sixth series, 1978
Seventh series, 1978
Eighth series, 1979
Ninth series, 1979

The Scientific Committee for Food was set up to advise on

problems arising from the composition of foodstuffs, food additives and processing aids.

OTHER PUBLICATIONS
Other recent publications include the following:

Study on radioactivity in consumer goods (Eur 5460), 1976

Problems posed by the growing use of consumer goods containing radioactive substances (Eur 5601), 1976

The judicial and quasi-judicial means of consumer protection, 1977

The European consumer: his preoccupation, his aspirations, his information, 1977

Consumer protection and information policy: first report, 1977

The consumer organizations and the public authorities, 1978

Proceedings of the symposium of consumer organizations on 2 and 3 December 1976, 1979

Consumer protection and information policy: second report, 1979

The rules governing medicaments in the European Community, 1978

Environment

There have been two reports on the *State of the environment*, the first in 1977 and the second in 1979. The second report contains a list of proposals adopted or being discussed by the Council on 31 March 1978. It also contains a list of the studies conducted and published by the Commission, 1976–77. There are thirty-nine studies listed which are nearly all *Eur* documents.

There is a substantial collection of documents in the collection *Environment and quality of life* of which the following have appeared recently:

System studies on recycling non-ferrous raw materials (Eur 5707), 1978

Environmental toxicology of chlorinated hydrocarbon compounds in the marine environment of Europe (Eur 5814), 1978

2nd CEC remote sensing campaign: Drax 1976; correlation spectrometry measurements (Eur 5809), 1979

Final reports on research sponsored under the first environmental research programme (indirect action) (Eur 5970), 1978

Noxious effects of dangerous substances in the aquatic environment (Eur 5983), 1978

An evaluation of economical consequences resulting from the application of directive proposal COM (75) 681. The use of low sulphur fuel oils with the aim of decreasing sulphurous emissions (Eur 6011), 1978

World TiO$_2$ industry projects and their environmental impact (Eur 6024), 1978

L'aménagement intégré du littoral dans la Communauté européenne (Eur 6105), 1978

Study of the contamination of continental fauna by organochlorine pesticides and PCBs (Eur 5888), 1978

Bathymetric map of Lake Lugano (Eur 5634), 1978

Third international symposium on ceramics (Eur 5956), 1978

Les problèmes d'environment propres aux centres des villes (Eur 5939), 1978

Pollution chimique due aux industries de l'énergie (Eur 5529), 1978

Classes of acoustical comfort in housing (Eur 5618), 1978

Study of the techniques for the determination of certain microbiological parameters in drinking water (Eur 6020), 1978

Ricerche condotte sul lago di Comabbio (provincia di Vares, Italia settentrionale) dal maggio 1976 al maggio 1977 (Eur 5890), 1978

Study of the techniques for the determination of the enteric viruses (Eur 6029), 1978

On the future average mercury content of air, soil and river sediments in the EEC and in the world's oceans (Eur 6023), 1978

Report of a feasibility study on the distribution and use of simulated water samples for comparative bacteriological analysis (Eur 6037), 1978

Environmental aspects of offshore mineral production in the European Economic Community (Eur 6034), 1978

Pollution problems resulting from the manufacture of nitrogenous and phosphate fertilizers (Eur 6081), 1979

Reliability conditions of Eh measurements in lake sediments (Eur 6035), 1979

Control of nitrogen oxide emissions from European cars (Eur
6028), 1979
*Möglichkeiten zur Verringerung der Stickoxidemissionen von
europäischen Personenkraftwagen* (Eur 6030), 1979
*Economic, technical and ecological aspects of the production, use
and marketing of compost in the Member States of the Euro-
pean Economic Community* (Eur 6000), 1979
*Studie über die Eigenschaften eines beschäftigungswirksamen
Umweltprogramms für die Gemeinschaft* (Eur 6204), 1979
*Proposal for a biotypological classification of water courses in the
European Communities* (Eur 6025), 1979
*Possibilités de valorisation et réutilisation des déchets de l'indus-
trie primaire du zinc et du plomb* (Eur 6191), 1979
*Exchange of information concerning atmospheric pollution by
certain sulphur compounds and suspended particulates in the
European Community: annual report for January to December
1976* (Eur 6472), 1979
*Collecte, élimination et récupération des emballages non bio-
dégradables* (Eur 6489), 1979
*Le marché des emballages de boissons dans la Communauté
européenne* (Eur 6490), 1979
*Umwelteinwirkung durch Gewinnung, Weiterverarbeitung und
Verbrauch von Kohle in der Bundesrepublik Deutschland*, 2
vols. (Eur 6562), 1979

Other publications on the environment include:

*Europe and its environment: programme for a better quality of
life*, 1975
*Intercomparison programme on atmospheric lead measurement
in Member States of the European Community*, 1976
*Results of environmental radioactivity measurements in the Mem-
ber States of the European Community for air—deposition—
water 1973–1974—milk 1972–1973–1974* (Eur 5630), 1977
*Council directive of 1 June 1976 laying down the revised basic
safety standards for the health protection of the general public
and workers against the dangers of ionizing radiation* (Eur
5563), 1977
*Results of environmental radioactivity measurements in the Mem-
ber States of the European Community for air—deposition—
water—milk 1975–1976* (Eur 5944), 1978

Migration phenomena in food packaging (Eur 5979), 1978
Ecological and economic necessity of waste recycling, 1979

There is a set of nine volumes, one volume for each of the member countries of the European Communities, on *The law and practice relating to pollution control* . . . which were published by Graham & Trotman in 1976 on behalf of the Commission.

AGRICULTURE

There were one hundred and sixty-nine studies in the series *Études—Série informations internes sur l'agriculture*, published between 1964 and 1975, mostly in French and German only. These studies were the results of research sponsored by the Commission in universities and other organizations into agricultural subjects, including the implementation of the common agricultural policy.

This series should not be confused with *Studies—Agricultural Series (Études—Série Agriculture)*. Twenty-three volumes were issued in this series between 1960 and 1966. The titles are listed in *Catalogue des publications 1952–1971*, Vol. 1, pp. 161–3. Nos. 11, 14, 15 and 21 were translated into English.

Such studies are now reported in the series *Information on Agriculture* which started in 1976. These are sales publications but are not necessarily translated into all the official languages.

Information on Agriculture

The following have been published:

Number	Title
1	Crédits à l'agriculture, 1976
2	Kredite an die Landwirtschaft, 1976
3	Crédits à l'agriculture, 1976
4	Credit to agriculture, 1976
5	Carte de la durée de la période de végétation dans les États membres des Communautés européennes, 1976

60	Critères supplémentaires de qualité pour les poulets et les oeufs, 1979
61	Microbiology and shelf-life of chilled poultry carcasses, 1979
62	Conséquences écologiques de l'abandon de terres cultivées, 1979
63	Situation de l'agriculture et de l'approvisionnement alimentaire dans certains pays arabes et méditerranéens et leur développement prévisible, 1979
64	Situation de l'agriculture et de l'approvisionnement alimentaire dans certains pays arabes et méditerranéens et leur développement prévisible, 1979
65	Projections for the agricultural sector: forecasts of the trends in farm structures and factor input in agriculture in the EC, 1979
66	Projections for the agricultural sector: forecasts of the trends in farm structures and factor input in agriculture in the EC, 1979
67	Water content of frozen or deep-frozen poultry. Examination of methods of determination: guinea-fowls and ducks, 1979
68	Possibilities of reduction of the quantities of phytosanitary products employed in agriculture, 1979
69	Dehydration of green fodder in the EC: technical and economic study, 1979
70	Development of uniform methods for pig carcass classification in the EC, 1979

Agricultural prices

DG VI publishes a wide range of data on agricultural prices outside the Eurostat series.

AGRICULTURAL MARKETS: LIVESTOCK
PRODUCTS (1962–)
This is an irregular series in the official languages. English has been used since No. 5, 1974. From 1979 it has been numbered

independently having previously been numbered with *Agricultural markets: vegetable products*. The main headings in use are:

pigmeat
eggs
beef and veal
milk and milk products

The following summaries have been published:

Date	Covering the years
1974	1967/8–1972/3
1975	1973–1974
1976	1973–1975
1977	1973–1976
1978	1973–1977
1979	1973–1978

AGRICULTURAL MARKETS: VEGETABLE PRODUCTS (1962–   )

This is an irregular series in the official languages. English has been used since No. 6, 1974. From 1979 it has been numbered independently having previously been numbered with *Agricultural markets: livestock products*. The main headings in use are:

cereals
rice
oils and fats
wine
sugar
isoglucose

The following summaries have been published:

Date	Covering the years
1974	1967/68–1972/73
1975	1973–1974
1976	1973–1975
1977	1973–1976
1978	1973–1977
1979	1973–1978

AGRICULTURAL MARKETS: PRICES RECEIVED BY FARMERS

This is an annual publication in the official languages. Each issue replaces the previous one. The issue of July 1979 contains data for 1959/60 to 1977/78 on the following:

common wheat
rye
barley
oats
maize
potatoes
sugar
beef cattle
pigs
milk
eggs

MARCHÉS AGRICOLES: ÉCHANGES COMMERCIAUX (1963–73)

This was an irregular limited distribution series in the four official languages. There were four sub-series:

Fruits, légumes, vin
Céréales et préparations à base de céréales
Viande de porc, viande de volaille, oeufs
Viande bovine, produits laitiers, riz

This series gave short-term import and export data.

Other publications

The following *Eur* documents on agriculture subjects have been published since 1976:

Laboratory manual for research on classical and African swine fever (Eur 5487), 1976
Diagnosis and epizootiology of classical swine fever (Eur 5486), 1976
Optimization of cattle-breeding schemes (Eur 5490), 1976

Improving the nutritional efficiency of beef production (Eur 5488), 1976

Differential diagnosis of avian lymphoid leukosis and Marek's disease (Eur 5494), 1976

Perinatal ill-health in calves (Eur 5603), 1976

Cross-breeding experiments and strategy of beef utilization to increase beef production (Eur 5492), 1977

Technical and physical aspects of energy saving in greenhouses (Eur 5679), 1977

Bovine leucosis: various methods of molecular virology (Eur 5685), 1977

Techniques for the separation of barley and maize proteins (Eur 5687), 1977

Utilization of manure by land spreading (Eur 5672), 1977

Protein quality from leguminous crops (Eur 5686), 1977

EEC Symposium on forest tree biochemistry (Eur 5885), 1977

Studies on the epidemiology and economics of swine fever eradication in the EEC (Eur 5738), 1977

Anatomical jointing, tissue separation and weight recording proposed as the standard method for beef (Eur 5720), 1978

Proceedings of a workshop: the use of ionizing radiation in agriculture (Eur 5815), 1978

Symposium on the transfer and interpretation of scientific and technical information in agriculture (Eur 5856), 1978

Report of the study group on vegetable proteins in foodstuffs for human consumption, in particular meat products (Eur 6026), 1978

Animal and human health hazards associated with the utilization of animal effluents (Eur 6009), 1979

Carbohydrate and protein synthesis (Eur 6043), 1979

Econometric models presented to the Beef–Milk symposium on 15–16 March 1977 (Eur 6101), 1979

Some current research on Vicia faba in western Europe (Eur 6244), 1979

Engineering problems with effluents from livestock (Eur 6249), 1979

AGREP: permanent inventory of agricultural research projects in the European Communities (Eur 5895), 2 vols., 2nd ed., 1979

Other recent publications on agricultural subjects include:

Directory of non-governmental agricultural organizations set up

at Community level, 1974
Language barriers in agriculture [etc], 1976
EAGGF: European Agricultural Guidance and Guarantee
Fund: importance and functioning, 1978
Reports of the Scientific Committee for Animal Nutrition: First
series, 1979

Older material can be found in Catalogue des publications,
1952–1971, Vol. 1, pp. 161–78.

TRANSPORT

There have been five titles in the series Studies—Transport Series
as follows:

Number	Title
1	Options in transport tariff policy, 1965
2	Problèmes posés par l'application pratique d'une tarification pour l'utilisation des infrastructures routières, 1970
3	Coordination of investments in transport infrastructures, 1973
4	The analysis of economic costs and expenses in road and rail transport, 1976
5	Étude de la structure de la navigation intérieure en Europe occidentale, 1978

Other recent publications include:

Proceedings of the European Motor Vehicles Symposium and the
Seminar on Accident Statistics, 2 vols., 1977
Report of an enquiry into the current situation in the major
Community seaports drawn up by the Port Working Group,
1978
Glossary: new transport technologies, 1978

ENERGY

Despite the assertion of national interest in energy matters there is a substantial literature from the Commission, especially research reports.

Community energy policy: texts of the relevant legislation was published in 1977. *Supplement No. 1–1978*, appeared in 1979.

First periodical report on the Community action programme for the rational use of energy (period 1975) and recommendations of the Council was published in 1977; *Second report on the Community programme for the rational use of energy: directive proposal and recommendations of the Council* was published in 1978.

The energy situation in the Community (La conjoncture énergetique dans la Communauté) (1963–)

This annual survey is published in the official languages. It was available in English from 1973. It gives an account of the situation in the previous year and makes forecasts for the current year. The report for 1967 was published as *Bulletin of the European Coal and Steel Community*, No. 67, 1967. The latest issue, published in 1979, describes the situation in 1978 and gives forecasts for 1979.

Eur documents

The following is a list of the *Eur* documents published since 1976:

Totem: a computer program for the stimulation of an electric power generation system (Eur 5421), 1976

Fifth symposium on microdosimetry, 2 vols. (Eur 5452), 1976

Towards fusion energy: the European programme (Eur 5462), 1976

Investigation of a TiO$_2$ electrolyte solar cell and the question of the photocatalytic water decomposition (Eur 5514), 1976

Superconducting and other high power cables for electric power transmission: state of the art and perspective (Eur 5520), 1976

High-output coal-mining districts (Eur 5600), 1976

The role of the demand–duration curve in the evaluation of power station installation policies (Eur 5599), 1977

Effects of fast breeders' characteristics on consumptions and expenditures related to electric power generation (Eur 5598), 1977

Chemical and physical valorization of coal (Eur 5692), 1977

Seminar on geothermal energy, 2 vols. (Eur 5920), 1977

Energetical and economical assessment of the waste heat problem (Eur 5724), 1977

Permanent directory of energy information sources in the European Community (Eur 5425), 1978

Photovoltaic conversion of solar energy using optical concentration systems (Eur 5894), 1978

Feinkoksherstellung aus Braunkohle (Eur 5742), 1978

Verbesserung der konventionellen Vortriebstechnik (Eur 5744), 1978

Vollmechanischer Flözstreckenvortrieb mit Teilschnittmaschinen (Eur 5745), 1978

New products and processes based on coal and materials derived from coal: resins and polymers (Eur 5765), 1978

A study of yield zones around roadways (Eur 5825), 1978

Development of heading/ripping systems and immediate roadway support (Eur 5827), 1978

Feststellung der an die Dauerfestigkeit von Drähten, Litzen und Seilen für Schachtfördereinrichtungen zustellenden Anforderungen (Eur 5830), 1978

Integration of face ends (Eur 5833), 1978

Benefication and utilisation of colliery (washery) tailings (Eur 5847), 1978

Untersuchung zum Einsatz vorerhitzter Kohle (Eur 5821), 1978

Verwertung von heissem, ungereinigtem Koksofengas (Eur 5823), 1978

Mechanisierung, Automatisierung und Rationalisierung der Förderund Versorgungstechnik unter Tage (einschl. Fahrung) (Eur 5781), 1978

Intergrierte Mechanisierung der Gewinnung, des Ausbaus und des Versatzes bei grosser Flözmächtigkeit. Schälende Gewinnung mit Schreitausbau und Blasversatz auf der Zeche Nordstern (Eur 5739), 1978

Pression de terrains et soutènements: prévisions et maîtrise des déformations dans les ouvrages miniers (Eur 5826), 1978

Misure di radioattività ambientale—Ispra 1976 (Eur 5805), 1978

Maîtrise du dégagement grisouteux (Eur 5579), 1978

Beherrschung der Ausgasung (Eur 5582), 1978

Maîtrise des dégagements grisouteux (Eur 5585), 1978

Chemische und physikalische Veredlung von Braunkohlenprodukten (Eur 5594), 1978

The comparison and coordination of national policies and programmes in the energy research and development sector (Eur 5911), 1978

Einfluss der Zusammensetzung von getrockneten oder vorerhitzten Kokskohlenmischungen auf Ofenführung und Koksqualität (Eur 5743), 1978

Ausschöpfung der Automatisierungsmöglichkeiten der Strebtechnik, 2 vols. (Eur 5832), 1978

Creusement conventionnel (Eur 5586), 1978

Valorisation physique et chimique des charbons (Eur 5596), 1978

Couloirs roulants (Eur 5578), 1978

L'application du process control à la ventilation des mines (Eur 5584), 1978

Round table meeting: chemical and physical valorization of coal (Eur 5954), 1978

Mécanisation du creusement des voies de chantiers et traçages en veine (Eur 5796), 1978

Amélioration des équipements de taille et de leur utilisation (Eur 5740), 1978

Transmission des ondes radio au fond (Eur 5741), 1978

Vollmechanisierung des Abbaustreckenvortriebs (Eur 5797), 1978

The development of mechanical equipment to assist in the reduction of effort employed in back-ripping (Eur 5798), 1978

Perfectionnement des techniques conventionnelles de creusement des galeries au rocher (Eur 5799), 1978

Utilisation de la radio dans les chantiers souterrains (Eur 5846), 1978

Propagation des ondes radioélectriques dans les milieux souterrains (Eur 5580), 1978

Research and development in respect of energy storage (Eur 5929), 1978

Study of mine climate (Eur 5985), 1978

A study of the relationship between the properties of the constituents of coke-oven blends and the size and strength of the coke product (Eur 5986), 1978

Rationalisation de méthodes de transport de personnel, de produits, de matériels (Eur 5921), 1978

Mise en oeuvre des méthodes de lutte contre le grisou (Eur 5958), 1978

Optimisation du traitement des eaux résiduaries de cokerie en fonction de la qualité exigée pour le rejet (Eur 5978), 1978

Automatisierung eines Walzenschrämladers (Eur 5962), 1978

Development of a method of measuring coke texture (Eur 5819), 1978

The charging of preheated coal (Eur 5820), 1978

Photovoltaic conversion of concentrated solar radiation (Eur 5723), 1978

Pollution chimique due aux industries de l'énergie (Eur 5529), 1978

Report on a collaborative investigation aimed at ascertaining the long term preservability of coal samples (Eur 6039), 1978

Application de la mécanique des terrains à la conduite des travaux miniers (Eur 5829), 1978

Gebirgsverfestigung (Eur 5984), 1978

Theoretical studies on the utilization of reciprocal salt pairs for solar heat storage (Eur 6044), 1978

Energy requirement for North Sea oil by secondary and tertiary production methods (Eur 6062), 1978

The separation of H_2SO_4 and Hi throughout the Bunsen reaction as a step in thermochemical cycles for hydrogen production (Eur 6092), 1978

Chemical and physical valorization of coal (Eur 6075), 1979

Untersuchungen an Messankern und anderen Messelementen zur Messung des Gebirgsverhaltens (Eur 6068), 1979

Creusement conventionnel de bouveaux circulaires avec revêtement en béton (Eur 6069), 1979

Improved industrial appliances for coal (Eur 6074), 1979

Benefication of coal by conversion to hydrocarbons (Eur 6073), 1979

Production, preparation and utilization of gas from coal (Eur 6072), 1979

Enfournements des fours à coke par entraînement à la vapeur du charbon fortement préchauffé (Eur 6070), 1979

Erfassung und Bekämpfung betrieblicher Schwachstellen und Engpässe (Eur 6096), 1979

Pollution atmosphérique en cokeries (Eur 6071), 1979

Valorisation des stériles (Eur 6093), 1979

Valorisation physique et chimique du charbon et de ses sous-produits (Eur 6210), 1979

Entwicklung einer Revierwarte (Eur 6238), 1979

FREDOCAN: a computer program for the analysis of energy policies in the household sector (Eur 6261), 1979

Solar gas turbine (Eur 6116), 1979

Round table meeting: coke oven techniques (Eur 6306), 1979

Automation and computer control of coal preparation plants (Eur 6254), 1979

A practical study of the application of a minicomputer to the collection and processing of management information coupled with the control of a transport system (Eur 6268), 1979

Utilization of colliery spoil in civil engineering (Eur 6253), 1979

Veredlung von Kohle durch Hydrierung: Hydrierverfahren mit Koksofengas-Wasserstoff (Eur 6260), 1979

Verkokungsversuche in einem mit Starkitsteinen ausgerüsteten Technikumsofen (Eur 6255), 1979

Meeting on heat pumps research, development and application (Eur 6237), 1979

Meeting on industrial processes—energy conservation R & D (Eur 6236), 1979

Optimierung der Ausbauarbeit in der Streckenauffahrung durch die Mechanisierung der Ausbauarbeit (Eur 6209), 1979

Mengen- und Energiebilanz beim Betrieb von Hochleistungskoksöfen (Eur 6239), 1979

Perfectionnement des moyens de lutte contre le grisou et les poussières (Eur 6298), 1979

Umsetzung von Koksofengas zu Reduktions und/oder Synthesegas (Eur 6256), 1979

Conversion of coal into raw materials for the chemical industry by the study of high-intensity chemical reactions (Eur 6252), 1979

Verbesserung der maschinellen Strebausrüstungen (Eur 6267), 1979

Steigerung der Förderleistung von Kettenkranzerförderern (Eur 6297), 1979

Round table meeting: chemical and physical valorization of coal (Eur 6576), 1979

Energy analysis as an economic tool (Eur 6387), 1979

Miscellaneous publications

Three volumes were issued in the series *Studies—Energy Series (Études—Série Énergie)* between 1968 and 1970. The titles are listed in *Catalogue des publications 1952–1971*, Vol. 1, p. 198. No. 2 was translated into English.

Forty-seven volumes in the series *Recueils de recherches 'charbon'* were issued between 1966 and 1973. The titles are listed in *Catalogue des publications 1952–1971*, Vol. 1, pp. 199–203, and *Catalogue of the publications of the European Community Institutions 1972–1973*, pp. 401–3. None were translated into English.

Some older material on nuclear energy is listed in *Catalogue des publications 1952–1971*, Vol. 1, pp. 205–10.

Other titles include:

The Community oil sector medium-term forecast and guidelines, 1974

Medium-term prospects and guidelines in the Community gas sector, 1974

Problems, resources and necessary progress in Community energy policy 1975–1985, 1974

Prospects of primary energy demand in the Community (1975–1980–1985), 1974

Twenty-five years of the common market in coal 1953–1978, 1978

INDUSTRY

There were six volumes in the series *Studies—Industry Series (Études–Série Industrie)* published between 1969 and 1971. The titles are listed in *Catalogue des publications 1952–1971*, Vol. 1, pp. 181–2. Nos. 4 and 6 were translated into English. The following have since been published:

Number	Title
7	Investigation on the development of software: report of the synthesis, 1973
8	Study of the European market for industrial nuclear power stations for the mixed production of steam and electricity: report, 1975

Investment in the Community coalmining and iron and steel industries (1956–   ) gives the results of the annual surveys of investments in these industries. It records actual expenditure, gives a forecast of future expenditure and examines the impact of investment on the production potential of the coal and steel industries. This series was published in the official languages and English from 1956 to 1972 and in the six official languages from 1973. From 1974 data relate to the enlarged Community. It is now a sales publication, but the report for 1970 was limited distribution in two volumes. A summary report covering 1956–65 was published in 1966 and another covering 1966–73 in 1974.

The *Financial report* (1956–   ) of the European Coal and Steel Community records its lending and borrowing operations for the year in question. It was published in the official languages and English from 1956 to 1972 and in the six official languages from 1973. No. 1, 1956 covers the period 1953–5; Nos. 2–24 are annual volumes covering 1956–78.

Iron and steel undertakings of the Community, 1976, is a list of the Community iron and steel producers giving both their addresses and their production programmes. There was a supplement in 1976 giving the basic prices for ECSC pig-iron and steel products.

Other recent publications include the following:

Review of studies carried out in the producer countries on the forecast consumption of the alloying elements Ni, Cr, Mo, V, W and Co for special steel production in the years 1980 and 1985, 1977
Study of deformation rate mechanisms in vanadium at temperatures (Eur 5980), 1978
Report on the ECSC experimental programme of modernization of housing, 1975
The ECSC price rules for iron and steel products. Position as at 1 May 1977, 1979
Transfer of information for industry (Eur 6104), 1979

Older material on industry and industrial research can be found listed in *Catalogue des publications 1952–1971*, Vol. 1, pp. 179–96; and *Catalogue of the publications of the European Community Institutions 1972–1973*, pp. 349–60 and 369–77.

There is a very large series of *Steel Research Reports* of which the following have been published since 1977:

Basic properties of high intensity electric arcs used in steel making (Eur 5716), 1977

Synthesis report on research into the thermomechanical treatments of steels (Eur 5828), 1977

Métallurgie physique: application des mesures de microplasticité à l'étude fondamentale des mécanismes de la déformation (Eur 5767), 1978

Étude du comportement d'assemblages types soudés soumis à des charges cycliques d'amplitude variable (Eur 5769), 1978

Gebrauchseigenschaften: Schweissbarkeit von Stahl; Untersuchung zur Frage der Schweisseigenspannungen (Eur 5771), 1978

Propriétés d'emploi: soudabilité des aciers; risque de fissuration à froid (Eur 5773), 1978

Mess- und Analysenverfahren: Ermittlung des Gefüges von Stählen mittels Ultraschall (Eur 5776), 1978

Propriétés d'emploi: soudabilité des aciers; étude structurale de la HAZ et propriétés du métal dans cette zone (Eur 5778), 1978

Gebrauchseigenschaften: Schweissbarkeit von Stahl; Untersuchung zur Kaltrissbildung von hochfesten Feinkornbaustählen (Eur 5779), 1978

Mesures: prélèvement de fonte et d'acier liquide et sa mécanisation (Eur 5788), 1978

Mise au point de nouvelles techniques d'exploitation dans le bassin ferrifère de l'Est de la France (Eur 5555), 1978

Walzwerke: Verbesserung von Anlagenelementen automatisierter Warmbreitbandstrassen; Steigerung von Leistung und Transportsicherheit am Auslaufrollgang (Eur 5713), 1978

Burden factors which influence blastfurnace regularity and productivity (Eur 5714), 1978

Entwicklung und Erprobung von Planheitsmessgeräten (Eur 5775), 1978

Verschiedenes: Entwicklung von Systemtechniken und Software-Grundlagen für ein EVD-gesteuertes System der Produktionsplanung und -lenkung in Betrieben mit vielstufiger Massensortenfertigung (Eur 5777), 1978

Mesures et analyses: étude du frottement dans l'intercylindre au cours du laminage à froid (Eur 5839), 1978

Propriété d'emploi: influence de facteurs climatiques et polluants sur la corrosion atmosphérique de l'acier; prédétermination en laboratoire (Eur 5840), 1978

Metallphysik: Bestimmung des Gefügeaufbaus in Legierungen durch äussere magnetische Felder (Eur 5838), 1978

Laminoirs: automatisation du préréglage des trains continus à larges bandes (Eur 5712), 1978

Aciérie: le procédé IRSID d'affinage continu, possibilités de refusion de ferrailles (Eur 5715/1), 1978

Transformation: aptitude des aciers à être mis en forme à froid (Eur 5770/1), 1978

Propriétés d'emploi: mécanique de la rupture (Eur 5772), 1978

Used properties: influence of the composition and microstructure on the mechanical properties of single pass weld metal obtained with two-run multipower submerged arc welding of 35 MM Fe 510 quality steels (Eur 5834), 1978

Mesures et analyses: analyse de produits sidérurgiques par spectrométrie 'X' à dispersion d'énergie (Eur 5860), 1978

Mess- und Analyseverfahren: Fehlersuche auf Kaltbandoberflächen mit opto-elektronischen Kontrollgeräten (Eur 5877), 1978

Mesures: mesure des dimensions des demi-produits et des profilés (Eur 5862), 1978

Verbesserung von Anlagenelementen automatisierter Warmbreitbandstrassen: Walguttemperaturen in Warmbreitbandfertigunstafeln, Grenzen hoher Walzgeschwindigkeiten und Möglichkeiten gezielter Walzgutkühlung (Eur 5713), 1978

Influence des facteurs métallurgiques sur différents critères d'évaluation de la fragilité des aciers (Eur 5871), 1978

Verfahren für die Korrekturberechnung bei der quantitativen Analyse mit der Mikrosonde (Eur 5870), 1978

L'aptitude des aciers au formage à froid—étirage des fils d'acier au carbone (Eur 5872), 1978

Verbesserung von Anlagenelementen automatisierter Warmbreitbandstrassen—Auftreten von Sekundarzundereinwalzungen (Eur 5713), 1978

Die Auswirkung der Bedingungen beim Einschwingen des Ermundungsanrisses (Eur 5880), 1978

Untersuchung des Einflusses von Anlagenausrüstung und Erzeugungsprogramm auf die Leistung von Kaltwalztandemstrassen (Eur 5993), 1978

Corrosion and self-protection of carbon steel in hot saline solutions (Eur 5864), 1978

Déformabilité et tenue à la fatigue d'aciers de construction (Eur 5975), 1978

Automatisation des fours de réchauffrage à voûte radiante (Eur 5992), 1978

Fatigue à programme des assemblages soudés (Eur 5989), 1978

Application industrielle du procédé de soudage ultrasonic à chaud au contrôle optimum du cisaillage des brames en acier effervescent (Eur 5987), 1978

Study on the blast-furnace coke grades used in the European Community (Eur 5968), 1978

Einfluss der chemischen Zusammensetzung und des Gefügezustandes auf Zähigkeitsverhalten und Langzeiteigenschaften von Chrom-Molybdän-Vanadin-Stählen mit 1% CR (Eur 6057), 1978

Correlation between admissable operating temperatures in a welded structure and the transition temperature in small samples (Eur 5859), 1978

Spectral analysis on liquid steel (Eur 5858), 1978

Transformation of cold-formed thin steel elements (Eur 5129), 1978

Influence du bore sur la trempabilité et la microstructure d'aciers Fe-NiCO, 12 (Eur 6056), 1978

Entwicklung und Erprobung von verfahrenstechnischen Möglichkeiten zur Vergleichmässigung des Schmelzergebnisses von Kupolöfen (Eur 5991), 1978

Machinability of steels (Eur 5132), 1978

Ermittlung der Bruchzähigkeit mit Hilfe von Rissaufweitungsmessungen (Eur 5988), 1978

Application des traitements thermomécaniques à haute température aux aciers soudables (Eur 6055), 1978

Contre-flexion des cylindres de laminoir (Eur 6052), 1978

Automatisation des aciéries à l'oxygène (Eur 6054), 1979

Deformation—induced cavitation in an austenitic stainless steel (Eur 6080), 1979

Casting and solidification of steel (Eur 5861), 1979

Amélioration des propriétés de fatigue des joints soudés: propriétés d'emploi (Eur 5974), 1979

Emboutissabilité des tôles minces (Eur 5990), 1979

Verbesserung von Anlagenelementen automatisierter Warmband-

strassen: Untersuchungen an Stossöfen; Walzwerke (Eur 5713), 1979

Improved mathematical models and control strategies for computerized process control (Eur 6022), 1979

Actions de recherches CECA pendant la période 1965 à 1977 sur la corrosion du fer et des aciers (Eur 6077), 1979

Probleme des stabilen Bandlaufes an neuzeitlichen Kaltwalz-Tandemstrassen (Eur 6066), 1979

Study of the structure of sinters (Eur 5717), 1979

Corrosion des tubes galvanisés dans l'eau chaude: mise au point d'un détecteur de corrosion (Eur 6132), 1979

Détermination des gaz dans les aciers et les fontes (Eur 6159), 1979

Coulée et solidification de l'acier (Eur 6136), 1979

Recristallisation et précipitation provoquées par la déformation à chaud d'aciers de construction soudables microalliés au Niobium (Eur 6150), 1979

Déformation d'aciers de traitement thermique (Eur 6147), 1979

Étude fondamentale de l'examen non destructif des pièces en acier par courant de Foucault (Eur 6139), 1979

Soudabilité des aciers—étude de la fissuration et des méthodes d'examen (Eur 6121), 1979

Chimie de surface de la tôle mince pour fer blanc (Eur 6050), 1979

Utilisation des calculateurs en sidérurgie (Eur 6137), 1979

Quality of products cold-formed at high temperature (Eur 5154), 1979

Temperature, a scattering parameter of creep-rupture (Eur 5139), 1979

Essai d'abattage par taille avec havage intégral en minerais siliceux (Eur 6188), 1979

Études de l'isoformation des échantillons pulvérulents pour la spectrométrie de fluorescence X (Eur 6143), 1979

Bestimmung des Kokillenfallstandes und des Ablösevorganges des Stranges von der Kokille mittels Ultraschall (Eur 6140), 1979

Fehlersuche auf Kaltbandoberflächen mit Opto-elektronischen Kontrollgeräten (Eur 6141), 1979

Untersuchung zur Verbesserung der Haltbarkeit von Hochofenblasformen (Eur 6138), 1979

Investigation of the strip feed and coiling quality on hot wide strip coilers (Eur 5713/IV), 1979

Unformbarkeit von Warmband (Eur 6124), 1979

Influence du manganèse sur les phénomènes de restructuration et de recristallisation ainsi que sur la formation des textures des aciers doux (Eur 6133), 1979

Traitements thermomécaniques des aciers (Eur 6131), 1979

Coulée et solidification de l'acier (Eur 6058), 1979

Fissuration sous les revêtements inoxydables des pièces pour cuves sous pression (Eur 6219), 1979

Acier à haute limite élastique pour cuves de fortes épaisseurs (Eur 6220), 1979

Automatisation des trains continus à chaud à larges bandes (Eur 6090), 1979

Étude du prélèvement d'acier et de fonte liquide et sa mécanisation (Eur 6126), 1979

The influence of the stress-strain diagram on the behaviour of steel structures (Eur 6223), 1979

Prüfen und Putzen von Knüppeln in einer rechnergesteuerten Durchlaufanlage (Eur 6052), 1979

Soudabilité des aciers (Eur 6186), 1979

Schweissbarkeit von Stahl—Festigkeit und Verformbarkeit hochfester schweissbarer Stähle unter Schweissbedingungen (Eur 5873), 1979

Einfluss der Blechdicke auf die Bruchzähigkeit (Eur 6226), 1979

Influence du zinc et des métaux sur la marche du haut fourneau (Eur 6275), 1979

Préparation de perles pour l'analyse par fluorescence X (Eur 6288), 1979

Contrôle de la propreté de peau des billettes de coulée continue par champs électromagnétiques glissants appliqués: niveau de la lingottière (Eur 6136), 1979

Mise au point d'essais industriels d'évaluation de la déchirure lamellaire (Eur 5875), 1979

Mise au point d'un essai pour déterminer la fissuration de la ZAT au cours d'un traitement de détente (Eur 5874), 1979

Poutres hybrides—soudabilités, comportement statique et fatigue (Eur 6190), 1979

Coulée et solidification de l'acier (Eur 6118), 1979

Untersuchung zur Dauerschwingfestigkeit des Stahles St 52–3 an geschweissten 1-Trägern (Eur 6193), 1979

Statische und dynamische COD-Messungen an Grossung Klein-problemen (Eur 6225), 1979

Anreicherung von Fremdatomen in Korngrenzen von Eisen und Stahl (Eur 6224), 1979

Études d'aciers soudables à haute limite d'élasticité pour tôles moyennes (Eur 6277), 1979

Appréciation du risque de rupture brutale des constructions contenant des défauts (Eur 6135), 1979

Microstructures et caractéristiques mécaniques d'aciers bainitiques à basse teneur en carbone (Eur 6199), 1979

Verbesserung von Anlagenelementen automatisierter Warmbreitbandstrassen: Untersuchung von Bandlauf und Wickelqualität an Warmbreitbandstrassen (Eur 5713), 1979

Sélection et utilisation optimales des sites d'essais de corrosion (Eur 6378), 1979

Microstructure et caractéristiques des aciers Mn-Mo à bas carbone (Eur 6195), 1979

Mesure et caractéristiques thermiques des aciers (Eur 6284), 1979

Étude et optimisation des dispositifs de refroidissement dans les laminoirs (Eur 6292), 1979

Propriétés structurales et mécaniques des aciers bainitiques à bas carbone (Eur 6294), 1979

Führungsmodell zur Optimierung des Elektrostahlprozesses (Eur 6217), 1979

Research into the corrosion of carbon steel by hot concentrated saline solutions (Eur 5128), 1979

Entwicklung und Erprobung spektrochemischer Analysenverfahren für nichtmetallische Stoffe mit Hilfe einer Glimmentladungstampe nach Grimm für den Routineeinsatz in der Stahlindustrie (Eur 6290), 1979

Analyse der Ultraschallfender bei der Impulsechoprüfung mit Transversalwellen (Eur 6198), 1979

Herstellen einer Generatorwelle mit 1900 mm Ballendurchmesser durch Zusammenschweissen von zwei Teilstücken nach dem Elektroschlacke-Schweissverfahren (Eur 6353), 1979

Cleavage fracture of structural steels (Eur 6295), 1979

Sampling of hot metal and liquid steel and its mechanization (Eur 5788), 1979

Einfluss der Schweissparameter und der Zusammensetzung von Schweisszusatzwerkstoffen auf die Heissrissneigung im Schweissgut austenitischer Stähle (Eur 6335), 1979

Betriebsnahe Untersuchung von Feuerfestmassen für Hochofenrinnen (Eur 6272), 1979

Kaltumformbarkeit von Stahl: Eignung von Stählen mit hohem Kohlenstoffgehalt zum Drahtziehen (Eur 6334), 1979

Verbesserung der mathematischen Modelle und Steuerstrategien für Prozessführungsrechner: Berechnung der Schadstoffverteilung in Luft für beliebig viele Punktquellen (Eur 6358), 1979

Fatigue des assemblages boulonnés (Eur 6134), 1979

Coulée et solidification de l'acier (Eur 6216), 1979

Automation of pre-setting of continuous wide-strip mills (Eur 5712), 1979

Mesure par ultrasons de la propreté inclusionnaire des aciers (Eur 6289), 1979

Soudabilité des aciers (Eur 6271), 1979

Messen des Durchsatzes von flüssigem und festem Metall (Eur 6296/1), 1979

SCIENCE AND TECHNOLOGY

Many scientific and technical publications have already been mentioned above. Much information is generated within the Commission's own research establishments and by research projects sponsored by the Commission. All this material, especially *Eur* documents should be readily traced through *Euro abstracts* (see below, p. 246).

From 1962 to 1974 there was a quarterly periodical entitled *Eurospectra: scientific and technical review of the Commission of the European Communities.* This was intended to provide information on key scientific and technical topics. It was published in the four official languages and in English. From 1962 to 1967 (Vols. I–VI) it was known as *Euratom bulletin.* In 1968 (Vol. VII) it was known as *Euratom review.* The last issue, Vol. XIII, No. 4, December 1974, contains an author and subject index, 1962–74.

The titles published in English since 1975 in two of the main series of *Eur* documents are listed below.

Information Management

Second report on the activities of the Committee for Information
and Documentation on Science and Technology of the European Communities (Eur 5597), 1977

Final report on project 2: extension and revision of the COST/
accounting scheme to interactive systems of the network (Eur
5627), 1977

Development and use of models for the prediction of costs for
alternative information systems, PT 1 (input model) and PT 2
(output model) (Eur 5693), 1977

Analysis of information marketing structures (Eur 5666), 1977

The connection to EIN packet switched (Eur 5874), 1978

Symposium on the transfer and interpretation of scientific and
technical information in agriculture (Eur 5856), 1978

Investigation of the present and future use of patent literature
(Eur 5952), 1978

Proceedings of the EURONET training workshop 1976 (Eur
5938), 1978

A descriptive model of an information marketing service applied
on the structure of technological services in Denmark (Eur
6003), 1978

Third report on the activities of the Committee for Information
and Documentation on Science and Technology of the European Communities (Eur 6158), 1979

Transfer of information for industry (Eur 6104), 1979

Nuclear Science and Technology

A method to solve the integral transport equation employing a
spatial Legendre expansion (Eur 5339), 1975

Simulation of transport equations with Monte Carlo (Eur 5347),
1975

Catalogue and classification of technical safety rules for light-
water reactors and reprocessing plants (Eur 5362), 1975

Fission gas release from HTR fuel compacts containing a known
quantity of free fuel (Eur 5363), 1975

Interaction between UO_2 kernel and pyrocarbon coating in
irradiated and unirradiated HTR fuel particles (Eur 5368),
1975

Systems analysis as a tool for optimal process strategy (Eur 5372), 1975

The angular gamma flux in an iron slab shield (Eur 5373), 1975

Stress analysis of BWR pressure nozzles (Eur 5374), 1975

LAM-16—a 16-channel low-level amplifier and multiplexer (Eur 5378), 1975

European Community light water reactor safety research projects, experimental issue (Eur 5394), 1975

On the determination of the Pu 240 in solid waste containers by spontaneous fission neutron measurements application to reprocessing plant waste (Eur 5158), 1976

Authorization procedure for the construction and operation of nuclear installations within the EEC Member States (Eur 5284), 1976

The gamma shielding of irradiated U^{235} (Eur 5335), 1976

Recommendations on the measurements of irradiation received by the structural materials of reactors (Eur 5274), 1976

R-curve analysis of burst test results of longitudinally cracked tubes in type AISI 304 stainless steel (Eur 5423), 1976

Use of staff for inspection, maintenance and repair work in the controlled area of nuclear power plants (Eur 5476), 1976

EUCRACK—a finite element mesh generation program for cracked pressure vessel nozzles (Eur 5446), 1976

Plutonium production and utilization forecast in Europe (Eur 5479), 1976

Application of atomic energy in agriculture: annual report 1974 (Eur 5442), 1976

Decontamination of the HFR dismantling cell (Eur 5468), 1976

Theoretical aspects of the eurodyn computer programs for non-linear transient dynamic analysis of structural components (Eur 5473), 1976

Eurodyn computer programs for the transient dynamic analysis of large-displacement, small-strain problems with material non-linearities (Eur 5474), 1976

Dicomics and algorithm for direct computation of minimal cut sets of fault trees (Eur 5487), 1976

On LMFBR Corrosion (Eur 5497), 1976

The Jet project (Eur 5516), 1976

J-integral measurements on various types of specimens in AISI 304 S.S. (Eur 5527), 1976

Removal of long-lived actinides from purex type HAW raffinates by solvent extraction: preliminary results on the use of the neotridecanohydroxamic acid (HX-70) extractant (Eur 5537), 1976

Removal of actinides from high activity wastes by solvent extraction: outline of the research work at Ispra JRC Laboratories (Eur 5527), 1976

Simulation possibilities of radiation effects in glasses used for conditioning high activity waste (Eur 5560), 1976

The motion of hydrogen isotopes in metals and intermetallic compounds (Eur 5465), 1977

Authorization procedure for the construction and operation of nuclear installations within certain non-member States of the European Communities (Eur 5525), 1977

Removals of actinides from high activity wastes by solvent extraction: outline of the research work at Ispra (Eur 5527), 1977

Handbook of materials testing reactors and ancillary hot laboratories in the European Community (Eur 5369), 1977

Stress wave emission: a biographical survey (Eur 5617), 1977

Prototype experiment of an irradiation facility for large HTR fuel specimens in the HFR Petten (Eur 5456), 1977

Authorization procedure for containers and modalities of transport of radioactive substances within the EC Member States (Eur 5663), 1977

Recalibration of high temperature thermocouples exposed to neutron flux (Eur 5648), 1977

Average unavailability of parallel systems composed of elements subject to failure with exponential laws and to periodic tests (Eur 5639), 1977

Post irradiation examination of the fuel discharges from the Trino Vercellese reactor after the 2nd irradiation cycle (Eur 5605), 1977

On the neutron multiplication problem in the passive neutron assay of plutonium bearing materials (Eur 5675), 1977

Programs AWE-1, AWE-2 and BRUNA for the calculation of systems reliability and availability, 1977

Fast pulse discriminator for photon counting at high photon densities (Eur 5631), 1977

The angular gamma flux in an iron shield due to a thin slab source (Eur 5684), 1977

Prediction for the high-level alpha-active waste to be generated by nuclear power stations in the Member states of the European Communities (Eur 5690), 1977

Neutron total and elastic scattering cross sections of ^6Li in the energy range from 0.1 to 3.0 MeV (Eur 5726), 1977

The delay function in finite difference models for nuclear channels thermohydraulic transients (Eur 5709), 1977

Calculation of nuclear reaction cross section with the statistical model (Eur 5722), 1977

The solubility of solid fission products in carbides and nitrides of uranium and plutonium (Eur 5766), 1977

Results of measurements of the thermal contact conductance (Eur 5443), 1977

The separation and recycling of Actinides (Eur 5801), 1977

The Jet project (Eur 5516), 1978

The Jet project (Eur 5791), 1978

ELISA: code for the calculation of systems reliability and availability description and how to use (Eur 5721), 1978

Application of heterogeneous method for the interpretation of exponential experiments (Eur 5658), 1978

Analytical evaluation of fission product sensitivities: mass number 80 to 86 (Eur 5701), 1978

Numerical method for computing partial ionization in gas dynamics (Eur 5761), 1978

The damage to activation ratio for graphite irradiations in the (Gamin technique) (Eur 5795), 1978

Catalogue and classification of technical safety standards, rules and regulations for nuclear power reactors and nuclear fuel cycle facilities (Eur 5849), 1978

The solubility of solid fission products in carbides and nitrides of uranium and plutonium (Eur 5766), 1978

The second Euratom sponsored 900°C HTR fuel irradiation experiment in the HFR Petten Project E 96.02 (Eur 5463), 1978

Prospects for plutonium recycling in light-water reactors in the European Communities (Eur 5936), 1978

A reference regional nuclear fuel centre (Eur 5955), 1978

Post-irradiation examination of a 1300°C-HTR fuel experiment: project J 96.M3 (Eur 5841), 1978

REXCO-EUR Code: user's manual (Eur 5813), 1978

ESP-TIMOC: code manual (Eur 5794), 1978

Automatic evaluation of isotope analysis of nuclear fuels including isotope dilution, mass spectrometry, alpha spectrometry and isotope correlation technique with an appropriate databank (Eur 5669), 1978

COVAL: a computer code for random variables combination and reliability evaluation (Eur 5804), 1978

Thermal desorption (outgassing) of inconel (Eur 5792), 1978

Self-adaptive numerical integrator for analytic functions (Eur 5803), 1978

Dynamic material properties of several steels for fast-breeder reactor safety analysis (Eur 5787), 1978

Modified Monte Carlo procedure for particle transport problems (Eur 5900), 1978

Safety assessment of radioactive waste disposal into geological formations: a preliminary application of fault tree analysis to salt deposits (Eur 5901), 1978

Long-term risk assessment of radioactive waste disposal in geological formations (Eur 5902), 1978

Authorization procedure for the construction and operation of nuclear installations within the EC Member States (Eur 5284), 1978

Surface dose rate contribution by actinides mixed in uranium-plutonium fuel elements (Eur 5917), 1978

Calculation of oxygen distribution in uranium-plutonium oxide fuels during irradiation (Programme CODIF) (Eur 5971), 1978

Report on swelling of MX-type fuels 1973/76: self diffusion in MX-type nuclear fuels out-of-pile and in-pile (Eur 5906), 1978

Removal of long-lived actinides from Purex type HAW raffinates: development of conceptual and experimental studies on solvent extraction (Eur 5816), 1978

Sensitivity analysis of the effect of various key parameters on fission product concentration (mass number 120 to 126) (Eur 5853), 1978

Measurements and observations on microscopic swelling in MX-type fuels (Eur 5907), 1978

Arisings of cladding wastes from nuclear fuel in the European Community (Eur 5969), 1978

Programme of research and development on plutonium recycling in light water reactors (Eur 6002), 1978

Sodium-fuel interaction: dropping experiments and subassembly test (Eur 5854), 1978

Ultra-high vacuum target assembly for charged particle irradiations in the materials research field (Eur 5908), 1978

Porosity in MX-type fuels and its stability (Eur 5812), 1978

Self-diffusion of plutonium in uranium-plutonium mononitride (Eur 5905), 1978

Thermal stresses in cracked nuclear fuel pellets (Eur 5973), 1978

Comparative analysis of a hypothetical loss of flow accident in a LMFBR using different computer models for a common Benchmark problem (Eur 5946), 1978

Users' report of HIP-TEDDI (Eur 6001), 1978

First technical meeting on the nuclear transmutation of Actinides, 1978

Recommendations to designers aimed at minimizing radiation dose incurred in operation, maintenance, inspection and repair of light water reactors (Eur 6005), 1978

Evaluation of long term leaching of borosilicate glasses (Eur 5947), 1978

The Community's R and D programme on radioactive waste management and storage (Eur 6128), 1979

The pressurized and boiling water loops BOWAL and PRIL for boiling mixing studies of the heat transfer division JRC/Italy (Eur 6045), 1979

A method for the quantitative metallographic analysis of nuclear fuels (programme QMA) (Eur 6111), 1979

First technical meeting on the nuclear transmutation of Actinides (Eur 5897), 1979

Monitoring of plutonium contaminated solid waste streams (Eur 6027), 1979

Preliminary design for a plutonium oxide storage unit (Eur 6087), 1979

Report 1 on swelling of MX-type fuels 1973–76: fabrication and characterization of MX-type fuels and fuel pins (Eur 6154), 1979

Description of a reference mixed oxide fuel fabrication plant (MOFFP) (Eur 6162), 1979

Sensibility analysis of the effect of various key parameters on fission product concentration (Eur 6059), 1979

Sensibility analysis of the effect of various key parameters on fission product concentration (Eur 6018), 1979

Proceedings of the colloquium 'The response of liquids to dynamic tension' (Eur 6046), 1979

Lecture notes on cross-section adjustment procedures (Eur 6041), 1979

A study on entrapment: splashing of liquid UO^2 over small sodium volumes (Eur 6113), 1979

List of reference materials for non-destructive assay of U, Th and Pu isotopes (Eur 6089), 1979

EEC-sponsored theoretical studies of gas cloud explosion pressure loadings (Eur 6119), 1979

Introduction of neutron metrology for reacter radiation damage (Eur 6182), 1979

SALP—3: a computer program for fault-tree analysis (Eur 6183), 1979

Testing and evaluation of the properties of various potential materials for immobilizing high activity waste (Eur 6213), 1979

High flux materials testing reactor HFR Petten (Eur 5700), 1979

Analysis of stress corrosion data by means of the statistic of extreme values (Eur 6063), 1979

Non-destructive assay of fissile materials by detection and multiplicity analysis of spontaneous neutrons (Eur 6309), 1979

Post-irradiation analysis of the Gundremmingen BWR spent fuel (Eur 6301), 1979

GENERAL INFORMATION

The Spokesman's Group issues frequent press releases as does the London office of the Commission. *Press review* consists of photocopies of press cuttings prepared by the Spokesman's Group.

Euroforum (1978–   ) appears about twenty times a year and is a general interest news magazine produced in Brussels. *European Community* (1957–   ) is a monthly produced in London. There are other general interest periodicals produced for other countries which are listed below (p. 133).

In 1979 there were fifty-three issues in the series *Background Report*. Each issue is devoted to a particular topic of interest. From 1970 until 1976 when it took its present title the series was called *Background Notes*. It is produced in London. *Community Topics* (1961–72) was a series of occasional publications on aspects of the work of the European Communities, also produced in London. Brief summaries on Community activities and policies can be found in the series *European File* (1979–). Longer summaries can be found in *European Documentation* (1975–). In 1979 the following titles appeared:

Number	Title
1	The European Community's budget
2	The agricultural policy of the European Community
3	European economic and monetary union
4	25 years of European Community external relations
5	The second enlargement of the European Community

Documentation européenne: série agricole was an irregular limited distribution series in the four official languages. The contents, 1968 to 1973, are listed in *Catalogue of the publications of the European Community Institutions 1972–1973*, pp. 454–5. Each issue consisted of a folder containing loose sections on the topics discussed.

Documentation européenne: série pédagogique was a quarterly limited distribution series in French. From 1966 to 1971 it was known as *Documentation européenne: dossiers pédagogiques*. The contents, 1966 to 1973, are listed in *Catalogue of the publications of the European Community Institutions 1972–1973*, pp. 441–3. In all there were fifty-six issues before it ceased publication in 1974. Each issue consisted of a folder containing loose sections on the topics discussed. From 1968 there were analogous series in the three other official languages and English. The English series was *European studies: teachers' series* which was published under the auspices of the Centre for Contemporary European Studies, University of Sussex. There had been twenty-two issues between 1968 and 1975.

Documentation européenne: série syndicale et ouvrière was a quarterly limited distribution series in the four official languages. The contents, 1968 to 1974, are listed in No. 74/4. The contents,

1968 to 1973, can also be found in *Catalogue of the publications of the European Community Institutions 1972–1973*, pp. 462–3. There were twenty-seven issues in all. Each issue consisted of a folder containing loose sections on the topics discussed.

Twelve issues of *Eurobarometre* have appeared since 1974. Reports of these opinion polls also appear in the *Bulletin of the European Communities*, see above p. 37. The data from these opinion polls is available in machine readable form at the Belgian Archives for the Social Sciences, Louvain-la-Neuve and also at the Inter-University Consortium for Political and Social Research, Ann Arbor, Michigan, USA.

The following reports of opinion polls have also been published:

Europeans and European unification, 1972

L'opinion des Européens sur les aspects régionaux et agricoles du Marché commun, l'unification politique de l'Europe et l'information du public, 1971

Satisfaction et insatisfaction quant aux conditions de vie dans les pays de la Communauté européene, 1974

L'Europe vue par les Européens, 1974

European men and women, 1975

European consumers, 1976

The perception of poverty in Europe, 1977

Science and European public opinion, 1977

The attitude of the working population to retirement, 1978

The European public's attitudes to scientific and technical development, 1979

European men and women in 1978, 1979

Chômage et recherche d'un emploi: attitudes et opinions des publics européens, 1979

The Community today published in 1980 is a valuable general book on the European Communities in an historical and political context.

The *Directory of the Commission of the European Communities* is revised regularly and lists Commission officials to the level A3.

Information (1972–)

This is an irregular series in the official languages. Each issue provides background information in one of the following areas:

Commercial policy
Competition
Consumers
Development
Economy and finance
Energy
Environment
External relations
Freedom of movement
Internal market
Political affairs
Regional policy
Research and development
Right of establishment
Social policy
Statistics
Transport

Information periodicals

As part of its information operation the Commission publishes a number of periodicals, which are directed at particular countries, as follows:

Avrupa toplulugu (Turkey)
Background information (USA)
Berichte und Informationen (Germany)
Borascáil (Ireland)
Comunità europee (Italy)
Communauté européenne: informations (France)
Communautés européennes: lettre d'information (Switzerland)
Community report (Ireland)
Comunidad europea (Spain)
Documentos de la Comunidad europea (Spain)
Dokumentation (Denmark)
EG Magazin (Germany)
EUR info (Belgium)
Europa (Denmark)
Europa-bericht (Belgium)

Europa-Informationen für die Jugendpresse (Germany)
Europa van morgen (Netherlands)
Die Europäischen Regionen (Germany)
Europe—magazine of the European Community (USA)
European Community/Communauté européenne (Canada)
European news (Thailand)
Guide (Denmark)
Informazioni e notizie sindicali (Italy)
News (USA)
Synspunkt (Denmark)
30 jours d'Europe (France)

Most of these titles are available gratis from the Information Offices of the Commission in the countries concerned.

There are a number of information periodicals of a slightly more specialized nature which in most cases circulate in all the Community countries.

Green Europe newsletter (1979–   ) is an irregular periodical on agriculture which in part replaces the *Newsletter on the Common Agricultural Policy* (1963–78). This was more detailed and usually included a summary of the annual report on the agricultural situation in the Community as special issues. No. 6, 1977 was the last to appear in English. Topics covered between 1963 and 1971 are listed in *Catalogue des publications 1952–1971*, Vol. 1, pp. 274–83; those covered during 1972 and 1973 in *Catalogue of the publications of the European Community Institutions 1972–1973*, pp. 471–6.

Integration: European studies review (1968–71) was an interdisciplinary journal on European integration. It appeared in twelve issues of which the last four were in English.

Industry and society (1968–   ) and *Trade union information* (1974–   ) are produced in Brussels, but *Trade union news* (1969–75) was produced in London.

Women of Europe (1978–   ) is a title on women's studies, with occasional supplements.

Miscellaneous information publications

The London office of the Commission issues a wide range of information publications gratis. Many of these are regularly updated. Some of the more recent publications include the following:

The Common Agricultural Policy, 1978
The Community and the common good, 1977
Europe and our food, 1978
The European Community: facts and figures, 1979
The European Community: today and tomorrow, 1979
The European Community: your future, 1979
The European Community and the third world, 1977
Everyday Europe: how the European Community helps consumers, 1975
Grants and loans from the European Community, 1979
The little citizens of Europe, 1979
Wales in the European Community, 1979
Working together: the Institutions of the European Community, 1979

DOCUMENTATION AND BIBLIOGRAPHY

Transatom bulletin: information on translations covering eastern nuclear literature (1960–   ) lists documents on nuclear and para-nuclear subjects written originally in eastern languages (that is Russian, Japanese, etc.) which are available in translation.

There is an annual classified list of recent additions to the Library of the Commission in Luxembourg; an irregular *Acquisitions récentes de la bibliothèque*, and an annual *List of periodicals*.

The Central Library of the Commission in Brussels publishes a valuable monthly *List of additions to the Library*. This was formerly arranged according to the Universal Decimal Classification, but since October 1978 has been arranged according to the OECD *Macrothesaurus*. Official publications of the European Communities as well as many research reports and other documents are included in this list.

Europäische Integration Auswahlbibliographie (1974–   ) is a periodical bibliography compiled in the Bonn office of the Commission. It includes both books and periodical articles. There had been forty-one issues by the end of 1979.

The London and Washington offices of the Commission produce useful short reading lists from time to time.

CHAPTER 5

Eurostat—Publications of the Statistical Office of the European Communities

THE STATISTICAL OFFICE OF THE EUROPEAN COMMUNITIES

The main concern of Eurostat is to provide a source of information and a 'practical tool' for the use of the Institutions of the European Communities and the member countries. Publication is to some extent a secondary activity. The current activities of Eurostat are described in the *Fourth statistical programme of the European Communities 1979–80*, *COM*(78) 124 final, of 3 April 1978. In describing the statistical work undertaken this document states that:

> considerable importance is . . . attached to the ideal of achieving a suitable balance between, on the one hand, those types of statistics which are largely intended to give an up-to-the minute picture of economic and social developments, particularly as regards employment, production, prices and external relations, and, on the other hand, those types of statistics which are intended more for use in describing structures or analysing society.

Many data are collected by the statistical offices of the member countries, especially the following:

—foreign trade statistics
—monthly, quarterly and annual industrial statistics

—employment and unemployment figures on a standardized basis

Considerable emphasis is placed on the harmonization and integration of data.

In recent years Eurostat has made increasing use of computers which are regarded as the 'essential means for the processing and storage of data, and sometimes of collection and dissemination'.

There are three main data bases and systems in use:

CRONOS   consists of about 600,000 regularly updated time series
OSIRIS   system for the production of statistical tables
AISE   archive of socio-economic information

In the long term it is hoped that the existence of Euronet will lead to improvements in the circulation and exchange of statistical information.

Eurostat is organized into six Directorates:

A   General statistics, statistical methods and liaison activities
B   National accounts
C   Demographic and social statistics
D   Agriculture, forestry and fisheries statistics
E   Industrial, environment and services statistics
F   External trade, ACP and non-member countries statistics

The ECSC had a statistical service from 1953. Eurostat was constituted in its present form in 1958 to serve the three Communities. Current information on Eurostat activities and publications can be found in the monthly *Eurostat news* (1976–).

GENERAL STATISTICAL PUBLICATIONS

Basic statistics of the Community (1958–)

Basic statistics of the Community is a useful little compendium of statistical information which has appeared in seventeen editions between 1958 and 1979. The seventeenth edition is sub-titled a 'comparison with some European countries, Canada, the United

States of America, Japan and the Union of Soviet Socialist Republics'.

The seventeenth edition is divided into fifteen sections as follows:

Population
Labour force
Research and education
National accounts
Agriculture
Energy
Industry
Transport
External trade
Prices
Earnings and hours of work
Social protection
Standard of living
Finance
Regional population and gross domestic product

The data in the seventeenth edition are mostly from 1977 but with some 1978 figures.

General statistics

In 1959 Eurostat brought out a monthly publication in French and German called *Notes statistiques rapides*. This was replaced in 1960 by the *General statistical bulletin* which was usually available in English as well as the official languages and appeared eleven times a year. In 1969 its title was changed to *General statistics*. It eventually ceased publication in 1978 with No. 4/6 and was replaced by *Eurostatistics: data for short-term economic analysis*.

There were various changes of format in *General statistics* over the years, but its purpose remained the same: to give a monthly survey of the most recent figures in order to indicate short-term economic developments. As the chosen indicators remained more or less the same, *General statistics* could be used in order to discern long-term trends.

From 1969 to 1972 data were arranged by country as well as by subject. The *General statistical bulletin* carried a 'special statistical report' from time to time which dealt with one or more subjects of topical interest. Since 1973, however, there were no special reports or features other than the subject tables.

Data were provided by the statistical offices of the member countries but in some cases were adjusted to ensure comparability.

In 1978 the main headings were as follows:

Population and employment
Industry
Internal trade and services
Transport
External trade
Price and wage indices
Finance
Balance of payments

In each issue could be found the most recent figures available and those of the eleven previous months together with the monthly averages for the two previous years.

Eurostatistics: data for short-term economic analysis (1979–)

This replaces *General statistics*. It is available in two separate editions. 'A' is in German, French and Dutch. 'B' is in Danish, English and Italian. Edition 'A' is sent to press on the second Tuesday of each month and 'B' on the fourth Tuesday. Data is updated not only from one month to the next but also from each edition to the next.

The object of this publication is to disseminate socio-economic statistical data in order to facilitate short-term economic analysis. It is divided into two main sections; 'community tables' and 'country tables' but it also includes articles and a list of recent statistical publications together with a one page summary of 'main developments'. In the section of community tables there are ten main headings:

National accounts esa
Employment

Unemployment
Index of industrial production
Opinions in industry
Output
External trade
Prices
Financial statistics
Balance of payments

The preface to No. 11B, 1979, states that the community tables:

contain the main indicators useful for following short-term
economic developments in the Community as a whole and in the
Member States, supplemented by a certain amount of structural
data relating to 1975. This part of the bulletin is intended to
make possible real comparisons between countries and therefore only contains data which has been harmonised by Eurostat
on the basis of common criteria, this explains many of the
differences from national series.

Statistical information (Informations statistiques) (1953–67)

Until it ceased publication in 1967 this was one of the most
important statistical publications, having articles on a wide range
of subjects. There is an index of the articles which were published
between 1953 and 1964, issued as a supplement under the title:
Index of articles published in 'Statistical information' 1953–64,
1965.

The last issue of Statistical information (No. 4, 1967) noted that:
'It has become apparent that the publications of the Statistical
Office need to be regrouped, and this will be done gradually'.

The role of reporting studies and surveys not covered by other
statistical serials was taken over by Statistical studies and surveys.

Statistical Studies and Surveys (Études et enquêtes statistiques) (1968–   )

This series contains accounts of surveys, articles on methodology and quantified results which are not part of any of the regular statistical series, except that for 1968 only *Études et enquêtes statistiques* replaced *Statistical information* and *Social statistics*. The contents of this series for 1968 to 1971 are listed in *Catalogue des publications 1952–1971*, Vol. 1, pp. 284–5. The contents of the more recent issues are given below.

Number	*Title*
1/1972	Le financement public de la recherche et du développement dans les pays de la Communauté: troisième rapport du groupe d'experts–statisticiens au groupe de travail 'Politique de la recherche scientifique et technique'
2/1972	Annual investments in fixed assets in the industrial enterprises of the member countries of the European Communities, 1964–70
3/1972	1. A system of integrated price and volume measures (indices), by T.P. Hill
	2. Enquête sur les prix de détail et taux d'équivalence de pouvoir d'achat à la consommation—1972
1/1974	Public expenditure on research and development in the Community countries, analysis by objectives 1969–73: 1st report from the sub-committee 'Statistics' to the 'Committee on Scientific and Technical Research' (CREST)
2/1974	Annual investments in fixed assets in the industrial enterprises of the member countries of the European Communities, 1970–2
1/1975	Public expenditure on research and development in the Community countries, 1974
2/1975	Annual investments in fixed assets in the industrial enterprises of the member countries of the European Communities, 1971–3
3/1975	The measurement of industrial concentration: a reassessment based on European data
4/1975	Commerce extérieur et approvisionnement en manganèse de la Communauté européenne: étude statistique dans le cadre du marché mondial

Miscellaneous publications

General statistical publications usually have an orange colour. Other recent documents of this colour include:

> *Confidentiality and business statistics in the European Communities*, 1977
> *Consumer price indexes in the European Community*, 1976
> *Survey of retail prices*, 1975

Two older publications which do not belong in any particular statistical series are:

> *The Common Market ten years on: tables 1958–1967*
> *Economic facts in figures 1955–1970*

Statistical reports of various kinds are carried in *Eurostat news* (1976–). There was a special number in 1978 which contained three papers on purchasing power parities.

FOREIGN TRADE STATISTICS CLASSIFICATIONS

There are a number of systems of classification, coding and nomenclature which have been used in the preparation of foreign trade statistics. NIMEXE is the most elaborate. CST has fewer codes and is equivalent to the United Nations Standard International Trade Classification (SITC). CCT was derived from the Brussels Tariff Nomenclature (BTN) which is now known as the Customs Co-operation Council Nomenclature (CCCN).

There were four editions of the *Classification statistique et tarifaire pour le commerce international* (CST) published as follows:

Edition	Year	Language
First	1960	in the official languages
Second	1961	in the official languages
Third	1963	in French only
Fourth	1964	in French only

Code numérique statistique de la nomenclature du TDC was published in 1976 in French only. It gives the CCT statistical codes used in *Tariff statistics 1975.* It replaces the loose-leaf *Code numérique statistique de la nomenclature du tarif douanier commun des Communautés Européennes* published in a version of 1970 and another of 1972 for which updating supplements had been published. Previous versions of the CCT which appeared between 1961 and 1969 were known as *Tableaux de concordance entre le code numérique statistique et la nomenclature du Tarif douanier commun des Communautés Européennes.*

A loose-leaf volume entitled *Tariff classifications* was published in the official languages in 1977.

The Nomenclature of goods for the external trade statistics of the Community and statistics of trade between member states has been published in three loose-leaf editions in the official languages:

First 1966   Second 1969   Third 1973

The third edition replaced a provisional English language edition also dated 1973. This version appeared first in French in the *Journal officiel*, No. L161, 17 July 1972. The NIMEXE has now appeared annually in the *Official journal* since 1975 as follows:

L331, 24 December 1975
L343, 13 December 1976
L325, 19 December 1977
L353, 18 December 1978
L346, 31 December 1979

The code itself has become more elaborate over time: it specified 4,828 items in 1966 but now specifies over 7,000.

Geonomenclature is an annual publication which standardizes the country nomenclature for the external trade statistics of the Community and statistics of trade between member countries. The 1979 version is reproduced from *Official journal*, No. L339 of 5 December 1978, pp. 6–11. It first appeared in 1962 when it was known as the *Standard country classification for foreign trade statistics of EEC member countries (Code géographique commun pour les statistiques du commerce extérieur des pays de la CEE).* From 1971 to 1975 its title was changed to the *Common country nomenclature for the foreign trade statistics of the member states of the European Communities* (NCP). It has always been available in the official languages. The GEONOM is not altered during the course of any one year, but may be altered from one year to the next after the Commission has consulted the Committee on External Trade Statistics. It is stressed that the GEONOM does not constitute an expression of opinion on the political status of any country or territory. Countries are represented by a three-figure code and various economic zones by a four-figure code.

Nomenclature douanière pour le commerce extérieur: codifications des marchandises et des pays was the trade classification in use for data prepared by the statistical division of the High Authority of the ECSC. It was published in the official languages in 1956.

List of chemicals in NIMEXE together with their tariff classification and NIMEXE code was published separately in 1978. This list provides all relevant information as to the tariff and statistical classification of the chemical products falling within chapters 28 and 29 of the Common Customs Tariff. It is also a multilingual list of 1,300 chemical terms in the six languages.

FOREIGN TRADE STATISTICS

In 1975 the Council passed a regulation ((EEC) No. 1736/75 of 24 June) which provides for the implementation of a standard methodology for the collection of trade statistics (*Official journal*, No. L183 of 1975). This was brought into effect on 1 January 1978 and has resulted in the harmonization of concepts and definitions, but it also means that comparisons with earlier years may not be strictly accurate.

Trade statistics are collected by the statistical offices of the member countries, and are sent to Eurostat in a standard form.

According to Article 39 of the regulation mentioned above the Commission is obliged to publish three sets of annual trade statistics:

1. analytical tables based on NIMEXE
2. analytical tables based on the statistical and tariff classification for external trade (CST) or on the standard international trade classification (SITC)
3. tariff statistics

Foreign trade statistics usually have a vermilion red-coloured cover.

The first foreign trade statistics appeared under the title *Foreign trade statistics: first series: synoptic tables*, and consisted of a retrospective volume which covered the trade of the member states of the EEC and associated countries, as well as other trading countries, published in 1959, and six issues published in 1960. The retrospective volume carried the title *Yearbook 1953–1958 of foreign trade by country of origin and destination* and was published in the official languages and in English. It was produced in order to facilitate comparisons before and after the creation of the Common Market. The six issues of 1960, again published in the official languages and English, gave detailed commodity statistics on the foreign trade of the member states of the EEC and associated countries for the period 1956 to 1959.

The *Monthly external trade bulletin* is designed to provide rapid information on short-term trends in the foreign trade of the European Communities, trade between member states and with third countries. The data are classified according to the Standard International Trade Classification (SITC) and the GEONOM. It provides monthly and quarterly results. From 1961 to 1975 this publication was known as *Foreign trade: monthly statistics (Commerce extérieur: statistique mensuelle)*. From 1961 to 1973 it appeared in French and German only but from 1974 the text has been presented in all the official languages. Parts are numbered to No. 12 in each year but in the past they have frequently been printed together so that in 1974, for example, there were actually only eight issues. Statistics relating to the enlarged Community have appeared since No. 5/6 of 1973 when some reduction in the quantity of cumulated data took place.

Beginning with 1975 there have been annual special numbers of the *Monthly external trade bulletin* which summarize the data on main trends in the trade of the European Communities since 1958.

Between 1969 and 1979 there were thirty-three supplements to the monthly trade statistics entitled *EC* [or *EEC*] *trade by commodity classes and main countries* [or *by areas*]. Two further supplements (to Nos. 4 and 5, 1969) were studies of the foreign trade of the Soviet Union and Eastern European countries, which were part of the series *Bloc oriental* (see below, p. 146).

Trade flows is a bi-monthly analysis of the external trade and related statistics of the trading partners of the European Communities, particularly with the state-trading countries.

Foreign trade of the Peoples' Republic of China 1974–1978, 1979 is an analysis of trade by both country and product with particular emphasis on trade with the European Communities. It is available in two editions, English and French, and German and Italian.

Bloc oriental: the foreign trade of the eastern European countries (1963–74). This was an irregular publication usually published in French and German only. Each issue dealt with the foreign trade of the Soviet Union or other eastern European countries. The following have been published:

1963	Nos. 1–5
1964	Nos. 1–2
1965	Nos. 1–5
1966	Nos. 1–5
1967	Nos. 1–2
1968	Nos. 1–4
1969	Nos. 1–6
1970	Nos. 1–3
1971	No. 1
1974	No. 1

There is a *Statistical telegram* (1975–   ) which is used to give a short summary of certain types of information such as a summary of foreign trade trends in a given period or some special aspect of the foreign trade of the European Communities.

Analytical tables

From 1958 to 1975 *analytical tables* were published of foreign trade according to the CST. They have usually only been available in a bilingual French/German edition. For 1976 onwards the 'Standard International Trade Classification rev. 2' has been used instead of the CST. The most recent set consists of eight volumes published in 1979 covering 1978; it is available both in hard copy and in microfiche.

Far more prominence is given to the *Analytical tables of foreign trade* (NIMEXE) which has been published in the official languages since 1966. From 1966 to 1969 there were twelve quarterly volumes each cumulating in each year. Since 1970 there have been thirteen annual volumes. There is now a microfiche as well as a printed edition; the microfiche is usually available two or three months before the hard copy. The contents of the volumes relating to 1978 are as follows:

A   Live animals and animal and vegetable products; fats and oils; foodstuffs, beverages and tobacco

B   Mineral products

C   Products of the chemical and allied industries

D   Plastics, rubber, raw hides and skins, leather, furskins and articles thereof; saddlery and harness; morocco leather goods; travel goods

E   Wood, cork, paper, paperboard and articles thereof; manufactures of plaiting materials and basketware

F   Textiles and textile articles; shoes; headgear; umbrellas and sunshades

G   Articles of stone, of plaster, of cement, ceramics; glass and glassware; pearls, precious stones, jewelry; coins

H   Iron and steel

I   Base metals (except iron and steel) and articles thereof

J   Machinery and mechanical appliances; electrotechnical apparatus

K   Means of transportation

L   Optical, photographic, cinematographic and medical instruments, apparatus and appliances; precision instruments; clocks and watches; musical instruments; sound recorders and reproducers; arms and ammunitions; miscellaneous articles

A–L   Corrigendum

Z   Countries—Products (revised version)

Although corrigenda to the printed volumes are published the fully corrected data are usually only available in the microfiche edition.

Tariff statistics

The third set of figures which Eurostat is obliged to publish is *Tariff statistics* (1961–   ). This was formerly a limited distribution publication in French and German only. From the volume for 1975 onwards it is a sales publication in four volumes but still available in French and German only. The following volumes were published between 1961 and 1973:

1961	Tableau 1	Import and Export
1962	Tableau 1–4	Import
	Tableau 1	Export
1963	Tableau 1–4	Import
	Tableau 1	Export
1964	Tableau 5	Import
1967	Tableau 1–3	Import
1968	Tableau 1–3	Import
1969	Tableau 1	Import
	Tableau 2–3	Import
1970	Tableau 1	Import
	Tableau 2–3	Import
1971	Tableau 1	Import
	Tableau 2–3	Import
1972	Tableau 1	
	Tableau 2–3	
1973	Tableau 1	
	Tableau 2–3	

For the years 1974 and 1975 there are four volumes relating to imports only which are numbered I–IV.

The Common Customs Tariff is now brought up to date annually. The most recent version is contained in *Official journal*, L342 of 31 December 1979.

European Coal and Steel Community

There is a separate yearbook of foreign trade in the products of the European Coal and Steel Community. Its full title is *Commerce extérieur de la Communauté [ECSC—CECA[: résultats par états membres* (1956–). It carries the cover title: 'Commerce extérieur: produits CECA'. Data are given on the foreign trade in iron and steel, iron and manganese ore, scrap iron, and coal. This series has been published in the official languages as follows from 1956 to 1958:

No.	Period covered	Published
1	January to December 1955	1956
2	April 1955 to March 1956	1956
3	July 1955 to June 1956	1956
4	1956	1957
5	January to March 1957	1957
6	January to June 1957	1957
7	July to December 1957	1958
8	1957	1958

From 1959–72 there were annual volumes covering 1958–71. 1973 data did not appear until 1977 and the data for subsequent years is available in microfiche only. The use of microform seems to have made the data available more rapidly, for example, 1978 figures were ready in 1979.

STATISTICS OF ASSOCIATED OVERSEAS COUNTRIES

Eurostat considers its task in this area to be one of supplying the Commission with statistics related to the implementation of the co-operation agreements which have been made with developing countries and preparing statistical files for use in negotiations with these countries. Two data bases have been created. ZCA1 contains foreign trade statistics. ZPVD contains data in the following areas:

  demography, social indicators and prices
  geography, food supply
  transport, services
  external aid
  debt
  public finance, exchange rates, external assets
  balance of payments
  agricultural and industrial production

Data are collected from the statistical offices in the countries concerned and from various international organizations, most notably:

Economic Commission for Africa
Food and Agriculture Organization
International Labour Office
International Monetary Fund
OECD
Unesco
United Nations
World Bank

The aim is to collect, analyse and disseminate this information as rapidly as possible in a standardized format. Even so it is recognized that there are anomalies when one makes comparisons between countries, though it is hoped that these will be reduced in future.

General statistics

The first publication of statistics relating to associated countries was *Bulletin général des statistiques AOM* (1963–4). It consisted of four numbers of which Nos. 1, 2 and 4 were in two parts. No. 1 was published in 1963 and the rest in 1964. It was available only in French. AOM (Associés d'outre-mer) includes all the overseas associated countries and territories before arrangements were much expanded by the signing of the Lomé Convention. The tables present such statistics as were available, hence any gaps.

Overseas associates: statistical bulletin (1963) continues the numbering of *Bulletin général des statistiques AOM*. No. 5a was a glossary or classification of the terms used. The other issues were Nos. 5, 6 and 7. It was published in the official languages and English. The main headings used were as follows:

Population and social statistics
Agricultural statistics: production and marketing
Industrial production and transport statistics
Public finance
Foreign trade

Data were presented according to the standard numerical code explained in the 'glossary'. No. 7 gave comparative data over several years for all the AOM countries—usually 1961 to 1964.

Overseas associates: yearbook of general statistics (1966, 1967) was a single volume in the official languages and English. It provided tables of general statistics for each of the AOM countries.

Overseas associates: statistical memento (1966, 1968) was a single pocket-size volume in the official languages and English. According to the preface to the 1966 volume its aim was to:

> provide in easily accessible form the general information needed by all those who are interested in the development of the associated countries, who need facts and figures on these countries and who are endeavouring to reach general conclusions on the basis of documentary material sometimes established only with considerable difficulty.

The main headings were:

Population
Agriculture
Mines, industry, transport
Public finance and prices
Foreign trade

Associates: general and foreign trade statistics (1961–71) was a quarterly published in French only. It was divided into two sections: general statistics and foreign trade statistics for the AOM countries. For trade statistics only it continued *Associés d'outre-mer: statistique de commerce extérieur*.

Annuaire statistique des AOM appeared once, in 1970, in the French language only. It was divided into two sections: 'Les états africains et malgache associés (EAMA)', and 'les territoires d'outre-mer (TOM) et les Départements d'outre-mer (DOM)'. The EAMA (AASM) were the countries associated by the Yaoundé Conventions. Both parts of this volume were arranged according to the headings used in *Annuaire statistique des EAMA*, 1969.

Statistical yearbook of the AASM (*Annuaire statistique des EAMA*) (1969, 1970, 1973) was published in French only for 1969 and 1970, but in the official languages for 1973. In the official catalogues it is actually described as a biennial. The volume for 1970 is the first part of *Annuaire statistique des AOM*, 1970. The main headings used in 1973 were:

Population, employment, education, health
National accounts
Agriculture, livestock, fishing
Energy
Industry
Transport
External trade
Prices and earnings
Public finance
European Development Fund

The publications described so far preceded the signing of the Lomé Convention. The first publication to give data for the ACP countries was *Selected figures for 'associables' countries*, (1974). The aim of this publication as stated in the introduction,

> is to help the structure of and latest developments in these countries to be more widely known. It is intended to assist in preliminary researches and to give an overall picture of the economies of these countries in particular with regard to trade with other countries principally the Community.

'Main statistical indicators' are given for each of the ACP countries, that is, population, national accounts, agricultural production and foreign trade.

The most recent statistical compilation is *ACP: statistical yearbook 1970–1976*. This was published in English and French in 1978. It includes sixteen tables for each of the fifty-two ACP countries and also summary tables.

Foreign trade statistics

There was a series of foreign trade statistics published in French and German only, entitled *Associés d'outre-mer: statistique du commerce extérieur* (1959–68). The pattern of publication was as follows:

Year	Frequency	Number of parts
1959	annual	2
1960	annual	2

1961	annual	2
1962	quarterly	6
1963	quarterly	8
1964–5	irregular	45 (see below)
1966	monthly	12
1967	monthly	11
1968	irregular	6

In the 1964–5 parts countries were dealt with as follows:

Country	Part(s)
Chad	1, 10, 19, 44, 45
Gabon	2, 11, 20, 44, 45
Central Africa	3, 12, 21, 44, 45
Congo (Brazzaville)	4, 13, 22, 44, 45
Togo	5, 26
Madagascar	6, 15
Cameroon	7, 14, 28, 35
Mauritania	8
Dahomey	9, 23, 44
Ivory Coast	16, 29, 44
Congo (Leopoldville)	17, 31
Guadeloupe, Guinea, Martinique and Réunion	18, 32, 44, 45
Curaco-Aruba	24, 38
Niger	25, 44
Senegal	27, 34, 40, 45
French Somaliland	36
Mauritius	30
Upper Volta	37
St. Pierre et Miquelon	39
New Caledonia	41
Comores	43

The series continued in *Associates: general and foreign trade statistics* for 1969–71. Much of the information contained in this series was consolidated in the fourteen-volume set *Associates: foreign trade* in 1968 and 1969.

There have been three issues of *Associates—foreign trade: yearbook* (1970–73), each in two volumes:

Date	Covering the years
1970	1967–9
1971	1969–70
1973	1970–1

The issues for 1970 and 1971 were written in the official languages and English, the issue for 1973 in the official languages. These yearbooks are part of a retrospective series of publications on the foreign trade statistics of the AASM countries. They continue from the series *Associates: foreign trade* of which the following were published in English and the official languages:

Title	Covering the years	Date
Mauritanie	1959–66	1969
Mali	1959–66	1969
Haute-Volta	1959–66	1969
Niger	1959–66	1969
Sénégal	1959–66	1969
Côte-d'Ivoire	1959–66	1969
Togo	1959–66	1969
Dahomey	1959–66	1969
Cameroun	1959–66	1969
République Centafricaine	1959–66	1968
Tchad	1962–66	1968
Gabon	1959–66	1968
Congo-Brazzaville	1959–66	1968
Madagascar	1959–66	1968

There were no volumes dealing with the following countries:

Democratic Republic of the Congo (Zaire)
Somalia
Rwanda and Burundi

because the detailed information required for complete statistical coverage, comparable with that carried out for the other countries, was not available. *Associates—foreign trade: yearbook* for 1970 and 1971 covers the same countries as *Associates: foreign trade*, but the 1973 volumes also cover Zaire. Products are coded according to the Statistical and Tariff Classification (CST). Each of the two volumes for 1973 is in two parts of which the first is common to both:

Synoptic tables of the Community of nine with the AASM
Synoptic and analytical tables of the foreign trade of each associated state

There have been two issues of *ACP: yearbook of foreign trade statistics*. The volume published in 1975 has the sub-title 'statistical abstract: 1968–1973'. A further volume published in 1977 covers 1968–76. Both volumes are in English and French only. They are divided into three sections:

the ACP countries and world trade
the trade of individual ACP countries
the ACP and the European Communities

Analysis of trade between the European Community and the ACP states is a special study which analyses the development and structure of the trade between the European Communities and the ACP states, particularly after the Lomé Convention. It includes a section on the trade between the ACP and the candidate countries (Greece, Spain and Portugal). This study was published in 1979 in English and French only.

The CRONOS file on external trade is used to produce a quarterly publication *EC trade with the ACP states and the South Mediterranean States* (1979–   ). This publication, in English and French only, classifies trade according to the SITC.

Although this had not been done consistently in the past, statistical publications about the associated countries now have an olive green-coloured cover.

ECONOMIC AND FINANCIAL STATISTICS

Economic and financial statistics usually have a purple-coloured cover. The main categories of published data are:

national accounts
input–output tables
regional statistics and accounts

balances of payments
tax statistics

As well as the main series, from 1975 there has been a monthly
entitled *Prices: press notice* which gives recent information.

National accounts

NATIONAL ACCOUNTS (1966–72)

Up to 1966 national accounts statistics were published only in the
General statistical bulletin. From 1966 to 1972 the following seven
annual volumes were published in the official languages and
English:

Date	Covering the years
1966	1955–65
1967	1959–66
1968	1958–67
1969	1958–68
1970	1959–69
1971	1960–70
1972	1961–71

The volume for 1967 is the first section (pp. 7–230) of a double
volume with *Balances of payments*. The volume for 1968 is Part I
of a two-volume set of which *Balances of payments* is Part II. In
the 1966 volume the data relate to the European Communities of
six, the UK and USA. The volumes of 1967 to 1971 also refer to
Japan. In the volume of 1972 the scope was increased to include
the nine. The system of national accounts on which the data are
based is that of the UN and the OECD. The volume for 1972 was
divided into five sections:

Comparative tables
Tables for the Community (of six)
Tables for the six member countries
Tables for the three acceding countries, the US and Japan
Tables on financial transactions

The first section gives comparative data for all the countries on an overall and a *per capita* basis. The second section consists of summary tables expressed in European Units of Account. The third section is the most detailed giving the data for each of the six expressed in the currency of the country in question. The fourth section contains tables on principal national accounts aggregates, aggregates per capita and the use and supply of goods and services for the three acceding countries, USA and Japan.

EUROPEAN SYSTEM OF INTEGRATED ECONOMIC ACCOUNTS

The European system of integrated economic accounts (ESA) is the European Communities version of the United Nations system of national accounts. This is regarded as an important development in the harmonization of economic and financial statistics. Eurostat hopes that all the individual member countries will adopt the system exclusively: though some, at the moment, use a national system as well as the ESA.

Eurostat went over to the ESA in 1973 in order to obtain a more complete and detailed knowledge of economic and financial structures and developments in the Community countries and also to ensure comparability of data between countries.

Data is now published in two forms:

aggregates
detailed tables

The second edition of the *European system of integrated economic accounts*, dated 1979, was published in 1980. The first edition, which was brought out in 1970, was not available in an English version.

AGGREGATES

National accounts: aggregates 1951–1972 was published in the official languages in 1973. Data were given at 1963 prices and current, that is to say 1973, prices. It is divided into two sections:

comparative tables
tables for the nine member countries of the European Communities, USA and Japan

The headings used in the comparative tables are as follows:

gross national product at market prices
gross domestic product at market prices
national income
compensation for employees
private consumption
public consumption
gross fixed capital formation
exports of goods and services
imports of goods and services
price indices
population and employment

The volume which is numbered 1–1974 is entitled *National accounts ESA aggregates 1960–1973*. The next annual volume is numbered 1–1975 but subsequent volumes were not numbered in this way (2–1974 and 2–1975 were the detailed tables). The 1978 volume covers 1960–77. It is divided into three sections:

country tables in national currencies
country tables in European Units of Account
comparative tables in purchasing power standards

The third section is arranged under the following headings:

gross domestic product at market prices
compensation of employees
consumption of fixed capital
net operating surplus of the economy
net national disposable income
net national saving
final domestic uses
final consumption on the economic territory
private consumption on the economic territory
collective consumption of general government
gross fixed capital formation
exports of goods and services
imports of goods and services
price indices
population and employment

There is a special study, published in 1977 in English and French, entitled *Comparison in real values of the aggregates of*

ESA, 1975. The aim of this study is to provide 'purchasing power parities' between the currencies of the nine. These are used instead of the official exchange rates in order to convert nominal values of each country of Gross Domestic Product and its uses into a common unit, the 'purchasing power standard'. Values expressed in these units are called 'real values' and make a direct comparison possible between the aggregates of the different countries.

DETAILED TABLES

National accounts—ESA: yearbook appeared in 1973 and 1974 covering the years 1970–2 and 1970–3 respectively. From 1975 to 1977 it appeared under the title *National accounts ESA detailed tables.* The volume published in 1977 covers the years 1970–6. These volumes complement the series on aggregates by providing more detailed figures and updating certain other figures. Data are given for each of the member countries under the following headings:

    simplified accounts for the nation
    gross value added at market prices by branch
    gross value added at factor cost, compensation of employees, gross operating surplus by branch
    occupied population, wage and salary earners, hours worked by branch
    final consumption of households on the economic territory by object
    gross fixed capital formation by product
    gross fixed capital formation by ownership branch
    sector and sub-sector accounts
    general government expenditure by purpose and by type of transaction
    gross accumulation and its financing by sector
    compensation of employees and its components
    actual social contributions by type and by receiving sector
    social benefits by type and by providing sector
    financial transactions of credit institutions
    main financial transactions
    financial assets and liabilities vis-à-vis the rest of the world

long-term bonds and medium- and long-term loans (gross recording)
table of the financial intermediaries

The ESA has been applied starting with data for the year 1970. In order to permit comparisons over time, the principal aggregates have been calculated from 1960. The base year for constant price data is 1970.

The 1978 issue of *National accounts ESA detailed tables*, which is only available in English, French and Dutch, appeared in two parts. No. 1 is divided into two sections. Section I contains the following headings:

gross value added at market prices by branch
gross value added at factor cost, compensation of employees, gross operating surplus by branch
occupied population, wage and salary earners, by branch
final consumption of households on the economic territory by object
gross fixed capital formation by product
gross fixed capital formation by ownership branch

Section II contains the following headings:

sector accounts, financial accounts
accounts of the rest of the world and sub-sectors, financial accounts
financial transactions of credit institutions
main financial transactions
financial assets and liabilities vis-à-vis the rest of the world
long-term bonds and medium- and long-term loans (gross recording)
table of the financial intermediaries

The second part (No. 2) gives the economic accounts of the institutional sectors as well as some supplementary tables. It is arranged according to the following headings:

simplified accounts for the nation
sector accounts
accounts of the rest of the world and sub-sectors

gross accumulation and its financing by sector
compensation of employees and its components
actual social contributions by type and by receiving sector
social benefits by type and by providing sector

There will be a further publication entitled *Accounts and statistics of general government.*

Public expenditure on research and development 1974–1976, 1976, is a summary report in the official languages which contains an analysis of trends in public expenditure on research and development in the member states.

Input–output tables

Eurostat has data which are designed to give a complete, consistent and detailed description of the flow of goods and services within a national economy and with the rest of the world. Harmonized input–output tables are available for 1959 and 1965 (the six) and 1970 (the nine). It is expected that 1975 data will be available in 1980 and that this will continue to be a five-yearly study. Data are available in the form of computer print-out and magnetic tape from Eurostat. Tables are prepared by the national statistical offices according to the ESA. (For further details see *Eurostat news*, No. 8-10, 1979, pp. 7–13.)

Tables were published for the six in 1970 under the title *Tableaux entrées-sorties 1965 (série spéciale)* in eight volumes as follows:

1. Méthodologie Communitaire des tableaux entrées-sorties
2. Italia
3. France
4. Belgique
5. Nederland
6. Deutschland
7. Communauté Économique Européenne
8. Communauté Économique Européenne: coefficients directs

A classification had been published in 1967 entitled *CLIO: Klassifikation und Nomenclature der input-output-Bereiche (Tabel-*

len 1965). Eurostat also published data for the EEC in *Tableaux 'entrées-sorties' pour les pays de la Communauté Économique Européenne (seconde version)*, December 1965, which replaced an earlier version of October 1964.

Input-output tables for 1970 have been published as follows:

1. Methodology 1970–1975
2. United Kingdom
3. Nederland
4. Italia
5. België/Belgique
6. B.R. Deutschland
7. France
8. The nine and the Community

A ninth volume will present coefficient tables and include a comparative analysis of the economic structure of the various countries. Vol. 1 is published in the official languages; Vols. 2–6 are in French and the language of the country in question; Vols. 7–8 are in English and French.

Regional statistics and accounts

Eurostat collects this kind of data in order to provide the information necessary for the implementation of the regional policy of the European Communities and sectoral regional policies. Data are broken down for the local government administrative units and the zones which benefit from regional aid, about 700 in all.

Eurostat co-ordinates, collects, analyses and disseminates regional statistics in the various statistical 'domains'. It presents regional accounts on the basis of the ESA for the administrative areas of the member countries.

REGIONAL STATISTICS

There were two issues of this yearbook as such. The 1971 volume which was published in the official languages and English contains data for 1968. The 1972 volume in French and English contains data for 1969. Both relate to the Community of six. The headings in the 1972 volume were:

population and employment
economic accounts
agriculture
industry
services
standard of living
the Community's financial participation in investment

The nomenclature was based on NACE—the general nomenclature of economic activities in the European Communities.

REGIONAL STATISTICS: COMMUNITY'S FINANCIAL PARTICIPATION IN INVESTMENTS (1975–)

This annual publication updates the last section of the yearbook *Regional statistics*. The 1975 volume gives the situation at the end of 1973. The 1976 volume gives data relating to 1972–4. The 1977 volume relates to 1975 and that of 1978 to 1977. The first three of these volumes were in the official languages but the 1978 volume is only available in English and French. The 1978 volume has the following tables:

general view
European Agriculture Guidance and Guarantee Fund (EAGGF)
European Regional Development Fund (ERDF)
European Coal and Steel Community (ECSC)
European Investment Bank (EIB)

REGIONAL STATISTICS: POPULATION, EMPLOYMENT, LIVING STANDARDS (1975–)

This annual publication updates the social statistics in the yearbook *Regional statistics*. The 1975 volume gives figures relating to 1973–4. The 1976 volume relates to 1975, the 1977 to 1976 and the 1978 to 1977.

The population figures include total population and population growth, births, deaths, trends in birth and death rates, age structures, trend of population, and inter-regional movement of population.

The employment figures include employment and the structure

of employment broken down by age, sex and categories of activity, and registered unemployment.

Living standards include indicators of environment, accommodation, education, health, standard of living and workers' hourly earnings by industrial activity.

REGIONAL STATISTICS: MAIN REGIONAL INDICATORS 1970–1977

This publication appeared in English and French in 1978. The main headings are:

population
activeness, employment and unemployment
production
Community's financial participation in investments

REGIONAL ACCOUNTS: ECONOMIC AGGREGATES, 1970

This publication appeared in the official languages in 1976. It represents the first attempt to present regional accounts according to the ESA, with the object of assessing more accurately the disparities between the regions in the European Communities. It contains the following tables:

principal regional economic aggregates
index of dispersion of gross value added at market prices per
    inhabitant
gross value added at market prices by groups of branches
localization quotient of gross value added at market prices
gross value added at market prices by branches
gross value added at factor cost by branches
compensation of employees by branches
gross operating surplus by branches
gross formation of fixed capital by groups of owner and pro-
    ducer branches
occupied population by branches
paid work by branches

It is planned that a second volume will present data for 1973 with a comparison for 1970, 1971 and 1972.

Balances of payments

BALANCES OF PAYMENTS: YEARBOOK
(1967–74)
From 1967 to 1972 this was published in the official languages and
English; the 1974 volume was in the six official languages. The
following volumes were published:

Date	Covering the years
1967	1962–6
1968	1958–67
1969	1958–68
1970	1958–69
1971	1960–70
1972	1961–71
1974	1963–73

The 1967 volume was the second section (pp. 231–311) of a
double volume with *National accounts*. The 1968 volume is Part II
of a two-volume set of which *National accounts* is Part I.

In the volumes for 1967 to 1970 the data relate to the six
Community countries, UK, USA and Japan. The 1971 volume
covers the nine Community countries, Norway, USA and Japan.
The 1972 and 1974 volumes cover the nine, USA and Japan.
Statistics are presented on the basis of a system which Eurostat
derived from that recommended by the IMF and the OECD.

The 1974 volume is divided into four sections:

comparative tables (abridged system)
country tables (detailed system)
tables for selected items (analysis by main geographical area of
    some selected items)
tables of outstanding amounts

BALANCES OF PAYMENTS: GLOBAL DATA
(1975–)

In 1975 it was decided to break *Balances of payments: yearbook*
into two parts of which *Global data* is one. The following have
been published in the official languages:

Date	Covering the years
1975	1961–74
1976	1961–75
1977	1970–6
1978	1970–7

The 1978 volume is divided into three sections:

comparative tables
analytical tables
tables of outstanding amounts

Data are provided of the global balances of payments and the external position of the monetary authorities for each of the countries of the European Communities, Spain, Greece, Portugal, USA and Japan.

BALANCES OF PAYMENTS: GEOGRAPHICAL BREAKDOWN (1975–   )

With *Global data* these data were reported formerly in the *Yearbook*. The following have been published:

Date	Covering the years
1975	1970–4
1976	1971–5
1977	1972–6
1978	1973–7

The 1975 and 1976 volumes were published in the official languages; the 1977 and 1978 volumes in three bilingual versions, English/French, German/Italian, Dutch/Danish. Each volume presents the most recent available data on the breakdown of the balance of payments of each of the countries of the European Communities, USA and Japan.

METHODOLOGY

There are studies of the methodology used by the statistical offices of the member countries in the construction of the balance of payments statistics of which the following have been published recently:

The methodology of the United Kingdom balance of payments,
   1976
*La méthodologie de la balance des paiements de L'Union
   Économique Belgo-Luxembourgeoise,* 1977
The methodology of Ireland's balance of payments, 1978

Tax statistics

The following volumes of the *Tax statistics (Statistiques fiscales)*
yearbook have been published in the official languages:

Date	Covering the years
1971	1965–9
1972	1965–71
1973	1968–72
1974	1968–73
1975	1969–74
1976	1970–5
1977	1970–6

Each volume presents the latest data on tax receipts and actual
social contributions in the countries of the European Communities.
Taxes are classified according to their economic nature into three
categories:

income and inheritance
capital
production and imports

and according to the collecting body. The classification is based on
the ESA. The 1977 volume is divided into four sections:

concepts and definitions of the ESA
statistical comments and comparative tables
summary tables by country
detailed tables by country

Revenue from taxation in the six EEC countries, 1967, is a study
of taxation in the six covering the years 1958 to 1965. Although
there is a foreword in the official languages and English the actual
text is in French only. The study was updated to 1967 by *Les*

recettes fiscales dans les pays-membres des Communautés européennes: résultats statistiques 1958–1967 which appeared as *Études et enquêtes statistiques*, No. 1, 1969.

AGRICULTURAL STATISTICS

Eurostat is concerned with agriculture, forestry and fisheries statistics, and its activities in this area are organized in two groups: agricultural accounts and structure, and agricultural balance sheets and products. Division D1 of Eurostat has responsibility for the following:

agricultural accounts
statistics of prices of agricultural products and of the means of production
surveys of the structure of agriculture and of agricultural holdings
statistics of agricultural manpower
methods to be applied to agricultural statistics

Division D2 covers:

statistics and balance sheets of crops
statistics and balance sheets of animal products
calculations of the supply of agricultural produce and food
statistics of forestry and timber
statistics on fisheries and fish products

The agricultural statistical publications have a green-coloured cover.

Yearbook of agriculture statistics (1970–   )

The *Yearbook of agricultural statistics* describes itself as a 'statistical vademecum containing the most important items given in *Agricultural statistics*'. It has appeared annually since 1970. Up to 1974 the text was available in French and German only; since then it has appeared in all the official languages.

The 1978 volume is arranged in six sections as follows:

general
agricultural and forestry accounts
structure
production
supply balance sheet
prices and price indices

Up to 1975 it was usually possible to make comparisons back as far
as 1958 which was taken as a reference point because it was the
first year of the Common Market. From the 1976 volume data are
usually given only for the last three years for which figures were
available. Although the data are presented in such a way as to
invite comparisons between countries as well as over time, the
data are collected from the statistical offices of the member
countries and are not necessarily strictly comparable.

Agricultural Statistics

From 1959 to 1975 this was a numbered annual series of agricultural statistics. From 1959 to 1972 it was published in French and
German only but from 1973 to 1975 in all the official languages.
From 1959 to 1960 it appeared under the title *Informations de la
statistique agricole* and there were eleven issues altogether. Each
issue was devoted to a separate topic. From 1961 to 1975 it was
irregular with between four and eleven numbers in a year, each of
which usually dealt with more than one topic. The contents of this
series from 1959 to 1970 are listed in the *Catalogue des publications
1952–1971*, Vol. 1, pp. 292–8.

From 1976 the series has been broken up into a number of
separate titles most of which appear annually.

The volumes listed below have appeared since 1976:

1976

Agricultural accounts
Agricultural price statistics, 1969–1975
Community survey of orchard fruit trees
Feed balance sheet: resources
Land use and production
Methodology of the EC-Index of producer prices of agricultural
products

Prices of fruit, vegetables and potatoes, 1974–1975
Production of vegetables and fruit
Statistics of animal production
Supply balance sheets

1977

Agricultural structure, 1950–1976
Economic accounts: agriculture, forestry, unit values
EC-Index of producer prices of agricultural products
Fisheries: fishery products and fishing fleet, 1974–1975
Fishery: catches by fishing region, 1964–1976
Forest statistics, 1970–1975
Land use and production, 1974–1976
Milk and milk products
Prices of fruit, vegetables and potatoes, 1975–1976

1978

Agricultural price statistics, 1969–1977
Animal production, 1968–1977
Community survey on the structure of agricultural holdings, 1975. Volume I. Introduction and methodological basis
Community survey on the structure of agricultural holdings, 1975. Volume II. Main results
Community survey on the structure of agricultural holdings, 1975. Volume III. Inventory of results by size classes of holdings
Community survey on the structure of agricultural holdings, 1975. Volume IV. Frequency distributions of selected results
Community survey on the structure of agricultural holdings, 1975. Volume V. Frequency distributions of selected results
Community survey on the structure of agricultural holdings, 1975. Volume VI. Frequency distributions of selected results
Economic accounts: agriculture, forestry, unit values
EC-Index of producer prices of agricultural products, 1970–1977
EC-Indices of purchase prices of the means of agricultural production, 1968–1977
Fishery: catches by region, 1968–1977
Community survey of orchard fruit trees, 1977
Land use and production, 1975–1977

Prices of fruit, vegetables and potatoes, 1976–1977
Production of vegetables and fruit, 1966–1977
Supply balance sheets, 1975–1977

1979

EC-Index of producer prices of agricultural products, 1971–1978
EC-Indices of purchase prices of the means of agricultural production
Fisheries: products and fleet, 1976–1977
Production of vegetables and fruit, 1967–1978

Agricultural prices: fruit, vegetables and potatoes (1974–5)

This was an annual internal information series of which the following were published:

Date	Covering the years
1974	1972–3
1975	1973–4

This now appears as a priced publication in the main series of *Agricultural statistics*.

Agricultural Statistical Studies (Études de statistique agricole) (1968–)

This was formerly a limited distribution series, but Nos. 19 and 20 have been sales publications. Nos. 1–13 are listed in *Catalogue of the Publications of the European Community Institutions 1972–1973*, pp. 241–4. The subsequent volumes are:

Number	Title
14	Statistiques dans le domaine de la production de porcs dans les États membres des Communautés européennes, 1968–1971, 2 vols., 1973

15   Ansätze zur Harmonisierung der Mengenstatistik für
            Eier und Geflügelfleisch in der Gemeinschaft, 1973
16   Zielsetzung, Aussagemöglichkeiten und Aussage-
            grenzen von mengen-und wertmässigen Gesam-
            trechnungen, 1974
17   Études sur les prix des terres, 1974
18   Einführung in die Diskussion über die Klassifizierung
            landwirtschaftlicher Betriebe, 1975
19   Medium-term forecasting of orchard fruit production
            in the EEC: methods and analysis, 1977
20   EC supply balance-sheets: detailed survey, 1978
21   Investigation into the forecasting of crop yields from
            meteorological data in the countries of the EC,
            1979

These studies are not necessarily translated into all six languages. No. 21 for example is available in English, French and
German.

Crop production (1963–   )

From 1963 to 1975 this was an irregular limited distribution series
(internal information) in French and German. Since 1976 it has
become a sales publication in the official languages. The following
numbers have appeared since 1976:

1976   Nos. 1–7
1977   Nos. 1–11
1978   Nos. 1–10, 11/12
1979   Nos. 1/2, 3/4, 5–10

It is divided into three sections:

summary of results
production statistics of vegetables and fruit
reports on agricultural meteorology

**EC-Index of producer prices of agricultural products
(1977–   )**

This is a quarterly sales publication in the official languages. The
following have been published:

1977   Nos. 1/2, 3/4, 5–6
1978   Nos. 1/2, 3, 4/5, 6

It presents data for the European Communities as a whole as well as for the individual member states on price indices for the agricultural means of production. Data are usually given for the most recent twelve-month period.

Enquête sur la structure des exploitations agricoles: résultats récapitulatifs (1966/7)

This was a major study of the structure of agricultural operations within the six. It consists of thirteen volumes published between 1971 and 1972 in the official languages as follows:

Volume	Title
1	Communauté États membres
2	Allemagne—régions
3	France-régions
4	Italie—régions
5	Benelux—circonscriptions d'enquête
6	Allemagne—circonscriptions d'enquête
7	Allemagne—circonscriptions d'enquête
8	France—circonscriptions d'enquête
9	France—circonscriptions d'enquête
10	France—circonscriptions d'enquête
11	France—circonscriptions d'enquête
12	Italie—circonscriptions d'enquête
13	Italie—circonscriptions d'enquête

Monthly statistics of eggs (1974–)

From 1974 to 1975 this was a limited distribution series (internal information) in French and German. Since 1976 it has become a sales publication in the official languages. The following numbers have appeared since 1976:

1976   Nos. 1–7, 8/9, 10, 11/12
1977   Nos. 1, 2/3, 4, 5/6, 7–12

1978   Nos. 1, 2/3, 4/5, 6–8, 9/10, 11–12
1979   Nos. 1–

In 1974 there was a provisional edition and monthly issues in 1975. The headings in use are as follows:

chicks placed
utilization of hatcheries
external trade in chicks
external trade in eggs and poultry meat

Monthly statistics of meat (**1968–**   )

From 1968 to 1975 this was a limited distribution series (internal information) in French and German. Since 1976 it has become a sales publication in the official languages. The following issues have been published:

1968   Nos. 1–12
1969   Nos. 1/7, 8–12
1970   Nos. 1/2, 3–12
1971   Nos, 1/2, 3, 4/5, 6/7, 8/9, 10–12
1972   Nos. 1–6, 7/8, 9–10, 11/12
1973   Nos. 1, 2/3, 4/5, 6–12
1974   Nos. 1/2, 3–4, 5/6, 7/8, 9/10, 11–12
1975   Nos. 1–12
1976   Nos. 1–3, 4/5, 6, 7/8, 9–12
1977   Nos. 1–6, 7/8, 9–12
1978   Nos. 1, 2/3, 4–5, 6/7, 8, 9/10, 11–12
1979   Nos. 1/2, 3–4, 5/6, 7/9

It is divided into two sections:

meat production by categories and external trade of animals
balance-sheets and external trade in meat

Monthly statistics of milk (**1972–**   )

From 1972 up to and including No. 1, 1976 this was a limited distribution series (internal information) in French and German.

Since then it has become a sales publication in the official languages. The following numbers have appeared since 1976:

1976	Nos. 1–7, 8/9, 10–11
1977	Nos. 12/1, 2–4, 5/6, 7/8, 9–12
1978	Nos. 1–7, 8/9, 10–12
1979	Nos. 1–4, 5/6, 7, 8/9

In 1972 there were two special editions covering 1968–70 and 1970–2 respectively and monthly numbers in 1974–5. There was a supplement on structure in 1978, and also in 1975.

It is divided into four sections:

weekly production
monthly collection and production
stocks at the end of the month
quarterly balance sheets

Monthly statistics: sugar (internal information) (1966–73)

This was a limited distribution series in French and German. The following were published:

1966	Nos. 1–11
1967	Nos. 1–11
1968	Nos. 1–12
1969	No. 1/12
1970	Nos. 1/4, 5–12
1971	Nos. 1/2, 3–12
1972	Nos. 1–6, 7/8, 9–10, 11/12
1973	Nos. 1/2, 3, 4/5, 6/10

Prix agricoles (informations internes de la statistique agricole) (1962–73)

This was a monthly limited distribution series in French and German. The following issues were published:

| 1962 | Nos. 1–12 |
| 1963 | Nos. 1–12 |

1964   Nos. 1–12 + special numbers with Nos. 5, 10
1965   Nos. 1–12 + special number with No. 5
1966   Nos. 1–12 + special number with No. 4
1967   Nos. 1–12
1968   Nos. 1–12 + special numbers with Nos. 2, 10
1969   Nos. 1–7, 8/12
1970   Nos. 1/6, 7, 8/9, 10–12
1971   Nos. 1–7, 8/9, 10–12 + supplements to Nos. 1, 5, 12
1972   Nos. 1/2, 3–4, 5/6, 7, 8/9, 10–12 + supplement to No. 1
1973   Nos. 1, 2/3, 4, 5/6, 7, 8/9, 10–12 + special nos. S1–S9

This series brought together information from the Community countries on the prices of the principal agricultural products and on the costs of means of production, and also data on certain processed foods. This series was replaced by two new series:

Purchase prices of the means of production
Selling prices of agricultural products

Purchase prices of the means of production

In 1974 Eurostat brought out a quarterly, limited distribution series (internal information) entitled *Agricultural prices: purchasing prices of the agriculture* which replaced in part *Prix agricoles*. It was published in French and German only. In 1976 it became a sales publication in the official languages entitled *Purchasing prices of the agriculture*. As from No. 3, 1977 its title was changed to *Purchase prices of the means of production*. From No. 1, 1979 it is only available in French, German, English and Italian. The following issues have been published:

1974   Nos. 1–4
1975   Nos. 1–4
1976   Nos. 1–4
1977   Nos. 1–4
1978   Nos. 1–4
1979   No. 1

The contents are as follows:

rates of the value added tax
straight feeding stuffs
compound feeding stuffs
straight fertilizers
compound fertilizers
fuels
seeds
pesticides

Selling prices of agricultural products

In 1974 Eurostat brought out a quarterly, limited distribution series (internal information) entitled *Agricultural prices: selling prices of agricultural products* which replaced in part *Prix agricoles*. It was published in French and German only. In 1976 it became a sales publication in the official languages. The following were published:

1974	Nos. 1/5, 6/8, 9, 10/12
1975	Nos. 1/3, 4/6, 9/12
1976	Nos. 1/3, 4/5, 6, 7/8, 9/10, 11/12

So that more price series could be included it was itself subdivided into two new publications:

Selling prices of animal products
Selling prices of vegetable products

EC-Index of producer prices of agricultural products, 1976 was an annual supplement to *Selling prices of agricultural products*, but subsequent volumes form part of the main series of *Agricultural Statistics* (see above, p. 170).

Selling prices of animal products (1977–)

This is a sales publication in the official languages which replaces in part *Selling prices of agricultural products*. The following have been published:

1977   Nos. 1–2, 3/4, 5/6

1978   Nos. 1–4, 5/6
1979   No. 1

Selling prices of vegetable products **(1977–)**

This is a sales publication in the official languages which replaces in part *Selling prices of agricultural products*. The following have been published:

1977   Nos. 1, 2, 3/4, 5/6
1978   Nos. 1–6
1979   Nos. 1/3

Quarterly bulletin of fisheries **(1978–)**

This is a sales publication in the official languages. The following have been published:

1978   Nos. 1/2, 3–4
1979   Nos, 1, 2

This contains monthly data on the landings of the more important fish species by quantity and value.

Miscellaneous publications

Other publications outside the main series of agricultural statistics produced by Eurostat have included:

Agricultural statistics: contribution à l'élaboration de statistiques comparables des prix des animaux de boucherie: étude sur les qualités des carcasses de bovins et porcins dans les pays de la Communauté Économique Européenne

Statistique des pêches 1950–1961: débarquements, commerce extérieur, approvisionnement en poisson, prix, membres d'équipage, flotte de pêche

Statistique agricole de la Norvège, 1950–1961

Agrarstatistik für Österreich, 1953–1963

DEMOGRAPHIC AND SOCIAL STATISTICS

Eurostat's work in the area of demographic and social statistics is divided into the following fields:

demographic statistics and household surveys
wages and incomes and research statistics
social accounts and indicators and health statistics
employment and education statistics

Demographic and social statistical publications have a yellow-coloured cover.

Social Statistics (1960–)

This is the main series in which Eurostat reports on the various social topics with which it is concerned. From 1960 to 1971 there were sixty-six issues of *Social Statistics*, the contents of which are listed in *Catalogue des publications 1952–1971*, Vol. 1, pp. 186–91. In addition, five issues of *Études et enquêtes statistiques*, 1968 (Nos. 2, 3, 4, 5 and Supplement) were devoted to social statistics. It is published in the official languages; there were no English texts before 1973. Up to 1975 it was a numbered series but from 1976 it has consisted of separately published titles, a number of which are regularly updated.

The more recent issues are listed below.

Year/number	Title
1972	
1	Statistiques harmonisées des gains horaires bruts, de la durée hebdomadaire du travail offerte et de l'emploi salarié dans l'industrie, X, 1971
2	Les comptes sociaux dans la Communauté euro-péene, 1962–70
3	Résultats de l'enquête communautaire par sondage sur les forces de travail, 1971

4   Les coûts de la main-d'oeuvre dans les banques,
           les assurances et le commerce de détail, 1970
5   Coûts de main-d'oeuvre des ouvriers dans l'in-
           dustrie, 1966–71. Statistiques harmonisées des
           gains horaires bruts, de la durée hebdoma-
           daire du travail offerte et de l'emploi salarié
           dans l'industrie, IV, 1972
6   Effectifivs scolaires et quelques aspects finan-
           ciers des systèmes d'enseignement dans les
           pays de la Communauté, 1960–71
6bis   Les accidents du travail dans l'industrie sidérur-
           gique, 1960–71
Supplement Les comptes sociaux dans la Communauté
           européenne: résultats préliminaires, 1962–71

1973

1   Harmonized statistics of gross hourly earnings,
           hours of work offered and number of em-
           ployees, X, 1972
2   Population, employment, unemployment, 1968–
           72
3   Les accidents du travail dans l'industrie sidérur-
           gique, 1960–72
4   Labour costs in industry, 1966–72. Harmonized
           statistics of gross hourly earnings, hours of
           work offered and number of employees, IV,
           1973
5   Schematic presentation of the educational sys-
           tems. Evolution of the numbers of pupils and
           students

1974

1   Labour costs in industry, 1966–73. Harmonized
           statistics of gross hourly earnings and hours of
           work offered, X, 1973
2   Labour costs in industry, 1966–72. Harmonized
           statistics of gross hourly earnings and hours of
           work offered IV, 1974
3   Social accounts in the European Community,
           1970–2

4   Coûts de la main-d'oeuvre dans l'industrie 1972:
           résultats préliminaires

1975

1   Labour force sample survey, 1973
2   Harmonized statistics of gross hourly earnings
           and hours of work offered, X, 1974
3   Social accounts in the European Community,
           1970–1973
4   General and vocational training: results of the
           specific survey on 'General and vocational
           training' annexed to the Community labour
           force survey conducted in 1973 in the six
           original member states of the Community
5   Earnings of permanent workers in agriculture,
           1974
6   Labour costs in industry, 1972–1975

1976

           Earnings in agriculture, 1975
           Education statistics, 1970–1975
           Harmonized statistics of gross hourly earnings
           and hours of work offered, IV, 1975
           Harmonized statistics of gross hourly earnings
           and hours of work offered, X, 1975
           Labour force sample survey, 1975

1977

           Censuses of population in the Community coun-
           tries, 1968–1971
           Demographic statistics, 1960–1976
           Earnings in agriculture, 1976
           Harmonized statistics of gross hourly earnings
           and hours of work offered, IV, 1976
           Harmonized statistics of gross hourly earnings
           and hours of work offered, X, 1976
           Labour costs in distributive trades, banking and
           insurance, 1974

Labour costs in industry, 1975, Vol. 1, Detailed results by industry

Labour costs in industry, 1975, Vol. 2, Structure of labour costs

Labour costs in industry, 1975, Vol. 3, Results by size classes of establishments

Labour force sample survey: methods and definitions

Population and employment, 1950-1976

Working conditions in the Community, 1975

Social accounts: accounts of social protection in the EC

Social indicators for the European Community, 1960–1975

1978

Demographic statistics, 1977

Education statistics, 1970/71–1976/77

Employment and unemployment, 1971–1977

Harmonized statistics of gross hourly earnings and hours of work offered, IV, 1977

Harmonized statistics of gross hourly earnings and hours of work offered, X, 1977

Labour force sample survey, 1977

1979

Employment and unemployment, 1972–1978

Harmonized statistics of gross hourly earnings and hours of work offered, IV, 1978

Labour costs in industry, 1975, Vol. 4, Results by regions

Harmonized statistics of gross hourly earnings and hours of work offered, X, 1978

Annuaire de statistiques sociales (1968–72)

There were three volumes of this yearbook; 1968, 1970 and 1972. They were published in the official languages. The chapter headings in the 1972 volume were as follows:

démographie
emploi et chômage
durée de travail et conflits de travail
salaires
niveau de vie
enseignement
comptes sociaux, securité sociale
accidents du travail

These topics are dealt with in individual statistical publications for the more recent years.

Special series of social statistics

Eurostat has produced a number of large-scale statistical studies. *Budgets familiaux* was a seven-volume study published in 1966 on family budgets in each of the six member countries of the European Communities; in all about 42,000 households were studied. For Germany the data relate to 1962/3 and for the other countries to 1963/4. This study follows one carried out for 1956/7 on behalf of the European Coal and Steel Community on the budgets of those employed in mining and iron and steel industries in the six countries. (*Informations statistiques*, No. 1, 1960, 'Budgets familiaux des ouvriers C.E.C.A. 1956/57'.)

Enquête sur la structure èt la répartition des salaires 1966 was an eight-volume study published in 1969/70 on wages in the six. The scope of the survey was limited to manual workers.

A second study was undertaken for the year 1972 and again involved only the six. The results have been published in thirteen volumes under the title *Structure of earnings in industry 1972*. It is published in the form of two volumes for each country, with an additional volume entitled 'Methods and definitions'. Volume *A* for each country gives an analysis and summary of the general results. Volume *B* for each country has detailed statistical tables for each of the headings of the NACE (which is more detailed than the NICE used in the 1966 study).

A complementary study is the *Structure of earnings in wholesale and retail distribution, banking and insurance in 1974*. This is the first of the surveys to be carried out in all nine countries of the

European Communities. Vol. 1 is entitled 'Methods and definitions', and there will be nine subsequent volumes, one dealing with each country.

It is planned to carry out a family budgets survey in 1981 for which it is hoped to produce harmonized statistics on the structure of household expenditure.

Rapid information

There was *Statistical telegram* (1976–8) which was an irregular series, available gratis, which gave an advance summary of data published in *Social statistics*. This has been replaced by the series *Rapid information* on the following topics:

Education and training
Employment and unemployment
Social protection
Wages and incomes

Selected figures

This is an occasional series of statistical reports, e.g. *Out-of-school vocational training, age and activity: Community 1973 and 1975.*

TRANSPORT STATISTICS
CLASSIFICATIONS

The *Nomenclature uniforme des marchandises pour les statistiques de transport (NST)* was published in 1961 following a recommendation by the Commission. It was subsequently revised and published in 1968 since when it has been known as NST/R. An English version, 'Standard goods classification for transport statistics', can be found as an annex to *Statistical yearbook transport, communications, tourism, 1976,* 1978 (pp. 137–44). There are 176 headings in use and there is said to be a 'complete correspondence between it and the Commodity Classification for Transport Statistics in Europe (CSTE)'. The CSTE was prepared by the UN and the Economic Commission for Europe.

TRANSPORT STATISTICS

Transport des produits du Traité de la CECA was published between 1957 and 1964 covering the years 1956 to 1963, in French and German only. The first two issues were published by the High Authority itself, subsequent issues by Eurostat. Issues covering the years 1964 and 1965 were numbered '1966, No. 2' and '1967, No. 2' respectively. They appeared in two bilingual editions; French and German, and Italian and Dutch.

There were two issues of *Statistiques de transport*, in French and German only. No. 1 covers 1962 and No. 2 covers 1963.

Issues of *Transport: statistique annuelle* covering the years 1964 and 1965 were numbered '1966 No. 1' and '1967 No. 2' respectively, and they were published in the official languages.

The following issues of *Statistiques de transport* were published in the official languages:

Year	Covering the year
1968	1966
1969	1967
1970	1968
1971	1969
1972	1970
1973	1971

Each volume was divided into three parts:

    railways, inland waterways and road transport
    sea and air transport and pipelines
    studies and surveys

Annual statistics transport and communications, tourism, 1972–1973, 1975, included data on posts, telecommunications and tourism for the first time.

The annual series is now entitled *Statistical yearbook transport, communications, tourism*. Volumes published 1976 to 1978 cover the years 1974 to 1976. The 1978 volume has the following section headings:

general tables
railways
road
inland waterways
merchant shipping
aviation
pipelines
posts and telecommunications
tourism
annex (NST/R)

There is also an index. Publication is in three bilingual editions; English/French, German/Italian, Danish/Dutch.

There was a special statistical study published in 1971 with the title: *The sea transport of the countries of the Community, 1968 and 1969.*

Transport statistical publications usually have a crimson-coloured cover.

Monthly tables of transport (1976–   )

The following have been published:

Year	Number
1976	Nos. 1/9, 10/11, 12
1977	Nos. 1/2, 3–6, 7/8, 9–12
1978	Nos. 1–2, 3/4, 5–6, 7/8, 9–12
1979	Nos. 1–6, 7/8, 9–10

The contents are as follows:

railways
road
inland waterways
merchant shipping
aviation
tourism

It was preceded by a limited distribution series (internal information) for 1975, entitled *Transport: monthly tables.*

INDUSTRIAL STATISTICS
CLASSIFICATIONS

A provisional edition of *Nomenclature des industries établies dans les Communautés européennes* (NICE) was published in 1961 in the official languages. This was replaced by a fuller version published in 1963 in the official languages. NICE has now been replaced by NACE.

The *Nomenclature du commerce* (NCE) was published in 1965 in the official languages. This too has been replaced by NACE.

The *General industrial classification of economic activities within the European Communities* (NACE) was published in 1970 in two editions. There is an English version and a multilingual edition in the official languages. The main classes are as follows:

Agriculture, hunting, forestry and fisheries
Energy and water
Extraction and processing of non-energy-producing minerals and derived products; chemical industry
Metal manufacture; mechanical, electrical and instrument engineering
Other manufacturing industries
Building and civil engineering
Distributive trades, hotels, catering, repairs
Transport and communication
Banking and finance, insurance, business services, renting
Other services

The *Common nomenclature of industrial products* (NIPRO) was published in a provisional English edition in 1976. This work complements NACE by classifying products according to the branch of industry producing them.

INDUSTRIAL STATISTICS

Industrial statistics usually have a dark blue-coloured cover.

Annual investments in fixed assets (1976–)

This annual series continues a feature which appeared in *Statistical studies and surveys.* Nos. 2/1972, 2/1974 and 2/1975 contained the data for 1964–70, 1970–2 and 1971–3 respectively. No. 2/1972 contained data for the Community of six only, subsequent issues covered the nine. No. 2/1972 contained a detailed description of the methodology used and information on the conditions under which the inquiries are carried out in the different countries. The inquiry is not carried out by Eurostat but by the statistical offices in the member countries.

The three issues of *Statistical studies and surveys* had the title 'Annual investments in fixed assets in the industrial enterprises of the member countries of the European Communities'. The 1976 publication which covers the years 1972–4 has the title *Investments in fixed assets*; and that of 1977 which covers the years 1973–5, *Annual investments in fixed assets*. Data are presented for individual countries and as aggregates for the Community as a whole.

Industrial short-term trends (1978–   )

This monthly replaces in part the *Quarterly bulletin of industrial production*. It gives data on short-term industrial indicators with comments and graphs; and contains indices of industrial production in about forty sectors as well as indices of turnover, new orders, employees, wages and salaries and hours worked. It is available in three language editions: French, English and German.

Industrial statistics: yearbook (1962–   )

The following volumes have been published in the official languages:

Year	Covering the years
1962	1953–61
1963	1954–62
1964	1955–63
1965	1956–64
1966	1957–65
1967	1958–66
1968	1958–67

1969	1958–68
1970	1958–69
1971	1958–70
1972	1958–71
1973	1958–72
1974/5	1958–74

The 1974/5 volume is divided into two parts:

indices of industrial production in the member countries of the
Community and certain other countries
data on the production in the Community of basic materials and
manufactured goods

Quarterly bulletin of industrial production

From 1959 to 1975 this was known as *Industrial statistics*. From
1976 to 1978, when it ceased publication, it was called *Quarterly
bulletin of industrial production*. It had always been published in
the official languages.

Data were given on the production of basic materials and
manufactured goods in the countries of the European Communities. Between 1959 and 1971 there were forty-three special reports
which gave data on the structure of industry, and basic statistics on
certain branches of industry in the Community.

The quarterly bulletin has been replaced in part by the monthly
Industrial short-term trends.

Structure and activity of industry. Coordinated annual
inquiry into industrial activity in the Member States

A volume entitled 'Methods and definitions' was published in
1978. There will be fifteen volumes of results covering the inquiry
for 1975. The object of this work has been to produce co-ordinated
and harmonized statistics of industrial activity in the member
countries of the European Communities which will be of value to
the Commission in the spheres of medium-term economic policy,
industrial policy and competition policy.

ENERGY STATISTICS

Energy statistics usually have a ruby-coloured cover.

Energy statistics: yearbook (**1964–**   )

The following have been published in the official languages:

Date	Covering the years
1964	1950–3
1965	1950–64
1967	1955–66
1968	1958–67
1969	1958–68
1970	1960–9
1971	1960–70
1972	1960–71
1973	1969–72
1974	1969–73
1975	1970–4
1976	1970–5
1979	1973–7

The main headings in use are as follows:

overall energy
solid fuels
petroleum
gas
electrical energy
world data

Coal statistics

There were annual volumes of *Coal statistics* in 1977 and 1978 covering the years 1976 and 1977 respectively. They were published in French, English and German, and included data on production, movement of stock and foreign trade.

Since 1977 there has been a monthly entitled *Coal: monthly bulletin*. This gives data on short-term trends in the coal industry. From 1971 to 1976 recent information could be found in *Coal: press notice*.

Electrical energy statistics

Statistiques de l'énergie électrique: production—échanges—consommation—équipement (Document de travail) covering 1970 and 1971 appeared in 1971 and 1972 respectively. In 1972 there was a study entitled *Electrical energy statistics of the three new member countries: United Kingdom—Ireland—Denmark: years 1969–1970 1971*. This was followed by *Electrical energy statistics 1972 (working paper)*, 1973 and *Electrical energy statistics 1973 (Internal information)*, No. 2, 1974.

There is now an apparently regular series of *Electrical energy statistics*. Data for 1975 appeared in 1977 and for 1977 in 1978. These volumes were available in English and French only.

Since 1977 there has been a monthly entitled *Electrical energy: monthly bulletin*. This gives data on short-term trends in the electrical economy in general and fuel consumption in power stations in particular. From 1969 to 1976 recent information could be found in *Electrical energy: press notice*.

Gas statistics

Gas statistics 1976, 1977, provides data on gas industry balance sheets for all combustible gases according to a harmonized methodology. It was published in French and English only.

Since 1977 there has been a monthly entitled *Hydrocarbons: monthly bulletin*. This gives data on short-term trends in the petroleum and gas industries.

Gas prices 1970–1976, 1977, is a study which gives the results of an inquiry into gas prices in the countries of the European Communities. This includes tariffs and taxes as well as a detailed analysis of prices. There is also an international comparison of the gas industry overall. This volume was available in two bilingual editions, English and French, German and Italian. More recent data are given in *Gas prices 1976–1978*, 1979. This study gives gas prices up to 1978 in thirty towns or conurbations in the countries of the European Communities for both domestic and industrial use. This volume is published in French, English, German and Italian.

From 1971 to 1976 recent information could be found in *Gas: press notice.*

Operation of nuclear power stations during . . . (1976–   )

This is an annual publication in English and French. The following volumes have appeared:

Date	Covers
1976	1975
1977	1976
1978	1977
1979	1978

Each volume is divided into two parts. The first part gives data on the main operating statistics for the year in question and also an outline of the structure of nuclear plant. The second part gives the monthly operating data for each nuclear power station of the Community as well as the yearly results since the first connection to the grid. The annual load diagrams are also included showing the main reasons for unavailability.

Overall energy balance-sheets (1977–   )

This is an annual series published in French only:

Date	Covering the years
1977	1963–75
1978	1963–76
1979	1970–7

It contains data on the energy balance sheets for each of the countries of the European Communities, expressed in tonnes of coal equivalent. The CRONOS programme is used which provides for unified balance sheets and balance sheets broken down by product.

Petroleum statistics

There were annual volumes of *Petroleum statistics* in 1978 and 1979 covering the years 1976 and 1977 respectively. They were published in French and English only, and included data on the various petroleum products expressed as energy flows, and on the structure of the petroleum industry.

Since 1977 there has been a monthly entitled *Hydrocarbons: monthly bulletin*. This gives data on short-term trends in the petroleum and gas industries.

From 1971 to 1976 recent information could be found in *Petroleum: press notice*.

Quarterly bulletin of energy statistics

From 1967 to 1975 this was known as *Energy statistics: quarterly bulletin*. In 1976 its title was changed to *Quarterly bulletin of energy statistics* but in that year it ceased publication. It had always been published in the official languages. Before 1967 data on energy appeared in the following:

Bulletin statistique: charbon, acier (1953–61)
Charbon et autres sources d'énergie (1962–4)
Statistique de l'énergie (1965–6).

In 1976 the chapter headings were:

overall energy
solid fuels
petroleum
gas
electrical energy

This series provided quarterly data on the overall energy balance sheet concerning major items of energy supplies and consumption for the whole of the Community and for each member country. It was replaced by three monthly series:

Coal: monthly bulletin
Electrical energy: monthly bulletin
Hydrocarbons: monthly bulletin

There were three supplements:

No. 1/2, 1971, entitled 'Prix du fuel-oil 1966–70' which updated 'L'évolution des prix du fuel-oil dans les pays de la CEE 1955–1965' (*Études et enquêtes statistiques*, No. 4/1969)
No. 1/2, 1972, entitled 'Oil tanker freight rates—1972 analysis'
No. 3, 1976, entitled 'Definitions of oil and oil products'

There were four special numbers:

No. 1–2, 1973, entitled 'L'évolution des prix du charbon dans les pays de la Communauté Européenne de 1955 à 1970'
No. 1, 1974, entitled 'A comparison of fuel prices—oil—coal—gas—Eur6 1955–1970'
No. 2, 1974, entitled 'The evolution of prices of oil fuels in the nine countries of the European Community from 1960 to 1974'
No. 1, 1975, entitled 'Prices of bunker oils Eur9 1965–1973'

Miscellaneous energy statistics

Other titles published by Eurostat on energy statistics include:

Bilan des transformations de combustibles dans les centrales électriques, 1970 (Document de travail), 1971
Quelques chiffres: l'énergie dans la Communauté, 1973
Useful-energy balance-sheets 1975, 1978

IRON AND STEEL STATISTICS

Iron and steel statistical publications usually have a turquoise blue-coloured cover.

Iron and steel yearbook (1964–)

The following have been published in the official languages:

Date	Covering the years
1964	1954–63
1966	1954–65
1968	1954–67
1970	1954–69
1972	1954–71
1973	1958–72
1974	1954–73
1976	1954–75
1977	1973–76
1978	1974–77

The two most recent volumes carry much less data than could be found in the earlier volumes.

The 1978 volume is arranged under the following headings:

main summary tables
production basis
  iron ore
  manganese ore
  pyrite residues
  pig-iron, spiegeleisen and high carbon ferro-manganese
  scrap
  coke
  energy
  independent steel foundries
production
  pig-iron
  crude steel
  special steel
  finished rolled steel and end products
  primary iron and steel processing
  by-products
works deliveries
foreign trade
  foreign dependence
  foreign trade of iron and steel
  direct foreign trade
  foreign trade of important third countries
  indirect foreign trade

   foreign trade of scrap
steel consumption
investments
prices, average values, wages
levy

Quarterly iron and steel bulletin

From 1962 to 1975 this appeared six times a year under the title
Iron and steel: statistical bulletin. Data for previous years appeared
in *Bulletin statistique: charbon, acier* (1953–61). *Méthodes at défini-
tions de base relatives aux données du bulletin sidérurgie* was
published in 1970.

Since 1976 it has appeared quarterly in the official languages
under its present title. The quantity of data presented was much
reduced in 1978. The following headings are used:

statistical note
production bases
    employment in the iron and steel industry
    other production bases
production
    pig-iron
    crude steel
    special steel
    finished steel products and end products
    primary iron and steel processing industries
works deliveries and receipts, stocks
trade
    foreign trade
    internal trade
steel consumption

Iron and steel: monthly bulletin (1978–   )

This monthly publication gives short-term trends for production,
consumption, stocks and trade.

From 1970 to No. 6, 177, recent information could be found in
Steel: press notice; for Nos. 9–12, 1977, the title was *Steel: monthly
bulletin.*

EUROPEAN COAL AND STEEL COMMUNITY: OLD SERIES

The following issues of *Bulletin statistique (charbon, acier)* were published:

1953	Nos. 1–4
1954	Nos. 5–8
1955–60	6 p.a.
1961	Nos. 1–4

It was replaced by *Energy statistics: quarterly bulletin* and *Iron and steel: statistical bulletin.*

Mémento de statistiques: énergie (charbon et autres sources d'énergie) was an annual publication in the official languages for the years 1959–60. It was replaced by *Basic statistics of the Community* (see above, p. 137).

Mémento de statistiques (charbon—sidérurgie: statistiques générales was an annual publication in the official languages for the years 1954–60. It was replaced by *Basic statistics of the Community.*

CHAPTER 6

Council of Ministers

REVIEW OF THE COUNCIL'S WORK

The *Review of the Council's work* is prepared by the General Secretariat of the Council of Ministers of the European Communities. It surveys the work of the Council during a given period, presenting without comment a general factual account of what has taken place. In a single volume it gives an overview of the most important secondary legislation in a given period. References to the *Official journal* are given where appropriate. Unlike many of the official publications of the European Communities it has an alphabetical subject index which makes it much easier to retrieve specific pieces of information. In the *Twenty-fifth review of the Council's work* there are the following chapter headings:

The work of the Institutions
Freedom of movement and common rules
Economic and social policy
External relations and relations with the Associated States
Agriculture
Administrative matters—Miscellaneous

This publication is only available in the official languages. Its French title is *Aperçu des activités du conseil.*
The following issues have been published:

First	October 1959 to April 1960
Second	April 1960 to September 1960
Third	October 1960 to March 1961
Fourth	April 1961 to September 1961

Fifth	October 1961 to March 1962
Sixth	April 1962 to September 1962
Seventh	October 1962 to March 1963
Eighth	April 1963 to September 1963
Ninth	October 1963 to March 1964
Tenth	April 1964 to September 1964
Eleventh	October 1964 to March 1965
Twelfth	April 1965 to December 1965
Thirteenth	January 1966 to June 1966
Fourteenth	July 1966 to December 1966
Fifteenth	January 1967 to June 1967
Sixteenth	July 1967 to July 1968
Seventeenth	August 1968 to July 1969
Eighteenth	August 1969 to July 1970
Nineteenth	August 1970 to December 1971
Twentieth	January to December 1972
Twenty-first	January to December 1973
Twenty-second	January to December 1974
Twenty-third	January to December 1975
Twenty-fourth	January to December 1976
Twenty-fifth	January to December 1977
Twenty-sixth	January to December 1978

GUIDE TO THE COUNCIL OF THE EUROPEAN COMMUNITIES

This is a loose-leaf directory prepared by the General Secretariat of the Council of Ministers, in the official languages and updated or re-issued from time to time.

It contains the following information:

List of representatives of the governments of the member states who regularly take part in Council meetings

A description of the function of some of the committees of the Council of Ministers

Details of the permanent representation of the member states

The organization of the General Secretariat of the Council of Ministers

Details of the Association and Co-operation Councils and the Council of Ministers of the ACP–EEC Convention together with a list of representatives of the ACP states

ASSOCIATION AGREEMENTS

The EEC has entered into various association agreements apart from the Yaoundé and Lomé Conventions. These are with:

Greece—signed at Athens, 9 July 1961
Turkey—signed at Ankara, 12 September 1963
Tunisia—signed at Tunis, 28 March 1969
Morocco—signed at Rabat, 31 March 1969
Eastaf (Tanzania, Uganda, Kenya)—signed at Arusha, 24 September 1969
Malta—signed at Valetta, 5 December 1970
Cyprus—signed at Brussels, 19 December 1972

The *Collected Acts* of the agreements between the EEC or European Communities and third countries or groups of countries have been made available in fourteen loose-leaf volumes. The material in these volumes is for the most part reprinted from the *Official journal*. As well as the association agreement itself, relevant EEC secondary legislation and the institutions of each association are given with the exception of those of a confidential nature. The following have been published:

	Number of volumes
Convention ACP–EEC of Lomé	2
Association between the European Economic Community and the Republic of Cyprus	2
Association between the European Economic Community and the United Republic of Tanzania, the Republic of Uganda and the Republic of Kenya	1
Association between the European Economic Community and Greece	2

All the above volumes are available in English. Some of the original versions were not available in English but only in the four official languages and the language of the country with which the association agreement was made. These limited distribution documents are described in *Catalogue des publications 1952–1971*, Vol. 1, pp. 42–3.

EUROPEAN PATENT

The European Patent Office opened for the receipt of patent applications in 1978 (see *Convention on the Grant of European Patents, European Patent Convention, with related documents, Munich, 5 October 1973*, Cmnd 5656, HMSO, 1974). This convention has been signed by a number of European countries including Sweden and Switzerland.

At a European Communities' level there have been other developments. In 1969 the 'six' convened an inter-governmental conference for the setting up of a European system for the grant of patents. The documents associated with this conference are listed in *Catalogue of the publications of the European Community Institutions 1972–73*, pp. 55–62. Subsequently a convention was signed which provides for the grant of a community patent by the European Patent Office which will have a unitary effect in all the countries of the European Communities, the object being to make it possible to file patent applications once only and in one language to have effect in each of the countries (see *Convention for the*

European Patent for the Common Market, Community Patent Convention, including Implementing Regulations and Final Act, Luxembourg, 15 December 1975, Cmnd 6553, HMSO, 1976). It appears that this latter convention is unlikely to be ratified by all the Community countries until 1981 or 1982.

There is a loose-leaf volume entitled *Draft guidelines for examination in the European Patent Office*, which was published in English, French and German in 1976.

LIST OF LAWS AND REGULATIONS ADOPTED IN THE MEMBER STATES OF THE COMMUNITIES IN APPLICATION OF ACTS ADOPTED BY THE COMMUNITIES (1973–)

This is a fortnightly publication which replaces the quarterly *Répertoire de dispositions législatives et réglementaires arrêtées dans les six États membres des Communautés*. The issues 1/1973 and 2/1973 appeared under the title *List of laws and regulations enacted in the Member States of the Communities*.

It is arranged firstly under subject headings and then under countries. Each entry consists of the citation of an Act of the European Communities, always in French, followed by the citation of the law, regulation or whatever, in the language of the country concerned. For example, 'the Customs Duties (Greece) (No. 3) Order 1977 (SI no 2056, 8.12.1977)' is listed under 'Décision du Conseil portant conclusion de l'accord créant une association entre la CEE et la Grèce (63/106/CEE) (JOCE no 26, 18.2.1963, p. 293)'.[1] For the UK entries are drawn from *Command papers* and *Public General Acts* as well as *Statutory Instruments*.[2] It does not cumulate in any way and there are no indexes. Heydt has condemned it in very forthright terms:

> This is an almost worthless publication, since obviously a systematic approach to such an enterprise is lacking and thus you just find a number of titles of legal acts without getting any information about the importance or about the Community acts to be mentioned; in addition, not all implementing acts are mentioned.[3]

EUROPEAN COMMUNITIES' GLOSSARY

It is possible to discover the official English equivalent to a corresponding French term from the French–English glossary. The most recent edition is the seventh of 1979. Presumably this will be kept up to date by supplements as was the previous edition it replaces. The need to standardize legal terminology is an obviously difficult problem despite the fact that many thousands of words and phrases have now been controlled. Cf. FitzGerald's comments noted above, p. 11.

Notes

1. Nov.–Déc. 1977, p. 17.

2. The other sources are: *Bundesanzeiger, Bundesgesetzblätter I und II, Belgisch Staatsblad, Gazzetta Ufficiale, Iris Oifigiùil, Journal officiel de la République française, Lovtidende, Moniteur Belge, Mémorial A du Grand-Duché de Luxembourg, Staatsblad, Staatscourant, Verordeningenblad Bedrijfsorganisaties.*

3. Volker Heydt, 'How to use the primary source material of the European Communities (EC)', *International journal of law libraries*, 5 (1), March 1977, pp. 57–63 at 62–3.

CHAPTER 7

European Parliament

DEBATES OF THE EUROPEAN PARLIAMENT

Beginning with the session 1968/69 the verbatim texts of the debates of the European Parliament have been published in the official languages in the *Annex* to the *Official journal* (see above, p. 25). For the period from 1952 to the session 1967/68 the *Débats* of the Common Assembly of the European Coal and Steel Community, and subsequently of the European Parliament (from 19 March 1958), were published in the four official languages by the organization itself. The hard copy of these earlier debates is now out of print but it is possible to acquire a set in microfiches.

The *Debates: report of proceedings* is a provisional version of the full text of the debates. Speeches are recorded only in the language in which they were delivered. More importantly, speakers do not have the opportunity to correct the texts. The provisional version appears a week or so after the debate in question and so is useful until a definitive version is available in the *Annex*. Regular readers of the *Annex* will know that it is not without its fair share of misprints anyway.

Appearing with the same frequency as the *Debates: report of proceedings* is the formal record of what took place, that is as opposed to what was said, which is the *Minutes of proceedings of the sittings of . . . .* Like the *Debates* this is in mimeographed form but is translated into all the official languages. It is also a provisional version of the minutes of proceedings until the final version appears in the *Information and notices* part of the *Official journal*.[1]

In order to make life easier for those undertaking a retrospective search through the minutes and the debates the Archives Department of the Directorate-General for Sessional and General Services have produced tables of concordances of the debates, minutes and indexes for the period 1952 to 1976/77. This is European Parliament document number PE 54.143 of June 1978. There might be something to be said for publishing all matters relating to the European Parliament in the *Annex* rather than allocating some to *Information and notices*.

As a concession to journalists there is a *Summary report* which is a multilingual publication of no official significance. Its value to journalists is that it provides an early translation of debates in another language. The *Debates: report of proceedings*, it should be remembered, is a source which gives a text only in the language in which a speech was delivered.

For general consumption there is a monthly summary of the proceedings of the European Parliament. Each issue is devoted to one of the week-long sessions. It is issued free of charge by the Directorate-General for Information and Public Relations of the Secretariat of the European Parliament. It was first issued in 1967 and until 1979 was known as *European Parliament information— the sittings*. From the first sitting of the directly elected European Parliament it was replaced by a tabloid newspaper called *EP News*. The monthly summary is not a substitute for the *Annex* to the *Official journal* but is useful for current awareness.

The London office of the European Parliament produces a number of information publications such as press releases and *European Parliament—report*, a broadsheet which first appeared in 1974.

From time to time the European Parliament holds joint meetings with other bodies most notably with the Parliamentary Assembly of the Council of Europe. These meetings which have been held regularly since 1953 take place alternately at Strasbourg and Luxembourg. The *Official report of debates* is published by both the European Communities and the Council of Europe.

A report of the meetings of the Consultative Assembly of the Lomé Convention (ACP–EEC) is carried in a pamphlet of a similar format to *European Parliament information—the sittings* in which the proceedings of the annual Parliamentary Conferences of the EEC/AASM Association had been reported.

RESOLUTIONS

The Secretariat of the European Parliament produces a list of all the resolutions passed in a given session. Lists exist for 1976–7, 1977–8 and 1978–9.

Each list is in four parts:

List of resolutions in chronological order of adoption
List of resolutions grouped by subject
Procedure without report
Texts of resolutions

WORKING DOCUMENTS OF THE EUROPEAN PARLIAMENT

Any document which is mimeographed within the European Parliament—that is produced in its own print shop—is given a number for internal use. This is done whether or not the document circulates outside the Parliament. The *Working documents* fall within this category but are more usually cited by the number assigned them in this series which consists of a running number and the year of the Parliament's session. For the session 1978/79 the *Working documents* were numbered from 1/78 to 683/78. The session actually runs from March to March.[2]

Working documents are listed in the index volume of the *Annex* both in the 'index of subjects' and in the numerical list. The numerical list contains the entries for *Working documents* presented during the session in question and also those accepted in that session though they were presented in the previous session. For the session 1973/74 a list was issued separately by the European Parliament and, more recently, a check list has been sent to those who are on the mailing list for the *Working documents*. The check list notes whether a document is available to all on the mailing list, Depository Libraries only, or no external distribution at all. Only the list for the session 1973/74 contained alternate references to the *Official journal* or cited *COM* document numbers. A list of this kind would be valuable because proposals from the Commission to the Council of Ministers are not present in the set of *Working documents* supplied to European Documentation Centres. Although every *Working document* which is distributed to Members of the European Parliament contains the text of the Commission proposal in question it is not a reprint of the *COM* document but merely the *COM* document original plus a new title page which has on the verso a copy of the formal letter to the President of the European Parliament from the Council of Ministers which invites the Parliament's opinion. Thus, for example, *Working document* 7/73 is actually *COM* (73) 330 final.

The importance of the *Working documents* lies in the fact that the subjects covered reflect the complete range of the Parliament's activities which is no less extensive than those of the European Communities themselves. So far as the business of the Parliament is concerned they include the reports of Parliamentary committees on Commission proposals as well as the Commission proposals themselves.

When the President of the European Parliament has received a Commission proposal from the Secretary-General of the Council of Ministers he will usually give responsibility for it to one of the committees. This does not prevent that committee from seeking expert views from one or more of the other committees, especially on financial and legal matters. In practice, it is not essential for a proposal to undergo detailed examination and many uncontroversial routine proposals can receive a favourable opinion without report or debate. In the case of the more important business or if a single Member of the European Parliament requires it, the business is discussed by the committee in charge of the proposal. It is usual to appoint a rapporteur who apart from drafting the report also steers the debate in committee and in plenary session.[3]

A typical report will consist of a 'motion for a resolution' together with an 'explanatory statement' and the opinions of the other committees consulted. The report of a committee is often known by the name of the rapporteur.

There are fifteen committees of the European Parliament:

Agriculture
Budgetary control
Budgets

Development and co-operation
Economic and monetary affairs
Energy and research
Environment, public health and consumer protection
External economic relations
Legal affairs
Political affairs
Regional policy and regional planning
Rules of procedure and petitions
Social affairs and employment
Transport
Youth affairs, culture, education, information and sport

The *Working documents* also include a wide selection of other documentation from the Commission and the Council of Ministers. It has become customary for the European Parliament to be consulted on a far wider range of matters than the Treaties demand. One supposes the recent direct elections will not affect this trend. This documentation includes certain papers which arising from relations with third countries, especially association agreements for which there is a different procedure for consultation,[4] and also 'communications' from the Commission to the Council of Ministers. Communications are consultative documents rather than firm proposals and indicate policy areas in which the Commission wishes to take an initiative.

Arising directly out of the Parliament's own activities are *Working documents* which give the text of questions which Members of the European Parliament intend to ask orally, motions for resolutions, and proposals for the administrative part of the budget of the European Communities. As well as considering draft legislation a committee of the European Parliament may have an investigative role analogous to that of a Select Committee of the House of Commons. For example, *Working document* 132/79 is a *Report drawn up on behalf of the Political Affairs Committee on respect for human rights in Ethiopia*, M. Zagari was rapporteur. This is an investigation initiated by the European Parliament itself.

Some of the documents which the Parliament receives from the Commission which are issued in the *Working documents* are amongst those which are for internal distribution only, most notably, . . . *general report on the activities of the European Communities.*

EUROPEAN PARLIAMENT BULLETIN

For the information of Members of the European Parliament there is a weekly information bulletin in the official languages which gives the necessary business information on forthcoming activities. This includes such matters as visits by foreign delegations, a calendar of official meetings in the European Parliament as well as the agenda for the plenary sessions. It also notes developments in the legislative process—such as modifications of Commission proposals to the Council of Ministers. It lists the *Working documents* and written questions and quotes the text of petitions from the 'European public'. Petitions are listed with the *Working documents* list in the index volume of the *Annex* to the *Official journal.*

Committee agendas which also list the documents to be discussed are published separately in the official languages.

DIRECT ELECTIONS

Understandably, the European Parliament has contributed to the already substantial literature on direct elections. There are the following major publications:

The case for elections to the European Parliament by direct universal suffrage, 1969

Elections to the European Parliament by direct universal suffrage, 1977

Electoral laws of Parliaments of the member states of the European Communities, 1978 (PE 50.159)

Laws or draft legislation for direct elections to the European Parliament: a comparative survey, 1978 (PE 54.676)

National electoral laws on direct elections. Texts of laws adopted by the Parliaments of Denmark, France and Ireland, 1978 (PE 54.524)

A Parliament for Europe, 1978

National electoral laws on direct elections. Texts adopted by the Parliaments of the Federal Republic of Germany and the United Kingdom, 1978 (PE 54.757)

National electoral laws on direct elections. Texts of laws adopted by the Parliaments of Denmark, France and Ireland, 1979 (PE 54.524)

Laws or draft legislation for direct elections to the European Parliament: a comparative survey. Situation November 1978, 1979 (PE 54.676/rev.)

National electoral laws on direct elections. Texts of laws adopted by the Parliaments of Belgium, Italy, Luxembourg and the Netherlands, 1979 (PE 57.047)

Manifesto of the European Movement on elections to the European Parliament by direct universal suffrage, 1979 (PE 57.767)

In addition to the above there are various information publications especially those produced by the London Office of the European Parliament of which the series *European elections briefing* is notable. There are other useful pamphlets which were produced centrally such as *Europe goes to the polls*, 1979. Although these are necessarily of a more ephemeral character they contain much valuable factual information.

OTHER PUBLICATIONS

The Directorate-General for Research and Documentation has been responsible for much original work such as *The effects, on the United Kingdom, of membership of the European Communities*, 1975. which is an expanded and updated version of *The effects, in 1973 on the United Kingdom of membership of the European Communities*, 1974.

A particularly useful source from this Directorate-General is *Europe today* which was first published in 1976 and is now in its third edition. It is in loose-leaf form in the official languages. To some extent it can be regarded as a digest of the secondary legislation of the European Communities. It is said 'to give an overall picture of the latest stage reached in the political and legal development of the Community'. If it has a tendency towards ellipsis this is the almost inevitable corollary of the attempt to encompass so much material in such a small space. Its value is enhanced by the comprehensive references to the *Official journal*, the Treaties, *Working documents* of the European Parliament, the . . . *general report on the activities of the European Communities* and the *Bulletin of the European Communities*.

Other major publications related to the work and interests of the European Parliament include:

L'université européenne, 1967

Les ressources propres aux Communautés européennes et les pouvoirs budgétaires du Parlement européen, 1970

Les ressources propres aux Communautés européennes et les pouvoirs budgétaires du Parlement européen. Les débats de ratification, 1971

The European Communities' own resources and the budgetary powers of the European Parliament, 1972 [an abridged version, in English, of the two previous titles]

The case for a European Audit Office, 1973

European integration and the future of parliaments in Europe, 1975

Terminology of human rights, 1976 (PE 43330)

Rules of procedure: European Parliament, 1979

Practical guide for members, 1979

Proceedings of the Round Table on 'Special rights and a charter of the rights of the citizens of the European Community' and documents, 1979

European documentation: a survey (1959–71) was a publication which was intended to describe the process of European integration which was going on outside the Institutions of the European Communities. From 1959 to 1964 it was a monthly published in the official languages (in 1959 there were only three issues). It was known in French as *Cahiers mensuels de documentation*. From 1965 to 1971 it was translated into English as the *Monthly bulletin of European documentation* or *European documentation: a survey*. In 1967 there were five issues, then it became quarterly. Previous publications were *Informations bimensuelles sur la Communauté européenne du charbon et de l'acier sur l'intégration européenne* (1954–5) and *Informations mensuelles sur la Communauté européenne du charbon et de l'acier sur l'intégration européenne* (1956–8).

There are various information publications of value, of which *Fact sheets on the European Parliament and the activities of the European Community*, 1979, is a collection particularly worth noting.

BIBLIOGRAPHIES

The European Parliament has been responsible for a number of bibliographies. The *Bibliographie méthodique trimestrielle* (1956–66) and its predecessor *Bulletin mensuel de bibliographie* (1953–5) were a subject listing of the stock of the European Parliament's Library. There is also a *List des publications periodiques dont les collections sont conservées à la Bibliothèque*, 1975, which has both an alphabetical and a subject sequence. A monthly *Library bulletin* lists recent accessions to the Library.

Other bibliographies to appear have included:

Bibliographie analytique du plan Schuman et de la CECA, 3 vols., 1955–9
Catalogue: marché commun, 1960, which updates and replaces *Le marché commun: bibliographie*, 3 vols., 1957–9
Zone de libre-échange, 1958
Euratom, 3 vols., 1958–9

In 1979 the Directorate-General for Research and Documentation produced *the European Parliament bibliography 1970–78*. It is proposed that the work will be kept up to date by annual supplements. It says that it has been compiled for: 'EC officials, parliamentarians and their staff, political scientists, teachers and students'. It excludes for reasons of space all but the more fundamental official publications as well as newspaper articles. Material is arranged under the following headings and then by year of publication:

general
powers
members
procedures and rules
sessions and activities
headquarters

direct elections
political groups
political parties
relations with other institutions

DIRECTORIES

The *Times guide to the European Parliament*, published in 1980, is probably the most accessible directory of members of the European Parliament. It includes election statistics, biographies and photographs of members and the manifestos of the political groupings within the European Parliament. Lists produced by the Parliament itself are much harder to come by, hence the commercial publication.

Notes

1. See above, p. 23.

2. The 1979/80 session started on 13 March 1979.

3. See Fitzmaurice, J., *The European Parliament*, Saxon House, 1978, pp. 17–22.

4. Ibid.

CHAPTER 8

Court of Justice of the European Communities

There is an increasing volume of case law issuing from the Court of Justice of the European Communities. Between 1953 and 1973 1,076 cases were brought before the Court, but it seems likely that this number will have more than doubled by the end of the present decade; indeed, in 1978 alone there were 256 cases. This is only a proportion of the cases involving questions of the law of the European Communities. Such litigation falls primarily within the competence of individual national courts. The judicial functions of the Court of Justice of the European Communities are exercised in the following specific areas:

Proceedings brought against states which fail to fulfil their obligations under the Treaties or Community secondary legislation
Review of the legality of Community Acts
Disputes involving the liability of the European Communities
Cases relating to failure to comply with the anti-trust legislation
Disputes between the Community and its officials
Interpretation of the rules of the law of the European Communities.[1]

REPORTS OF CASES BEFORE THE COURT

Judgments are reported in the *Official journal*, but law reports including the Opinions of Advocates-General are published in

Reports of cases before the Court. Reports are published in the official languages and, at the insistence of the Irish judge, in Irish. These are the languages in which Court proceedings may take place. The 'authentic' language version of a report is the one in which the case in question took place.[2] There are rules for determining what the language of the proceedings should be.[3]

The translation of the case law 1953 to 1972 into Danish and English is now complete in twenty volumes. Translation has obviously created particular problems in this area above all: the blank pages and spaces at the foot of columns in the English text result from the attempt to maintain the same pagination in the various language editions. There are considerable delays in the dissemination of law reports. Reports usually appear about six months after the judgments.

The judgments and the Opinions of Advocates-General are available to interested parties after the public hearing. They were available free to some libraries but are now sold to subscribers to *Reports of cases before the Court* for an annual subscription which is equal to that of *Reports of cases before the Court.* It is also possible to buy single cases in the same cyclostyled format.

There is a preferred method of citation for judgments (as is usual with law reports). In the case of an English text the legal citation would be as follows:

'Case 13/72 Netherlands v. Commission 1973 E.C.R. 27.'

This means that a judgment in Case No. 13 of 1972 can be found on page 27 of the 1973 volume of *Reports of cases before the Court.*

Annual indexes are provided and there is a cumulative index covering 1973–5.

Ninty-five per cent of the Court's publications budget is devoted to *Reports of cases before the Court.*

OTHER SOURCES OF CASE LAW

The main unofficial series is *Common Market law reports* (1962–   ) which is one of a number of titles published by the European Law Centre Ltd. It is issued weekly with four-monthly bound volumes. From 1962 to 1977 418 cases in the Court of Justice of the European Communities were reported. This series differs from

Reports of cases before the Court by reporting, in the same period, 402 decisions in national courts. Since 1970 it has also reported judgments in the procedural language of the case. A measure of the importance of this series is that it was itself used by the Court in the preparation of the retrospective translation of the case law into English. A companion publication of note is *European law digest*.

Some important cases are reported in *The Times* newspaper and sometimes in the 'European practitioner' section of the *New law journal* (monthly).

The Court publishes a weekly summary of its work entitled *Proceedings of the Court of Justice of the European Communities* (1975–). This is published in the official languages by the Information Office of the Court. It has two regular sections: judgments and opinions. No. 26/79 also gives the composition of the Court for the legal year 1979/80.

A valuable unofficial source is *Common market reports* published by Commerce Clearing House in the United States.

COURT OF JUSTICE OF THE EUROPEAN COMMUNITIES: LIST OF JUDGMENTS GIVING THEIR CITATIONS 1954–1972, 1973

This list is arranged in chronological order according to the date of the judgment given. It sets out the names of the parties, the type and subject matter of the action, and the language of the case. The citation of each report is given in the French language, and also in English if a translation was available at the time the list was prepared. As well as the references to *Recueil de la jurisprudence de la cour*, it is an index to the main English-language sources of case law which were available prior to the British accession.

BIBLIOGRAPHY OF EUROPEAN CASE LAW: DECISIONS RELATING TO THE TREATIES ESTABLISHING THE EUROPEAN COMMUNITIES

This publication is a subject bibliography of judicial decisions not only of the Court of Justice of the European Communities but also of the national courts. Its subject headings are in French only, because this is the working language of the Court. Other legal questions are dealt with in *Publications concerning European integration*. Each volume has four indexes at the back:

A numerical index to articles in the Treaties and Regulations
Decisions and Directives for the volume in question
An alphabetical index to authors for the volume in question
A chronological table of judicial decisions covering the whole set of volumes

There is also a table of contents.
The following volumes in the series have been published:

		pages
Bibliography	1965	1–261
Supplement 1	1967	263–370
Supplement 2	1968	371–475
Supplement 3	1969	477–628
Supplement 4	1970	629–775
Supplement 5	1973	777–1091
Supplement 6	1976	1093–1559

All the volumes carry the cover title in English, *Bibliography of European judicial decisions*. The work has been produced by the Library and Documentation Service of the Court.
The bibliography is continued by:

BULLETIN BIBLIOGRAPHIQUE DE JURISPRUDENCE COMMUNAUTAIRE

This has the same format as the *Bibliography of European case law*. No. 77/1 covers the period February 1976 to November 1977. No. 78/1 covers December 1977 to June 1978. It is produced by the Library and Documentation Service of the Court.

PUBLICATIONS CONCERNING EUROPEAN INTEGRATION

A new edition of this bibliography was published in 1967 and covered the years 1952 to 1966. From 1968 to 1971 four annual supplements appeared and a fifth supplement which appeared in 1975 brought the work up to date to August 1974. It was produced by the Library and Documentation Service of the Court.

SELECTED INSTRUMENTS RELATING TO THE ORGANIZATION, JURISDICTION AND PROCEDURE OF THE COURT

The third edition of this work appeared in 1976. It contains all the provisions relating to the organization, jurisdiction and procedure of the Court of Justice of the European Communities 'to be found in the Treaties establishing the European Communities, the Protocols and Conventions annexed thereto and in the implementing regulations made under those Treaties'. It contains the Rules of the Court.

MISCELLANEOUS PUBLICATIONS

A calendar of public hearings is drawn up in French each week and is available from the Court Registry.

Information on the Court of Justice of the European Communities (1968–)

This is a quarterly which summarizes the more important cases before the Court and important cases involving the law of the European Communities before national courts. Nos. 1–7, 1968–70 were published in French only as *Informations sur la Cour de justice des Communautés européennes*. Since 1971 it has been available in the official languages.

Synopsis of the work of the Court of Justice of the European Communities in . . . (1968–)

This is an annual publication issued free of charge and giving a brief account of what was done in each year; that is not only the case load but other associated activities. From 1969 it appeared in English but otherwise only in the official languages.

Formal hearings of the Court of Justice of the European Communities . . .

This is a free publication giving the formal speeches made at the opening sessions. It has appeared in most years usually in the official languages. The title in French is *Audiences solennelles de la Cour de justice en* . . .

MECHANIZED INFORMATION RETRIEVAL

As the use of interactive on-line information retrieval becomes more widespread it can be expected that developments will take place in the exploitation of the law of the European Communities. The Legal Service of the Commission has developed CELEX which is now one of the CIRCE files (see below, p. 241). Unfortunately CELEX is not at present offered on EURONET Diane.

The European Law Centre Ltd is in the process of offering a whole-text service known as EUROLEX which will include *Common Market law reports*. It does not seem that LEXIS will have any European content.

The Italians have undertaken most of the pioneering work in this field. The case law of the Court of Justice is available on the CEE file from CED (Centro Elettronico di Documentazione Giuridica). CED is a EURONET Diane host.

Notes

1. See 'The Court of Justice of the European Communities', *European documentation*, 1976, p. 4 (Commission of the European Communities).

2. Article 31 of the Rules of the Court.

3. Articles 29–31 of the Rules of the Court.

CHAPTER 9

Other bodies

COURT OF AUDITORS

The Court of Auditors began operating in October 1977. Having audited the accounts of the Institutions it makes a report to that body. The *Annual report concerning the financial year [e.g. 1978] accompanied by the replies to the institutions transmitted to the authorities responsible for giving discharge and to the other institutions on [e.g. 30 November 1979]*, is a substantial document which appears in the *Official journal*. The first report appeared in *Official journal*, No. C313 of 30 December 1978 and the second in No. C326 of 31 December 1979.

The Court has published separately its *Comments concerning the financial year 1978 sent to the Commission*, 1979, and an information publication entitled *Court of Auditors of the European Communities*, 1978.

ECONOMIC AND SOCIAL COMMITTEE

The Economic and Social Committee exists to express 'Opinions' on Commission proposals before a final decision is taken by the Council. The Treaties may require that the Committee be consulted; the Council or Commission may invite an Opinion; or the Committee may decide to express an Opinion on its own initiative. The Division for Research and Documentation of the General Secretariat of the Committee issued in 1977 *The right of initiative of the Economic and Social Committee: documentation* which describes the possibilities open to the Committee to influence the legislative process.

Up to the end of 1978 the Committee had met in 164 plenary sessions and since 1958 had produced no fewer than 1,136 opinions, information reports and studies.

A twenty-one member 'Bureau' elected from within the membership of the Committee arranges business but much of the work is carried out in the nine Sections:

Agriculture
Transport and Communications
Energy and Nuclear Questions
Economic and Financial Questions
Industry, Commerce, Crafts and Services
Social Questions
External Relations
Regional Development
Protection of the Environment, Public Health and Consumer
    Affairs

In some respects the Sections are analogous to the Committees of the European Parliament and are responsible for drafting the Opinions.

Documents

In 1974 the total number of documents relating to the work of the Committee reached 12,000. Obviously, very little of this large volume of documentation is generally available to the public. Some documents are circulated on a limited distribution basis and these can be identified by a code in the bottom left-hand corner of each page. The code consists of the letters *CES*, a serial number and year, and a suffix, e.g.:

CES 993/78 rév. 1 (novembre 1979)

which is one of the lists of the *Bureau of the Economic and Social Committee*.

Publications

The Economic and Social Committee has made use of the Official
Publications Office in the past but now tends to issue material in its
own right. Invariably the publications which are intended for
widespread circulation are distributed free.

The *Annual report* (1973–   ) is the best overview of the
activities of the Committee in a given year. It gives an account of
activities, describes any changes which have taken place in the
organization, and attempts to assess what impact the opinions
expressed have had on the decisions eventually taken. The annual
report lists the opinions, studies and information reports issued
during the year in question, together with the name of the
rapporteur.

From 1962 to 1973 there was an *Information bulletin* which was a
quarterly periodical published in the official languages which gave
an account of the discussions in the plenary sessions and described
other Committee activities. There were frequent delays in publication so that often several numbers were run together.

Since 1974 there has been a monthly *Bulletin* presenting similar
information. From No. 2, 1979 it was reduced from A4 to A5 size
which is more convenient, and is now generally an up-to-date
source of information. The *Bulletin* gives an account of the
discussion on a particular proposal but the text of the opinion itself
can be found in the *Information and notices* section of the *Official
journal*, e.g., the 'proposal for a Council Regulation extending and
modifying Council Regulation (EEC) No. 2829/72 of 28 December
1972, regarding the Community quota for the carriage of goods by
road between Member States'. The Commission proposal was
published in the *Official journal* on 12 June 1974 (No. C68, 1974,
p. 6). It was discussed in the 124th Plenary Session of the
Economic and Social Committee held on 18 October 1974. The
discussion is reported in *Bulletin*, No. 10/1974, pp. 15–16. The text
of the ESC opinion is published in the *Official journal*, No. C142,
1974, pp. 12–13. The proposal was eventually enacted by the
Council on 19 December 1974 and became 'Regulation (EEC) No.
3256/74 of the Council' (*Official journal*, No. L349, 1974, p. 5).

*Opinions delivered by the Economic and Social Committee of the
European Economic Community and the European Atomic Energy
Community* is an irregular list of the opinions set out in tabular

form. Each stage in the legislative process is noted and appropriate document numbers and *Official journal* references are given. It is a useful guide to the progress of a particular legislative proposal from the time it first appears in the *Official journal* to the final enactment.

A *Directory* appears annually which contains a list of Bureau members by nationality and by Group; a list of members of the Economic and Social Committee classified by country, qualifications and Group; and the composition of the Sections by Group and nationality.

Various lists of members are circulated and revised from time to time. They include:

Members of the Committee (Functions)
List of members in alphabetical order (with addresses)
List of Committee members according to nationality
Composition of the sections (by group and nationality)
Members of the sections of the Economic and Social Committee (alphabetical order)
Bureau of the Economic and Social Committee
Liste des membres du Comité avec indication d'appartenance aux organes de travail du Comité (Bureau—Sections)

A number of opinions and other documents have appeared separately. They include:

The economic and Social Committee, 1975
European Union: opinion, 1975
Systems of education and vocational training in the member countries of the European Community: study, 1976
The situation of small and medium-sized undertakings in the European Community: study 1975, 1976
Objectives and priorities for a common research and development policy: study May 1976, 1977
EEC's transport problems with East European countries: opinion, 1977
Small and medium-sized enterprises in the Community context: opinion, 1978
Youth unemployment: education and training: 5 opinions of the Economic and Social Committee, 1978
Employee participation and company structure: opinion, 1978

Monetary disorder: opinion, 1978
20th Anniversary of the Economic and Social Committee, 1978
Agricultural structural policy: opinion, 1979
Community nuclear safety code, 1977

Earlier publications of the Economic and Social Committee are listed in *Catalogue des publications 1952–1971*, Vol. 1, pp. 243–6 and *Catalogue of the publications of the European Community Institutions 1972–73*, p. 435.

CONSULTATIVE COMMITTEE OF THE EUROPEAN COAL AND STEEL COMMUNITY

Whereas the Economic and Social Committee has a separate Secretariat and organization, the Consultative Committee is, in the words of the Treaty, 'attached to the High Authority' with a Secretariat which is a part of the Secretariat-General of the Commission. Membership of the Consultative Committee, of its Bureau and Sub-committees is reported in the *Information and notices* section of the *Official journal*.

The Treaty provides that the minutes of proceedings shall be forwarded to the High Authority and the Council at the same time as the opinions of the Committee (Article 19).

The publications of the Consultative Committee are usually free or limited distribution. An exception is the annual *Handbook*. Publications are listed in *Catalogue des publications 1952–1971*, Vol. 1, pp. 231–2, and *Catalogue of the publications of the European Community Institutions 1972–1973*, pp. 429–30.

EUROPEAN INVESTMENT BANK

The European Investment Bank was established for the purpose of granting long-term loans or guarantees in order to contribute to a balanced development of the Common Market. It is particularly active in the area of regional development and energy. The various association and co-operation agreements into which the European Communities have entered have greatly extended the number of

countries in which the bank can operate. In 1978 it provided
1966.5 million u.a. in the Community countries (from which Italy,
the largest single beneficiary, received 688.7 million u.a.). Outside
the Community it provided 221.7 million u.a.

The most detailed information on the activities of the Bank can
be found in the *Annual report of the European Investment Bank*
which has appeared annually since 1958. This report contains both
detailed financial statistics and commentary on the Bank's operations. From time to time it has issued a newsletter entitled
Information and there are also press releases, though UK projects
are often mentioned in press releases from the London Office of
the Commission. The Luxembourg press releases of the Bank give
quick information about new loans and other developments of
significance.

For the years 1972 to 1976 the Research Department has
brought out annual surveys of investment and the financing of
investment entitled *Investment in the Community in [e.g. 1976]
and its financing*.

The Research Department was also responsible for *The European Investment Bank and the problems of the Mezzogiorno*. The
Mezzogiorno is an area in which the Bank has taken a considerable
interest.

There are a number of summaries of the Bank's operations:

*European Investment Bank operations under the Lomé conven-
tion*, 1976
Financing outside the Community: Mediterranean countries,
1979
*Loans and guarantees in the member countries of the European
Economic Community*, 4th ed., 1977
Operations in Turkey, 1974

From time to time there has been an overall summary of which
the most recent is *European Investment Bank: 20 years 1958–1978*,
1978.

The 'Statute of the European Investment Bank' is an annex to
the Treaty of Rome (EEC) but has been published separately in
European Investment Bank: statute and other provisions, 1978.

All the publications of the European Investment Bank have to
be obtained from the organization itself. Nothing is issued by the
Official Publications Office and there are no priced publications.

They can usually be traced in *Publications of the European Communities*.

Earlier publications from the Bank are listed in *Catalogue des publications 1952–1971*, Vol. 1, p. 249; and, *Catalogue of the publications of the European Community Institutions 1972–1973*, pp. 437–9.

MONETARY COMMITTEE

The Monetary Committee was established by Article 105 of the Treaty of Rome (EEC) in order to keep under review the monetary and financial situation of the member countries and of the Community as a whole. No important decision on monetary policy is taken without the Monetary Committee having been consulted beforehand.

There are two members of the Committee from each member country: they are usually central bankers or civil servants. In addition there are three Commission officials from DG II Economic and Financial Affairs. The Secretariat of the Committee is also located in DG II.

The . . . *report on the activities of the Monetary Committee* is an annual report of the activities of the Committee which also gives the texts of its opinions, any special reports and general observations on the monetary situation in the Community. This report is printed separately for limited distribution, the first issue relating to the year 1959. It has been available in English since the *Fourth report* relating to the year 1962. Since the *Second report* of 1960 it has been first published in the *Official journal* (e.g. 'Sixteenth report on the activities of the Monetary Committee', *Official journal*, No. C174, 1975).

From time to time a *Compendium of Community monetary texts* is published of which the latest is dated 1979. It aims to collect together the major legal texts on Community monetary affairs since the EEC was founded.

There is usually no separate heading in the official catalogues for publications of the Monetary Committee. In the *Catalogue des publications 1952–1971*, Vol. 1, they are listed under the general heading, 'Questions monétaires et financières', pp. 108–9, and are not identified as coming from the Monetary Committee. In the

Catalogue of the publications of the European Community Institutions 1972–1973 they appear under the heading 'Economic, monetary and financial affairs', pp. 171–84, but again they are not specifically identified.

OTHER COMMITTEES

As well as the Institutions of the European Communities and the other bodies which have been mentioned in this chapter and elsewhere the Treaties provide for a number of committees of which the Committee of Permanent Representatives (COREPER) is one of the more notable. There are also a large number of advisory committees and the like, many of which can be traced through the index and pages of the *Official journal*.

The composition, functioning and activities of forty-six of the most important advisory committees with a socio-economic interest are described in *Les comités consultatifs communautaires à composition socio-économique*, Editions Delta, 1979.

Here is a list of some of the committees:

Administrative Commission for the Social Security of Migrant
  Workers
Advisory Committee for Beef and Veal
Advisory Committee for Eggs
Advisory Committee for Milk and Milk Products
Advisory Committee for Pigmeat
Advisory Committee for Poultrymeat
Advisory Committee for Public Contracts
Advisory Committee for Wine
Advisory Committee of the Euratom Supply Agency
Advisory Committee on Cereals
Advisory Committee on Customs Matters
Advisory Committee on Feedingstuffs
Advisory Committee on Foodstuffs
Advisory Committee on Freedom of Movement of Workers
Advisory Committee on Industrial Research and Development
Advisory Committee on Joint Data Processing Projects
Advisory Committee on Live Plants
Advisory Committee on Medical Training

Advisory Committee on Milk and Milk Products
Advisory Committee on Questions of Agricultural Structure Policy
Advisory Committee on Safety, Hygiene and Health Protection at Work
Advisory Committee on Social Questions affecting Farmers and Members of their families
Advisory Committee on Social Security for Migrant Workers
Advisory Committee on Training in Nursing
Advisory Committee on the Training of Dental Practitioners
Advisory Committee on Veterinary Training
Advisory Committee on Vocational Training
Advisory Veterinary Committee
Article 113 Committee
Committee of Central Bank Governors
Committee of Experts of the European Foundation for the improvement of living and working conditions
Committee of Experts on Radioactive Wastes
Committee of the European Social Fund
Committee of Senior Officials on Public Health
Committee on Transport Infrastructures
Consumers' Consultative Committee
Economic Policy Committee
European Agency for Trade with Developing Countries
European Centre for the Development of Vocational Training
European Foundation for the Improvement of Living and Working Conditions
Joint Committee on Social Problems in Sea Fishing
Joint Committee on Social Problems of Agricultural Workers
Mixed Committee on the Harmonization of Working Conditions in the Coal Industry
Nuclear Research Consultative Committee
Regional Policy Committee
Scientific Advisory Committee to examine the toxicity and ecotoxicity of chemical compounds
Scientific and Technical Committee
Scientific and Technical Research Committee
Scientific Committee for Animal Nutrition
Scientific Committee for Food
Scientific Committee for Pesticides

Scientific Committee on Cosmetology
Scientific Committee on Plant Health
Shipbuilding Committee
Standing Committee on Employment
Standing Committee on Zootechnics
Transport Committee
Tripartite Conference
Waste Management Committee

CHAPTER 10

Bibliographic aids

OFFICIAL PUBLICATIONS CATALOGUES

Up to 1969 various official catalogues were produced. Among the more notable ones was *Publications des Communautés européennes*, July 1962, which was intended to provide a complete list of the publications of the European Coal and Steel Community. There was a supplement available in English as *Publications of the European Communities: bibliographical supplement to the catalogue*, March 1964. This supplement was correct to the beginning of 1964.

The European Economic Community issued five catalogues up to 1965, three of which were available in English.

Up to 1966 the Publications Department of the European Communities issued various sales catalogues of items in print. The 1966 issue was made more useful by the inclusion of an index. It was not intended that these catalogues should list free publications or limited distribution documents.

In 1967 *Publications of the European Communities: catalogue*, covering the period March 1964 to July 1967, was issued. For its scope this is probably the best official publications catalogue produced by the European Communities. It was well designed and has some lasting value because of its subject index. A supplement, *Publications des Communautés européennes: supplément*, was issued in 1969, which covered the period August 1967 to December 1968.

None of these earlier catalogues have been completely superseded by later works especially in the case of listing free publications.

Catalogue des publications 1952–71, Vol. 1

This was issued in 1972 as a special supplement to the *Bulletin of the European Communities*. Unlike the catalogue of 1967 it is not available in English nor has it been indexed. A good deal of patience has to be exercised to get the best out of this catalogue and some references have undoubtedly been omitted. The scope is all material published by the European Communities up to 1971 except scientific and technical material. Some limited distribution documents and free publications are included but no *COM* or *SEC* documents are described.

It had been planned that there should actually be a second volume to this catalogue. Its proposed scope was: 'les "publications EUR," publications scientifiques et techniques, pour la plupart d'intérêt nucléaire, issues des programmes d'Euratom et, depuis la fusion, du programme plus vaste des Communautés européennes.' There would have been about 5,000 records for what are in the main Euratom technical reports.

The contents of Vol. 1 are arranged in the following order: Publications of the European Communities; European Parliament; Council; Commission; Court of Justice; Economic and Social Committee; and European Investment Bank. References are then grouped under subject headings. The contents of various periodicals are listed in annexes at the end of the catalogue.

List of the publications of the European Communities in English: supplement to the French edition of the 'Catalogue of publications of the European Communities 1952–71', 1972

This is described as a 'provisional edition for the internal use in the departments of the Commission of the European Communities'. A notice on p. 11 states: 'This document is an extract from the

French edition of the "Catalogue of publications 1952–71," Vol. 1. It lists, by groups, the titles of all works and periodicals *still available*, published in English during the period mentioned above.' It follows the same arrangement as *Catalogue des publications 1952–71*, Vol. 1, and is probably best used in conjunction with it.

Catalogue of the publications of the European Community Institutions 1972–73, 1974

There are two versions of this catalogue. The first is sub-titled 'provisional edition for the internal use in the departments of the Commission of the European Communities'. The second version, like the first, is dated 1974, but has no sub-title and has printed on the back cover 'Edit2/1974'.

The use of the first version should be avoided because it suffers from many imperfections. The second version is expanded, though it is still not without flaws.

This is probably the most difficult to use and needlessly complicated of all the official publications catalogues which the European Communities have produced. It is multilingual—entries appear in all the official languages of the Communities and it has no index. The arrangement is broadly similar to *Catalogue des publications 1952–71*, Vol. 1, although there are a number of departures. For example, Eurostat publications are divided under the various subject headings instead of being kept together. Despite its title, this catalogue does include entries for works published before 1972. It may be that it was intended to be to some extent a catalogue of material in print.

Publications of the European Communities (1974–   )

Since the issue of January 1974 the last part of the *Bulletin of the European Communities* has included a section entitled 'Publications of the European Communities'. This feature is the continuation of the practice which began with issue No. 12, 1961, of the *Bulletin of the European Economic Community*, and which was continued in the *Bulletin of the European Communities*, of listing new publications. The present list is printed on yellow pages and is available as a separate offprint.

A multilingual format is used, similar to *Catalogue of the publications of the European Community Institutions 1972–73*, which makes the list very difficult to use. Further confusions arise because it is stated that the list contains 'both official and unofficial publications'. One presumes that only those works which are properly publications of the European Communities (see chapter 2 above) are considered to be official publications. It is not clear how many free publications and limited distribution documents are included. Under the heading 'General remark' we are told that:

> Publications not bearing a sales price whose circulation is given as 'limited' are generally only for the attention of administrations of the Member States, Community departments and, where relevant, the authorities concerned.

Nevertheless many of these works are circulated to European Documentation Centres and only some limited distribution documents are listed anyway. Again, *COM* documents do not appear.

It is difficult to understand why the multilingual format is persisted with when the annual cumulations are divided into language sections. The annual cumulation also has a simple index. Cumulations for 1974, 1975 and 1976 have appeared so far.

List of additions to the Library, No. 10/11/12, 1979

This is a 'Catalogue of European Community publications and documents, 1978–1979, received at the Commission Library'. It is a particularly valuable work, being so much more up to date than the sales catalogues and broader in scope. The criterion for inclusion is simply whether the work in question has been received in the Central Library. It is arranged according to the OECD *Macrothesaurus*, with an author and title index.

It should be noted that this catalogue includes works sponsored in the first place by the Commission but handled by commercial publishers. Although this issue is regarded as experimental it is to be hoped that the catalogue will be carried on in future years since it is very much better than anything else available.

HMSO CATALOGUES

HMSO acts as an agent, in the UK, for a number of international agencies and overseas organizations, among them the European Communities. Confusion often arises because HMSO has the triple function of printer, publisher and bookseller. So far as the official publications of the European Communities are concerned HMSO is acting exclusively as a bookseller. The HMSO catalogues are a major bibliographic source so far as priced publications are concerned but they handle no others.

In *Government publications 1954* publications of the European Coal and Steel Community were listed for the first time; they appear on pp. 875–6. In 1955 and 1956 the only entry to be found is for the *Official gazette* (i.e. the *Official journal*). In 1957 this entry too was deleted. From 1955 to 1964 the entries for agency publications were transferred to the supplement *International organisations publications*. In 1959 entries for publications of the European Economic Community first appeared. In 1964 publications were grouped under the heading 'European Communities' which remained the practice up to 1975. From 1965 the title of the supplement had been changed to *International organisations and overseas agencies publications*. In February 1977 HMSO went over to a new system for the construction of the catalogue entries which was made retrospective to 1976. This involved the use of the *Anglo-American Cataloguing Rules* and the choice of highly specific headings. It is no longer possible to find the publications of the European Communities listed together.

The *Daily list* continues to list publications according to the old format but in the *Monthly list* the new format is adopted.

There are a number of difficulties now in using the HMSO catalogues. In the first place the choice of headings is very hard to comprehend, 'Division Youth, Schools and Universities' being among the more arcane, going to the third level of organization even within the Commission. There is also a preference for the French form of the heading for documents in French. The treatment of serials is inconsistent. A monthly periodical might be listed under the name of a Directorate (the second level of organization within the Commission) but a document in a series sometimes under the series heading. Other publications may appear under the name of a Directorate-General (the first level of organization within the Commission). The indexing tends, on the whole, to be rather inadequate and publications do not often appear under more than one heading in the body of the catalogue. There are cross-references but seldom of a very helpful kind.

In the past HMSO circulated a *Weekly list of government publications from Her Majesty's Stationery Office: a selection of interest to local authorities*, which was a useful current awareness service with a high European content.

Headings in use for European Communities' publications in *International organisations publications 1978:*

Administration of the Customs Union (European Communities Commission)

Agricultural statistical studies (eurostat)

Agriculture [series] (European Communities Commission)

Biological sciences [series] (European Communities Commission)

Centre for European Studies (Catholic University of Louvain)

Court of Justice of the European Coal and Steel Community

Demography and Household Surveys Division (eurostat)

Direction générale des relations extérieures (Communautés européennes commission)

Directorate for Agricultural Economics (European Communities Commission)

Directorate for National Economies and Economic Trends (European Communities Commission)

Directorate-General for Agriculture (European Communities Commission)

Directorate-General for Competition (European Communities Commission)

Directorate-General for Economic and Financial Affairs (European Communities Commission)

Directorate-General for Information (European Communities Commission)

Directorate-General for Research and Documentation (European Parliament)

Directorate-General for Social Affairs (European Communities Commission)

Division Youth, Schools and Universities (European Communities Commission)

Environment and quality of life [series] (European Communities Commission)

Esone Committee (European Communities Commission)

European Agricultural Guidance and Guarantee Fund Directorate

European Centre for the Development of Vocational Training

European Communities

European Communities Commission

European Communities Commission programmes: regional policy series

European Communities Commission studies: commerce and distribution series

European Communities Commission studies: competition: approximation of legislation series

European Communities Commission studies: education series

European Communities Commission studies: evolution of concentration and competition series

European Communities Commission studies: labour law series

European Communities Commission studies: regional policy series

European Communities Commission studies: social policy series

European Regional Development Fund

eurostat

Information on agriculture (Directorate for Agricultural Economics (European Communities Commission))

Mines Safety and Health Commission (European Communities Commission)

Nuclear science and technology [series] (European Communities Commission)

Physical sciences [series] (European Communities Commission)

Port Working Group (European Communities Commission)

Scientific Committee for Food (European Communities Commission)

Terminology Office (European Communities Commission)

BULLETIN ON DOCUMENTATION

This has had a particularly complicated publishing history, having gone through a number of changes of title and format. In 1964 the

Service Central de Documentation (which is now known as Central Archives and Documentation Service or SCAD-DG IX/D/1) brought out *Articles sélectionnés*. Its purpose was to list documents and articles which would be of interest to officials of the Commission of the European Economic Community. It was in fact a current awareness service. Material was catalogued, classified by the Universal Decimal Classification and microfilmed. Any official, having seen a reference which interested him, could then request a photocopy. *Articles sélectionnés* appeared fortnightly, the last issue being No. 20, 1972.

Between 1971 and 1973, SCAD also produced a series of bibliographies on specific subjects numbered 1 to 13. These were selections of official texts, publications and documents of the European Communities, relating to a particular topic. Most of these have been updated subsequently by *Supplement B* of the *Bulletin on documentation* described below.

During 1973, twenty-four issues and nine supplements of the *Internal bulletin on documentation* appeared. This was divided into three parts, though not necessarily were all three represented in each issue. Part I contained references to Community documents. Part II contained references to Community publications and studies, and also a selection of periodical articles. Both these parts were arranged according to the Universal Decimal Classification. Part III was called 'Outlines of archive-files', and listed references to official documents, 'prepared in such a way as to reflect the various aspects of the matter in question'.

The supplements were of two kinds. Some were cumulations of references over a given period on a particular subject from the *Internal bulletin on documentation* itself. Others were revisions of the SCAD bibliographies mentioned above. From time to time the *Internal bulletin on documentation* listed recent official publications in an annex. The last issue appeared on 12 July 1973 and was No. 24, 1973.

The first issue of the *Bulletin on documentation* was numbered 25, 1973, and although it had a different style of cover from its predecessor, the *Internal bulletin on documentation*, issues 25–7 were of similar content and arrangement. The next three, 28–30, contained only two sections; Part I—'Community documents and instruments'; and Part II—'Community publications and studies'. Selections of periodical articles went into a supplement. In issues

31–6 Part III—'Outlines of archives-files' was brought back. Bibliographies and cumulative lists of references also appeared as supplements.

From No. 37, 1973, until the end of 1976 there was a fortnightly *Bulletin on documentation* which was in two sections, though not necessarily did both appear in each issue. Part I—'Community documents and instruments' was arranged by the Universal Decimal Classification with general subject headings, up to No. 18/75 when the use of UDC was abandoned. Part II—'Community publications and studies' was a subject bibliography of the official publications of the European Communities. This part was particularly useful because it listed articles in periodicals as well as separately published material: the method of arrangement was the same as for Part I.

There was a fortnightly *Supplement A* which listed 'periodicals and articles on international economic activity or on national policies having a bearing on the European, international or world economy'. Entries were in the language in which the material was first written with brief annotations in that language. There was an irregular *Supplement B* which consisted of individual bibliographies on subjects of interest to the European Communities. Sometimes they were updated versions of earlier bibliographies. Some included periodical articles and some were confined to official publications and documents. The irregular *Supplement C* also consisted of individual bibliographies on particular subjects of interest to the Communities but in this case the entries were cumulated from the entries in the *Bulletin on documentation* and *Supplement A* during a stated period. In 1973 there were two issues of a *Supplement D* which was described as 'other documentary material' but seems to have been intended as a current contents service of periodicals received in the Central Library of the Commission. This was abandoned because of internal difficulties.

In 1977 the format of the *Bulletin on documentation* was simplified. It now consists of three series called *A*, *B*, and *C*. *A* contains official publications and periodical articles selected by SCAD and the documentation service of the European Parliament. It appears weekly. Material is arranged according to the following headings:

Customs matters and free movement of goods
Competition
Taxation
Right of establishment and freedom to provide services
International, public and private law
Economic, monetary and financial matters
Regional planning and development
Social affairs and sociology
Agriculture and fisheries
Industry, technology and scientific research
Energy
Transport
Environment
International policy and trade
Community institutions
Financing of Community activities
Integration movements
Education, culture and youth
General statistics. Demography
Domestic policy
International organizations
Information, press, public opinion

There is a *Guide du lecteur*, 1979 which explains the method of arrangement in more detail, expands abbreviations and lists the periodicals consulted. It replaces an earlier version which appeared as a special supplement in 1976.

B consists of bibliographies on the following subjects which are updated from time to time:

1   Community legislation relating to the elimination of technical barriers to trade in industrial products
2   Energy
3   Transport
4   Women's work
5   Fiscal matters
6   Community legislation relating to the removal of technical barriers to trade in foodstuffs
7   Veterinary and zootechnics matters

8   Approximation of the legislation on plant health, seeds,
       forestry
9   Education
10 Promotion of consumer interests
11 Protection of the environment
12 Competition policy
13 Regional policy
14 Community relations with the Mediterranean countries
15 Company law
16 Economic, monetary and financial matters
17 Free movement of persons and services
18 North–south dialogue

C is an irregular series of bibliographies which lists the entries
from A on a given subject which have appeared since the previous
cumulation.
The following were published in 1979:

1   Les mouvements d'intégration
2   Les organismes internationaux
3   Les marchés agricoles
4   Le droit communautaire

MECHANIZED INFORMATION RETRIEVAL

In 1979 it was reported that 'data processing at the Commission
which, a few years ago, was basically limited to statistical applications and pay has since been extended and diversified considerably
and the applications currently being developed or already adopted
cover virtually all the Commission activities'.

CIRCE is a major documentary application but the Commission
has taken a leading role in the establishment of EURONET Diane
(Direct Information Access Network for Europe). The Commission is itself a EURONET host and data base provider. ECHO
service (European Community Host Organization) plans the following data bases:

AGREP   Permanent Inventory of Agricultural
                 Research Projects in the Community
EABS   Euro abstracts

ENDOC   Environmental Centres in the Com-
                    munity
ENREP   Current environment research projects
                    in the Community
EURODICAUTOM   Multilingual terminology data bank
EUROFILE   Inventory of data bases and banks avail-
                    able in Europe

DG XIII publishes *Euronet Diane news* (previously *Euronet news*) which provides current information on developments in EURONET.

CDIC, the Steering Committee on data processing at the Commission was established in 1976. There is an *Annual report of the data-processing departments of the Commission*. The report for 1978, from which the quotation in the first paragraph is taken, is *COM*(79) 678 final of 28 November 1979. The report for 1977 is *COM*(78) 347 final of 21 July 1978.

The Commission has taken an interest in on-line information retrieval over a number of years. The latest thinking is described in depth in *European society faced with the challenge of new information technologies: a community response*, *COM*(79) 650 final, 26 November 1979.

The report of a workshop on the European information industry held in Luxembourg in June 1979 and sponsored by the Commission appears in a supplement to *Aslib proceedings*, January 1980.

CIRCE

CIRCE is the Information and Documentary Research Centre of the European Communities. The acronym stands for the French, Centre d'information et de recherche documentation des Communautés européennes. It was set up in December 1976 with the object of merging two earlier systems—ECDOC which was managed by the Secretariat-General and CELEX managed by the Legal Service. It provides an information service to the Commission only, except that CELEX and also the Statistical Office data base CRONOS are available to the other Institutions. It is planned that both CELEX and CRONOS should ultimately become available publicly.

CELEX was set up in 1971 and the initial work on the system is described in Thomas, J.E.F., *The problem of legal information in the European Economic Community* (unpublished dissertation), University of Sheffield, 1974. At the moment the scope of the information in the system includes:

Treaties
Legal acts resulting from the external relations of the European
    Communities
Secondary legislation
Judgments of the Court of Justice
Questions and answers in the European Parliament

It is intended that CELEX should eventually provide coverage for the whole of the law of the European Communities, in full text, in all the official languages. It is planned to include coverage of the decisions of national courts and national measures relating to Community law as well as draft legislation and opinions from the European Parliament and the Economic and Social Committee.

Apart from a confidential file of staff records there are four Commission data bases in CIRCE:

ECO1
PRC
ACTU
ASMODEE

ECO1 was started in 1974 and now includes data on the following:

Meetings' papers of the Commission and minutes
Documents sent to the Commission
Records of Council decisions
Secretariat-General's summary of the records of the Council
    and COREPER meetings
Commissioned studies
Written procedures
Questions and answers in the European Parliament

The documents themselves are stored in microfiche and ECO1 acts as an on-line index to the contents of the microfiche set. The indexing is extremely detailed with about 45,000 descriptors in use. Many of the documents are on-line in full text.

PRC is a file of proposals, recommendations and communications. It is designed to provide information on the progress of the inter-Institutional examination of proposals, recommendations and communications to the Council, and Council decisions. It is regarded as the most politically sensitive of the CIRCE data bases.

ACTU, short for 'actualités', is updated daily and covers any document sent by the Secretariat-General to the Commission. It includes information on the progress of written and delegated procedures, inventories of decisions by type and related statistics.

ASMODEE has been designed to monitor the progress of directives.

Although there is a lot of confidential information in the CIRCE system the problem of confidentiality arises not so much from the content of the data but the inferences that can be drawn from its manipulation. Nevertheless there are a number of 'products' which can be derived from it:

> A half-yearly list of Commission proposals, amendments to or withdrawls of proposals, opinions of the European Parliament and Economic and Social Committee, items adopted by the Council of Ministers
> A half-yearly list of proposals pending before the Council of Ministers on which the European Parliament has delivered an opinion
> A list of directives due to enter into force in the Member States of the European Communities
> A list of regulations enacted after the opinion of the European Parliament which are about to expire

Work has begun on the compilation of a multilingual index of secondary legislation in force.

EUROPEAN BIBLIOGRAPHY

This was a multilingual card bibliography covering the years 1965 to 1973. It was produced in DG X.

The scope of this work was publications relating to the study of European integration. It consisted mainly of books and pamphlets but also listed a substantial number of official publications and documents. There is an author index but the cards themselves are in classified order. The classification scheme has been adopted by a number of European Documentation Centres and is given below:

420   European integration

     420.1   History
     420.2   Economics and social sciences
     420.3   Politics
     420.4   Education—Culture—Technology
     420.5   Legal aspects of integration—European civil service
     420.6   Public opinion polls—Information
     420.7   Geography
     420.8   Defence
     420.9   Bibliographies

421–427   European Communities—Institutional structure

     421   European law—Community law
     422   Treaties
     423   European executives
     423.1   Commissions—High Authority
     423.2   Council of Ministers
     424   European Parliament
     425   Court of Justice
     426   Economic and Social Committee—Consultative Committee
     427   European Investment Bank

430   European Communities—General Activities

     430.1   European Economic Community
     430.2   European Coal and Steel Community
     430.3   Euratom

441–499   European Communities—Activities by sector

     441   External relations
     441.1   International organizations
     441.2   Non-member countries and associated countries
     441.3   Commercial policy

442 Economic policy—Finance
442.1 Trade—Cycle policy—Programming
442.2 Regional economic policy—National economies
442.3 Finance—Currency—Capital
443 Internal market
443.1 Customs—Free movement of goods
443.2 Coal and steel industries
443.3 Other industries—Crafts—Commerce
443.4 Right of establishment
443.5 Nuclear research and its applications
444 Competition—Taxation
444.1 Competition
444.2 Taxation
445 Social questions
445.1 Vocational training—Technical research
445.2 Manpower—Employment—Labour movements
445.3 Wages
445.4 Social security
445.5 Social services—Housing
445.6 Labour—Trade Unions
446 Agriculture
447 Transport
448 Associated overseas countries
449 Energy problem

450 European Communities and the rest of the world

450.1 Western Europe
450.2 Eastern Europe
450.3 North America
450.4 Latin America
450.5 Africa
450.6 Asia
450.7 Australia

460 European international organizations

460.1 EFTA
460.2 Benelux

460.3   Council of Europe
460.4   Comecon
460.5   OECD
460.6   NATO
460.7   WEU
460.8   Nordic Council

This card file should not be confused with *The European bibliography* compiled by the European Cultural Centre, Geneva, under the editorship of H. Pehrsson and H. Wulf, Sijthoff, 1965; or with *European bibliography* compiled by L. L. Paklons, (Cahiers de Bruges, N.S. 8), College of Europe, 1964.

SCIENTIFIC PUBLICATIONS

Bibliographies of scientific publications produced under the auspices of the European Communities appear in the following publications. From 1962 to 1967 scientific literature was listed in the . . . *general report on the activities of the Community* (Euratom). In the *Fifth general report* a list of 'scientific and technical publications resulting from the Euratom research programme and publications of a more general character', appears on pp. 235–63.

In the *Sixth general report* 'scientific and technical reports stemming from the Euratom research programme and published by the Commission', covering 1 April 1962 to 28 February 1963, are listed on pp. 283–98.

From 1964 to 1967 there was a second volume of the report entitled *Documentation attached to . . . general report on the activities of the Community* with a section devoted to the 'scientific and technical publications stemming from the Euratom research programme':

Seventh, pp. 169–91, covers 1 March to 31 December 1963.
Eighth, pp. 173–214, covers 1 January to 31 December 1964.
Ninth, pp. 171–248, covers 1 January to 31 December 1965.
Tenth, pp. 189–277, covers 1 January to 31 December 1966.

EURO ABSTRACTS

Since 1963 there has been an abstracting service covering documents that are numbered with the prefix *Eur*. These include reports, lectures, articles, proceedings of scientific and technical conferences and patents. This material had been the product of the Euratom research programme and since the Treaty of Brussels, which merged the executives, the wider scientific and technical research programme of the European Communities.

From 1963 to 1969 this service was known as *Euratom information* and was published in the official languages and English. There were four issues in Vol. 1 and twelve in Vols. 2 to 7. There was an annual index in each volume. Publications listed here were the result of three kinds of activities:

Euratom Joint Nuclear Research Centre (JNRC)
research conducted by firms or organizations working under contract to or in association with Euratom
Euratom/United States Joint Research and Development Program

The indexes were organized in three sections:

publications
patents
contracts

For all years there were author and subject indexes for publications, and an inventors index for patents. There was a patent owners index 1963–6 and a subject index 1968–9. For all years there was a subject index to contracts, and an index of contract holders for all years except 1967.

In 1970 the title was changed to *Euro abstracts* although the volume numbering was continued. There were twelve issues to each volume and an annual index. Publications were listed with an abstract in the original language and/or in English. The indexes were organized in two sections:

publications
patents

For all years there were author and subject indexes for publications, and in 1974 a programmes index as well. There were subject and inventors' indexes to patents for all years.

From 1975 *Euro abstracts* has been divided into two sections:

Section I. Euratom and EEC research: scientific and technical

publications and patents
Section II. Coal and Steel. Research programmes and agreements, scientific and technical publications and patents

In *Section I* there are three headings in use:

scientific and technical publications
patents
training courses and seminars—conferences and symposia in
  preparation

Although there is a title page in each of the official languages, entries appear only in English together with the language of the original publication if different from English. Each issue has an author index for publications and an inventors index for patents.

In *Section II* there are five headings in use:

research programmes
research agreements
scientific and technical publications
patents
training courses and seminars—conferences and symposia in
  preparation

The first four of these headings are each sub-divided further:

coal
steel
research of a social nature (industrial hygiene, safety and
  medicine)

Again, there are title pages in each of the official languages but the rest of the material is presented in English, French and German.

It is planned to offer *Euro abstracts* as an on-line data base through ECHO with the name EABS (see above, p. 240).

PATENT LITERATURE

The patents listed in both sections of *Euro abstracts* are those published in the usual way in the member countries of the European Communities but derived from the implementation of the research programmes of the Commission or one of the Commission's contractors or associates.

The information contained in *Euro abstracts* appears about eighteen months after the priority date. The abstracting is done by the Commission's Patent Bureau.

The 'European patent' is a different question (see above, p. 201).

APPENDIX I

Addresses to which orders for publications should be sent

FREE PUBLICATIONS

Requests for free publications including limited distribution documents should be sent to the originating Institution. Free publications are not normally available from the Information Offices of the Commission and certainly not from sales offices. This is a list of the addresses of the Institutions to which requests should be sent:

Commission
Division IX-D-1
Rue de la Loi 200
1049 Bruxelles
Belgium

Council of Ministers
Sécrétariat général du Conseil
Direction 'Information et
   documentation'
Rue de la Loi 170
1048 Bruxelles
Belgium

Court of Justice
Service intérieur
Plateau du Kirchberg
Boîte postale 1406
Luxembourg

**Economic and Social
   Committee**
Division 'Presse, information
   et publications'
Rue Ravenstein 2
1000 Bruxelles
Belgium

European Investment Bank Service information 2 place de Metz Luxembourg	**Court of Auditors of the** **European Communities** 29 rue Aldringen Boîte postale 43 Luxembourg

INFORMATION OFFICES OF THE COMMISSION

The Information Offices of the Commission supply their own publications free of charge. They do not deal in sales publications, except in the case of the Washington Office, and cannot usually supply the limited distribution documents of other Institutions. This is a list of the offices in Community countries:

Belgium
Rue Archimède 73
1040 Bruxelles

Italy
Via Poli 29
00187 Roma

Denmark
Gammel Torv 6
Postboks 144
1004 København K

Luxembourg
Centre européen
Bâtiment Jean Monnet B/O
Plateau du Kirchberg
Luxembourg

France
61 Rue des Belles-Feuilles
75782 Paris
Cedex 16

Netherlands
Lange Voorhout 29
Den Haag

Germany (Federal Republic)
Zitelmannstrasse 22
5300 Bonn

United Kingdom
20 Kensington Palace
  Gardens
London W8 4QQ

Kurfürstendamm 102
1000 Berlin 31

4 Cathedral Road
Cardiff CF1 9SG

Ireland
29 Merrion Square
Dublin 2

7 Alva Street
Edinburgh EH2 4PH

OFFICES OUTSIDE THE COMMUNITY COUNTRIES

Canada
Inn of the Provinces
Office Tower
Suite 1110
Sparks' Street 350
Ottawa
Ont. KIR 7S8

Chile
Avda Ricardo Lyon 1177
Santiago de Chile 9
Adresse postale: Casilla 10093

Greece
2 Vassilissis Sofias
T.K. 1602
Athina 134

Japan
Kowa 25 Building
8–7 Sanbancho
Chiyoda-Ku
Tokyo 102

Switzerland
Case postale 195
37–39 rue de Vermont
1211 Genève 20

Turkey
13 Bogaz Sokak
Kavaklidere
Ankara

United States
2100 M Street, NW
Suite 707
Washington DC 20037

1 Dag Hammarskjöld Plaza
245 East 47th Street
New York NY 10017

Venezuela
Quinta Bienvenida
Valle Arriba
Calle Colibri
Distrito Sucre
Caracas

SALES OFFICES

Belgium
Moniteur belge
Rue de Louvain 40–42
1000 Bruxelles

Denmark
J. H. Schultz—Boghandel
Møntergade 19
1116 København K

France
Service de vente en France
  des publications des
  Communautés européennes
26 rue Desaix
75732 Paris
Cedex 15

Germany (Federal Republic)
Verlag Bundesanzeiger
Breite Strasse
Postfach 10 80 06
5000 Köln 1

Ireland
Government Publications
Sales Office
G.P.O. Arcade
Dublin 1

Italy
Libreria dello Stato
Piazza G. Verdi 10
00198 Roma

Luxembourg
Office des publications
  officielles des
  Communautés européennes
5 rue du Commerce
Boîte postale 1003

Netherlands
Staatsdrukkerij- en
  uitgeverijbedrijf
Christoffel Plantijnstraat
's-Gravenhage

Spain
Libreria Mundi-Prensa
Castelló 37
Madrid 1

Sweden
Librairie C. E. Fritze
2 Fredsgatan
Stockholm 16

Switzerland
Librairie Payot
6 rue Grenus
1211 Genève

United Kingdom
HMSO
49 High Holborn
London WC1V 6HB

United States
European Community
  Information Service
2100 M Street, NW
Suite 707
Washington DC 20037

European Documentation Centres and Depository Libraries

ARGENTINA

Biblioteca del Congresso de la
    Nación Argentina
Rivadavia 1850
Buenos Aires

Universidad Catolica
Trejo 323
Cordoba

AUSTRALIA

La Trobe University
Library
Bundoora
Victoria 3083

National Library of Australia
Processing Branch
Canberra
A.C.T. 2600

University of Tasmania
Box 252 C, GPO
Hobart
Tasmania 7001

State Library of Victoria
304–328 Swanston Street
Melbourne 3000
Victoria

Public Library of New South
    Wales
Macquarie Street
Sydney
New South Wales

AUSTRIA

Secrétariat général de la
    Fédération Internationale
    des Maisons de l'Europe
Tuchlauben 8/1
1011 Wien

Zentrale Verwaltungs-
  Bibliothek und Dokumen-
  tation für Wirtschaft
  und Technik
Stubenring 1
1011 Wien

BELGIUM

Europees Studie- en
  Informatie- Centrum
Toulousestraat 49
200 Antwerpen

Collège d'Europe—Europa
  College
Dijver 11
8000 Brugge

Vrije Universiteit Brussel
Faculteit der
  Rechtgeleerdheid
Seminarie Europees Recht
Pleinlaan 2
1050 Brussel

Université Libre de Bruxelles
Institut d'Études
  Européennes
Bibliothèque
Av. Franklin Roosevelt 39
1050 Bruxelles

Bibliothèque Royale Albert
  1er
Boulevard de l'Empereur 4
1000 Bruxelles

Institut Royal des Relations
  Internationales
Av. de la Couronne 88
1050 Bruxelles

Rijksuniversiteit Gent
Faculteit van de Economische
  Wetenschappen
Korte Meer 48
9000 Gent

Université de Liège
Faculté de Droit
Avenue Rogier 12
4000 Liège

Katholieke Universiteit te
  Leuven
Centrum voor Europees
  Studies
1 Place de l'Université
1348 Louvain La Neuve

Université Catholique de
  Louvain
Institut de Recherche
  Économique—IRES
Place Montesquieu 1
1348 Louvain La Neuve

Facultés universitaires
N.D. de la Paix
Rue de Bruxelles 61
5000 Namur

BRAZIL

Universidade de Brasília
Biblioteca
Agência Postal 15
70.000 Brasilia D.F.

Fundaçao Getúlio Vargas
186 Praia de Botafogo
Caixa Postal 4081-ZC-05
Rio de Janeiro, R.J.

BULGARIA

Cyril and Methodius National
    Library
Official Publications Section
Boul. Tolbuhin 11
Sofia

CANADA

University of New Brunswick
Harriet Irving Library
P.O. Box 7500
Fredericton
New Brunswick E3B 5H5

Dalhousie University
Library
Documents Section
Halifax
Nova Scotia B3H 448

Queen's University
McDonald Hall
Law Building
UN & International
    documents
Kingston
Ontario

Université de Montréal
Centre d'Études et de
    Documentation
    européennes
5255 rue Decelles
Montréal 250
Québec

McGill University
University Libraries
3459 McTavish St.
Montreal 2
Quebec H3A 1Y1

Bibliothèque nationale du
    Canada
Dons et échanges
395 rue Wellington
Ottawa
Ontario K1A ON4

University of Ottawa
Institute for International
    Cooperation
190 rue Laurier Est
Ottawa
Ontario K1N 6N5

Carleton University
The Library
Documents Division
Colonel By Drive
Ottawa 1
Ontario K1S 5B6

Brock University
The Library
St Catharines
Ontario L2S 3A1

Université Laurentienne
Département de Science
   Politique
Centre de documentation et
   de Recherche européennes
Sudbury
Ontario P3E 2C6

York University
Government Documents
Scott Library
4700 Keele Street
Downsview
Toronto
Ontario M3J 2R6

Wilfrid Laurier University
Library
Waterloo
Ontario N2L 3C5

CHILE

Biblioteca Escuela
   Latino-americana de
   Ciencia Politica y
   Administración Pública
Casilla 3212
Santiago de Chile

Biblioteca de Congresso
   Nacional
Calle Compañía, F, 1883
Santiago de Chile

COLOMBIA

Universidad del Valle
Bibliotecas
Apart. Aéreo 6641
Cali

CUBA

Universidad de La Habana
Centro de Informacion
   Cientifica y Tecnica
Apartado 6022
La Habana 6

CZECHOSLOVAKIA

Institut des Relations
   Internationales
Bibliothèque
Nerudova 3
Praha 1—Malá Strana

GERMANY (FEDERAL REPUBLIC)

Freie Universität Berlin
Fachbereich Politische
   Wissenschaften
Otto-Suhr-Institut
Ihnestrasse 22
1000 Berlin 33

Freie Universität Berlin
Universitätsbibliothek
Garystr. 33
1000 Berlin 33

Technische Universität Berlin
Institut für
   Wirtschaftwissenschaften
Uhlandstrasse 4–5
1000 Berlin 12

Europäische Akademie Berlin
Bibliothek
Bismarckallee 46–48
1000 Berlin 33

Staatsbibliothek Preussischer
   Kulturbesitz
Abt. Amtsdruckschriften und
   Internationaler Amtlicher
   Schriftentausch
Postfach 59
1000 Berlin 30

Universität Bielefeld
Fachbereich
   Rechtswissenschaft
Universitätsstrasse
4800 Bielefeld

Universität Bochum
Universitätsbibliothek
Im Lottental–Zeche
Klosterbusch
4630 Bochum–Querenburg

Deutsche Gesellschaft für
   Auswärtige Politik
Dokumentationsstelle
Adenauerallee 133
5300 Bonn

Deutscher Bundestag
Bibliothek
Sachgebiet Internationale
   Organisationen
Bundeshaus
5300 Bonn

Technische Hochschule
   Darmstadt
Fachbereich Gesellschafts-
   und
   Geschichtswissenschaften
Abt. Wissenschaftliche Politik
Schloss
6100 Darmstadt

Gesamthochschule Duisberg
Bibliothekzentrale
Zeitschriftenstelle
Bürgerstrasse 15
4100 Duisberg 1

Universität Frankfurt/Main
Institut für ausländisches und
   internationales
   Wirtschaftsrecht
Senckenberganlage 31
6000 Frankfurt/Main

Deutsche Bibliothek
Stiftung des Öffentlichen
Rechts
Zeppelinallee 8
6000 Frankfurt/Main

Universität Freiburg
Institut für öffentliches Recht
Werthmannplatz
7800 Freiburg i. Brsg.

Universität Giessen
Fachbereich
Rechtswissenschaft
Abt. Öffentliches Recht IV
Licher Str. 74
6300 Giessen

Universität Göttingen
Sozialwissenschaftliche
Bibliothek
Abt. Europäisches Recht
Kreuzbergring 12 A
63400 Göttingen

Universität Hamburg
Abteilung Europäisches
Gemeinschaftsrecht
Seminar für öffentliches
Recht und Staatslehre
Schlüterstr. 28 III
Rechtshaus
2000 Hamburg 13

Universität Hamburg
Institut für europäische
Wirtschaftspolitik
Verfügungsgebäude IV
Von-Melle-Park 5
2000 Hamburg 13

HWWA-Institut für
Wissenschaftsforschung
Bibliothek
Neuer Jungfernstieg 21
2000 Hamburg 36

Max-Planck-Institut für
ausländisches Recht und
Völkerrecht
Bibliothek
Berliner Strasse 48
6900 Heidelberg

Institut für Weltwirtschaft an
der Universität Kiel
Bibliothek
Mecklenburger Str. 2–4
2300 Kiel

Universität Köln
Institut für das Recht der
Europäischen
Gemeinschaften
Gottfried-Keller-Str. 2
5000 Köln 41

Universität Köln
Universitäts- und
Staatsbibliothek
Universitätsstr. 41
5000 Köln-Linenthal

Universität Konstanz
Universitätsbibliothek
Sonderakzession
Giessberg
7750 Konstanz

Europa-Institut der
  Universität Mannheim
  (WH)
Schloss/Westflügel (Jur. Fak.)
6800 Mannheim

Universität München
Institut für internationales
  Recht
Europäisches und
  internationales
  Wirtschaftsrecht
Ludwigstr. 29/III
München 22

Bayerische Staatsbibliothek
Erwerbungsabteilung
Ludwigstrasse 16
München 22

Universität Regensburg
Europäische
  Dokumentationsstelle—
  Teilbibliothek Recht
Universitätsstrasse 31
8400 Regensburg

Universität des Saarlandes
Universitätsbibliothek
St. Johanner Stadtwald
6600 Saarbrücken 15

Universität des Saarlandes
Europa-Institut/Bibliothek
Stadtwald
6600 Saarbrücken

Universität Hohenheim (LH)
Abteilung für öffentliches
  Recht, Agrarrecht und
  Umweltrecht
Garbenstrasse 17
Postfach 106
7000 Stuttgart 70

Württembergische
  Landesbibliothek
Konrad-Adenauer-Str. 8
7000 Stuttgart 1

Universität Tübingen
Universitätsbibliothek
Zeitschriftenstelle
Wilhelmstrasse 32
7400 Tübingen

Universität Würzburg
Institut für Öffentliches
  Recht, Europarecht und
  Internationales
  Wirtschaftsrecht
Franziskanerplatz 4
8700 Würzburg

DENMARK

Handelshøjskolen i Aarhus
EF—Biblioteket
Funglesangsallé 4
8210 Aarhus V

Statsbiblioteket
Aarhus

Copenhagen School of
  Economics and Business
  Administration
The Library
Julius Thomsenplads 10
1925 København V

Københavns Universitet
Institut for international Ret
  og Europaret
Pilestraede 58/4
1112 København

Het Kongelike Bibliothek
Kontorst for Internationale
  Publikationer
Christians Brygge 8
København K

EGYPT

Council of Arab Economic
  Unity
The Library
20 Aisha El-Taymouria Str.
Garden City
Cairo

FIJI

University of the South Pacific
Lancala Bay
P.O. Box 1168
Suva

FINLAND

Eduskunnan Kirjasto
Library of the Parliament
00102 Helsinki 10

Turku University
Institute of European Market
  Law
Law Faculty
20500 Turku 50

FRANCE

Université d'Aix-en-Provence
Centre des Institutions
  Internationales et des
  Communautés européennes
3 av. Robert Schuman
13621 Aix-en-Provence

Université de Picardie
Faculté de Droit
Chemin du Thil
Le Campus
80044 Amiens Cedex

Université d'Angers
Faculté de Droit et des
  Sciences Économiques
Centre de Documentation et
  de Recherche européennes
Bld. Beaussier
49005 Angers Cedex

Université de Besançon
Faculté de Droit et des
    Sciences économiques et
    Politiques
Centre de Documentation et
    de Recherche européennes
Av. de l'Observatoire
25030 Besançon Cedex

Université de Bordeaux I
CDRE de la Faculté de Droit
    et des Sciences
    économiques
Av. Louis Duguit
33604 Pessac,
Bordeaux

Université de Bretagne
    occidentale
Faculté de Droit et des
    Sciences économiques
Centre de Documentation et
    de Recherche européennes
1 av. Foch
B.P. 331
29273 Brest Cedex

Université de Caen
Faculté de Droit et des
    Sciences Politiques
Centre d'Études et de
    Recherche européennes
Esplanade de la Paix
14032 Caen Cedex

Université de
    Clermont-Ferrand
Faculté de Droit
Centre d'Études et de
    Recherche européennes
41 Bld. Gergovia
63002 Clermont-Ferrand
    Cedex

Université de Dijon
Institut de relations
    internationales
Centre de Documentation et
    de Recherche européennes
4 Bld. Gabriel
21000 Dijon

Institut Européen
    d'Administration des
    Affaires
Bibliothèque et Centre de
    Documentation
Bld. de Constance
77305 Fontainebleau

Université de Grenoble II
Centre Universitaire de
    Recherche européenne et
    Internationale (CUREI)
B.P. 47
38040 Grenoble Cedex

Centre Universitaire du Mans
Centre de Documentation et
    de Recherche européennes
Bureau d'études économiques
    et juridiques
Campus—Route de Laval
72000 Le Mans Cedex

Université des Sciences et
 Techniques Lille I
Centre de Documentation et
 de Recherche européennes
U.E.R. de Sciences
 Économiques et Sociales
Bâtiment 5 Cité Universitaire
B.P. 36
59650 Villeneuve d'Ascq
Lille

Université de Lille II
Faculté des Sciences
 Juridiques, Politiques et
 Sociales
Centre de Documentation et
 de Recherche européennes
Campus—Rue de Lille
B.P. 19
59650 Villeneuve d'Ascq
Lille

Université de Limoges
Faculté de Droit et des
 Sciences économiques
Centre de Documentation et
 de Recherche européennes
Place du Présidial
87100 Limoges

Université de Lyon III
Faculté de Droit
Centre de Documentation et
 de Recherche européennes
15 Quai Claude Bernard
B.P. 155
69224 Lyon Cedex 1

Université de Lyon II
Institut d'Études politiques
Centre d'Études de Science
 Politique et de
 Documentation
 européenne
1 rue Raulin
69365 Lyon Cedex 2

Université de Montpellier I
Centre de Droit de
 l'Entreprise
Centre d'Études et de
 Recherche européennes
39 rue de l'Université
34060 Montpellier Cedex

Université de Nancy II
Centre Européen
 universitaire
15 Place Carnot
54042 Nancy Cedex

Université de Nantes
U.E.R. Sciences juridiques
Chemin de la Sensive du
 Tertre
44036 Nantes Cedex

Université de Nice
Institut du Droit de la Paix et
 du Développement
Centre de Documentation et
 de Recherche européennes
34 av. R. Schuman
06000 Nice

Université d'Orléans
Faculté de Droit et des
  Sciences économiques
Domaine Universitaire
Route de Blois
45045 Orléans Cedex

Université de Paris I
Centre Universitaire d'Études
  des Communautés
  européennes
Panthéon–Sorbonne
12 Place du Panthéon
75231 Paris Cedex 05

Université de Paris IX–
  Dauphine
Centre de Documentation et
  de Recherche européennes
6e étage—Bibliothèque
Place du Maréchal de Lattre
  de Tassigny
Paris Cedex 16

Université de Paris X–
  Nanterre
U.E.R. de Sciences juridiques
Centre de Documentation et
  de Recherche européennes
2 rue de Rouen
92000 Nanterre
Paris

Université de Paris XII–Val
  de Marne
Faculté de Droit et des
  Sciences politiques et
  économiques
Centre de Documentation et
  de Recherche européennes
58 av. Didier
94210 La Varenne St Hilaire
Paris

Université de Paris-Nord
  (XIII)
Faculté de Droit et de
  Sciences politiques
Avenue J.B. Clément
93430 Villetaneuse
Paris

Université de Paris
Bibliothèque de la Faculté de
  Droit et des Sciences
  économiques
Service des Publications
  internationales
2 rue Cujas
75 Paris 5e

École Nationale
  d'Administration
56 rue des St. Pères
75007 Paris

Centre Judiciaire de
  documentation européenne
Bibliothèque de la Cour
  d'Appel de Paris
34 Quai des Orfèvres
75001 Paris

Bibliothèque Nationale
Service des publications
  officielles
Département des Entrées
Rue Richelieu 58
75 Paris 2e

Université de Pau et des Pays
  de L'Adour
Faculté de Droit et des
  Sciences économiques
Avenue du Doyen Poplawski
64000 Pau

Centre Universitaire de
  Perpignan
Faculté Pluridisciplinaire des
  Sciences humaines et
  sociales
Centre de Documentation et
  de Recherche européennes
Chemin de la Passio Viéla
66025 Perpignan Cedex

Université de Poitiers
Faculté de Droit et des
  Sciences sociales
Centre d'Études européennes
93 av. du Recteur Pineau
86022 Poitiers

Université de Reims
Faculté de Droit et des
  Sciences économiques
Centre de Documentation et
  de Recherche européennes
57 bis rue Pierre Taittinger
B.P. 97
51054 Reims Cedex

Université de Rennes I
Faculté des Sciences
  juridiques
Centre de Documentation et
  de Recherche européennes
9 rue Jean Macé
35042 Rennes Cedex

Université de Rouen
Faculté de Droit et des
  Sciences économiques
Centre de Documentation et
  de Recherche européennes
Bld. André Siegfried
76130 Mont Saint Aignan
Rouen

Université de Strasbourg III
Institut de Recherches
  juridiques, politiques et
  sociales
Centre d'Études
  Internationales et
  Européennes
Place d'Athènes
67084 Strasbourg Cedex

Université de Strasbourg III
Institut des Hautes Études
  européennes
5 rue Schiller
67000 Strasbourg

Centre Universitaire de
  Toulon
Faculté de Droit
Château Saint-Michel
R.N. 38
83130 La Garde
Toulon

Université de Toulouse I
Centre de Documentation et
    de Recherche européennes
Place Anatole France
31070 Toulouse Cedex

Université de Tours
Faculté des Sciences
    juridiques et économiques
Centre de Documentation et
    de Recherche européennes
116 Bld. Béranger
B.P. 312
37 Tours

HUNGARY

Institute of Economics
Hungarian Academy of
    Sciences
Münnich Ferenc u. 7
1351 Budapest V

INDIA

National Library
Belvedere
Calcutta 27

Indian Council of World
    Affairs
Sapru House
Barakhamba Road
New Delhi 1

Library of Parliament
Parliament House
11001
New Delhi

Servants of India Society's
    Library
Poona 4
Maharashtra

IRAN

Université de Téhéran
Centre des Hautes Études
    Internationales de la
    Faculté de Droit et des
    Sciences Politiques
43 av. Anatole France
Teheran

IRELAND

The Library
University College
Cork

The Library
University College
Dublin 4

The Library
Trinity College
Dublin 2

Library of the Oireachtas
Dail Eireann
Kildare Street
Dublin 2

The National Library of
   Ireland
Kildare Street
Dublin 2

The Library
University College
Galway

National Institute for Higher
   Education
Plassey House
Limerick

ISRAEL

The Hebrew University of
   Jerusalem
Centre for European Studies
P.O. Box 503
Jerusalem

University of Tel Aviv
Library
Leon Recanati Graduate
   School of Business
   Administration
Ramat-Aviv
Tel Aviv

ITALY

Università di Bari
Istituto di diritto
   internazionale e scienze
   politiche
70100 Bari

Università di Bologna
Biblioteca Facoltà Economia
   e Commercio
Via Belle Arti 33
40126 Bologna

Università di Bologna
Istituto Giuridico 'A. CICU'
Via Bamboni 27/29
40126 Bologna

Centro Informazioni e Studi
   sulle Comunità europee
Croso Garibaldi 53
72100 Brindisi

Università di Cagliari
Facoltà di Giurisprudenza
Viale S. Ignazio 17
09100 Cagliari

Università di Catania
Istituto di Diritto
   Internazionale
Biblioteca
Villa Cerami
95100 Catania

Università di Ferrara
Istituto di Economia e
   Finanza
Centro di Documentazione e
   Studi sulle Comunità
   europee
Via Savonarola 9
44100 Ferrara

Istituto Universitario
  Europeo
Biblioteca
Badia Fiesolana
Via dei Roccettini 5
50016 San Domenico di
  Fiesole
Firenze

Biblioteca Nazionale Centrale
Piazza dei Cavalleggeri 1
50122 Firenze

Università di Genova
Istituto di diritto
  internazionale
Via Balbi 30
16126 Genova

Università di Genova
Facoltà di Economia e
  Commercio
Istituto di Politica Economica
  e Finanziaria
Via Bertani 1
Genova

Università di Macerata
Istituto di Economia e
  Finanza
Facoltà di Giurisprudenza
Via Crescimbeni 14
62100 Macerata

Università di Messina
Facoltà di Economia e
  Commercio

Biblioteca
Via dei Verdi
98100 Messina

Università Cattolica del Sacro
  Cuore
Biblioteca
Largo Gemelli 1
20123 Milano

Università Commerciale
  'Luigi Bocconi'
Biblioteca di Economia e
  Commercio
Via R. Sarfatti 25
20136 Milano

Centro Internazionale di Studi
  e Documentazione sulle
  Comunità Europee
Via dei Mercanti 2
20121 Milano

Centro di Documentazione e
  Ricerche sulle Comunità
  europee
Corso Canale Grande 33
41100 Modena

Università di Napoli
Centro di Specializzazione e
  Ricerche economico-
  agrarie per il Mezzogiorno
Facoltà di Agraria
80055 Portici
Napoli

Società Italiana per
l'Organizzazione
Internazionale
Villa Pignatelli
Riviera di Chiaia 200
80121 Napoli

Biblioteca Nazionale Vittorio
Emmanuele III
Palazzo Reale
80100 Napoli

Università di Padova
Centro di Studi Europei
Facoltà di Giurisprudenza
Via III Febbraio
35100 Padova

Università di Palermo
Biblioteca
Facoltà di Lettere
Viale delle Scienze
80128 Palermo

Università di Parma
Scuola di Specializzazione in
Diritto ed Economia delle
Organizzazioni
internazionali
Via Università 12
43100 Parma

Università di Pavia
Centro Studi sulle Comunità
Europee
Fac. Giurisprudenza, Sc.
Politiche Economia e
Commercio
Corso Strada Nuova 65
27100 Pavia

Università di Perugia
Biblioteca Centrale
Piazza dell'Università
06100 Perugia

Università di Chieti
Istituto di Diritto
Comparado
Economato 'Gabrielle
d'Annunzio'
Via Gramsci 12
65100 Pescara

Università di Pisa
Istituto di diritto
internazionale
'D. Auzilotti'
Via S. Maria 32
56100 Pisa

Istituto Superiore Europeo di
Studi Politici
Via Torrione 101/F
89100 Reggio Calabria

Università di Roma
Facoltà di Economia e
Commercio
Scuola di perfezionamento in
Studi europei
Piazza Benedetto Cairoli 3
00100 Roma

Università di Roma
Facoltà di Scienze Politiche
Istituto di Diritto Pubblico e
dottrina dello Stato
Città Universitaria
00100 Roma

Centro Italiano di Studi
  Europei 'Luigi Einaudi'
Piazza SS. Apostoli 80
00187 Roma

Società Italiana per
  l'Organizzazione
  Internazionale
Biblioteca
Via di San Marco 3
00186 Roma

Scuola Superiore della
  Pubblica Amministrazione
Corso Vittorio Emanuele 116
Palazzo Vidoni
Roma

Centro Studi e Formazione
  Europea
Ufficio Studi delle ACLI
Via Monte della Farina 64
00100 Roma

Università di Salerno
Biblioteca delle Facoltà di
  Giurisprudenza e di
  Economia e Commercio
Via Prudente
84100 Salerno

Università di Siena
Facoltà di Giurisprudenza
Piazza S. Francesco
53100 Siena

Università di Torino
Istituto Universitario di Studi
  Europei
Corso Vittorio Emmanuele 83
10128 Torino

Società Italiana per
  l'Organizzazione
  Internazionale
Centro Internazionale di
  perfezionamento
  professionale e Tecnico
Corso Unità d'Italia 140
10127 Torino

Università di Trieste
Istituto di Diritto
  Internazionale e
  Legislazione Comparata
Piazzale Europa I
34100 Trieste

Centro Informazioni e Studi
  sulle Comunità Europee
Accademia 1056
30123 Venezia

Università di Padova
Istituto di Politica Economica
  e Finanziaria
Facoltà di Economia e
  Commercio
Via dell'Artigliere 8
37100 Verona

JAPAN

Seinan Gakuin University
6–2–92, Nishijn, Nishihu
Fukuoka 814

Doshisha University
Faculty of Law
Kyoto 602

Nagoya University
Faculty of Economics
Library
Furch-cho, Chikusa-Ku
Nagoya 464

Sophia University
Socio-Economic Institute
4 Yonbancho, Chiyoda-ku
Tokyo 102

National Diet Library
Nagato-cho
Chiyoda-ku
Tokyo

LUXEMBOURG

Centre international d'Études
et de Recherches
européennes
Institut universitaire
international
162a avenue de la Faïencerie
Luxembourg

Bibliothèque Nationale
14a Boulevard Royal
Luxembourg

MALTA

Royal University of Malta
59 Old Mint Street
Valetta
Malta

MEXICO

Universidad del Nuevo Leon
Faculdad de Economia
Ario Garza Mercado
Abasolo 907 OTE
Monterrey

NETHERLANDS

Universiteit van Amsterdam
Europa Instituut
Bibliotheek
Herengracht 506–508
1002 Amsterdam

Vrije Universiteit
Economisch en Sociaal
  Instituut
De Boelelaan 1105
Amsterdam-Buitenveldert

T.M.C. Asser Instituut
Interuniversitair Instituut
  voor Internationaal Recht
Alexanderstraat 20–22
's-Gravenhage
Den Haag

Technische Hogeshool Delft
Julianalaan 134
Delft

Rijksuniversiteit te
    Groningen
Juridische Faculteit
Broerestraat 7
Groningen

Europa Instituut
Rijksuniversiteit te Leiden
Hugo de Grootstraat 27
Leiden

Europees Studie- en
    Informatiecentrum
Wilhelminasingel 56
Maastricht

Katholieke Universiteit te
    Nijmegen
Faculteit der
    Rechtsgeleerdheid
Afdeling Europees Recht
Oranje Singel 72
Nijmegen

Katholieke Universiteit te
    Nijmegen
Fakulteit der Soziale
    Wetenschappen
Instituut Politicologie
4 Van Schaeck Mathonsingel
Nijmegen

Erasmusuniversiteit
Centrale Bibliotheek
Burgemeester Oudlaan 50
Rotterdam

J. F. Kennedy Instituut
Katholieke Hogeschool
Hogeschoollaan 225
Tilburg

Europa Instituut
Rijksuniversiteit te Utrecht
Janskerkhof 16
Utrecht

NEW ZEALAND

Auckland Public Libraries
Central Library
Wellesley Street, E
Auckland C.1

General Assembly Library
Parliament House
Wellington C.1

NORWAY

Det Norske Nobelinstituut
Biblioteket
Drammensvn. 19
Oslo 2

POLAND

Instytut Zachodni
Departement de
    documentation
St. Rynk 2
61–772 Poznan

Szkola Glowna Planowania i
   Statystyki
Centres d'Études sur les
   Organisations
   Internationales
UL. Rakowieska 24
Warszawa 12

Polish Institute of
   International Affairs
UL. Warecka 1a
00-950 Warszawa

PORTUGAL

Universidade de Coimbra
Centro interdisciplinar de
   estudos
   juridico-economicos
Rua de Aveiro
11 Estudio A
Coimbra

Universidade Tecnica de
   Lisboa
Instituto Superior de
   Economia
Rua do Quelhas 6
Lisboa 2

ROUMANIA

Biblioteca centrala de Stat
Str. Ion Ghica 4
70018 Bucaresti I

SOUTH AFRICA

South African Library
Queen Victoria Street
Cape Town 8001

Johannesburg Public Library
Market Square
Johannesburg 2001

SOVIET UNION

Institut Mirovoj Ekonomiki
   i Mezhdunarodnich
   Otnoshenij ANSSR
Jaroslavskaja 3
Moscow

SPAIN

Escuela Superior de
   Administracion y Direccion
   de Empresas
Ava. de la Victoria 60–62
Barcelona 17

Universidad Autonoma de
   Madrid
Facultad de Derecho
Departamento de derecho
   internacional
Seminario de Estudios
   Europeos
Cantoblanco
Madrid 34

Universidad Complutenza de
  Madrid
Facultad de derecho
Ciudad universitaria
Madrid 3

Universidad de Oviedo
Facultad de derecho
Institutos de Estudios
  europeos
San Francisco 1
Oviedo

SWEDEN

University of Lund
Juridiska Fackulteten
Avdelningen för
  internationell rätt
Box 1165
22105 Lund

Stockholms Universitet
Juridiska Institutionen, rum
  960
Fiskartorŝvägen 160 c
Fack
10405 Stockholm

SWITZERLAND

Institut für Internationales
  Recht und Internationale
  Beziehungen
Steinenring 23
4051 Basel

Universität Bern
Lehrstuhl für Europarecht
Hochschulstr. 4
3000 Bern

Université de Fribourg
Rectorat
Miséricorde
1700 Fribourg

Institut Universitaire
  d'Études européennes
122 rue de Lausanne
1211 Genève

Centre d'Études Juridiques
  européennes
5 Cours des Bastions
1211 Genève 3

Centre de Recherches
  européennes
1 rue de la Louve
1000 Lausanne

Université de Neuchâtel
Faculté des Sciences
  économiques
Av. de 1er mars 26
2000 Neuchâtel

Institut für Europäisches und
  Internationales Wirtschafts-
  und Sozialrecht
Hochschule St Gallen
Bodanstr. 4
St Gallen

Universität Zürich
Institut für Völkerrecht und
   ausländisches
   Verfassungsrecht
Hirschgrabenstr. 40
8001 Zürich

TRINIDAD

University of the West Indies
Institute of International
   Relations
St Augustine
Trinidad

TUNISIA

Université de Tunis
Faculté de Droit et des
   Sciences politiques et
   Économiques
Campus Universitaire
Belvedere
Tunis

TURKEY

Union des Chambres de
   Commerce de l'Industrie et
   des Bourses de Turquie
Ataturk Bulvari 149
Bakanliklar
Ankara

Avrupa Ekonomik Topulugu
   Enstitusu
Akademi Sitesi
Eskisehir

Iktisadi Kalinma Vakfi
Fondation de Développement
   Économique
Ali Han, Kat 5 no. 501–512
Sahne Sok
Galatasaray
Istambul

Istambul Universitesi
Centre d'Études et de
   Recherches de Droit
   européen
Bayezit
Istambul

EGE University
Faculty of economic and
   commercial sciences
Izmir

UNITED KINGDOM

The Library
The University
Aberdeen AB9 2UB

The Library
The Univeristy
Claverton Down
Bath BA2 7AY

The Library
Queen's University
Belfast BT7 1LS

Commerce Centre Library
Birmingham Polytechnic
Aston Street
Gosta Green
Birmingham B4 7HA

The Library
The University
PO Box 363
Birmingham B15 2TT

British Library Lending
   Division
Boston Spa
West Yorkshire LS23 7BQ

The Library
The University
Bradford BD7 1DP

The Library
University of Sussex
Falmer
Brighton BN1 9QZ

The Library
The University
Queen's Road
Bristol BS8 1RJ

The Library
The University
Cambridge CB3 9DR

The Library
University of Kent at
   Canterbury
Canterbury CT2 7NU

The Library
University College
PO Box 78
Cardiff CF1 1XL

The Library
University of Essex
PO Box 24
Colchester CO4 3UA

The Library
New University of Ulster
Coleraine BT52 1SA

The Library
University of Warwick
Coventry CV4 7AL

The Library
Lanchester Polytechnic
Priory Street
Coventry CV1 5FB

The Library
The University
Perth Road
Dundee DD1 4HN

The Library
The University
Palace Green
Durham DH1 3RN

The Library
Centre of European
   Government Studies
University of Edinburgh
Old College
South Bridge
Edinburgh EH8 9YL

The Library
Faculty of Law
University of Exeter
Amory Building
Rennes Drive
Exeter

The Library
The University
Glasgow G12 8QE

The Library
University of Surrey
Guildford GU2 5XH

Brynmor Jones Library
The University
Cottingham Road
Hull HU6 7RX

The Library
The University
Keele ST5 4BG

The Library
The University
Bailrigg
Lancaster LA1 4YH

The Library
Leeds Polytechnic
Calverley Street
Leeds LS3 3HE

The Library
The University
Leeds LS2 9JT

The Library
The University
Leicester LE1 7RH

Liverpool and District
    Scientific Industrial and
    Research Library Advisory
    Council
Central Libraries
William Brown Street
Liverpool L3 8EW

Centre for Advanced
    European Studies
Royal Institute of
    International Affairs
Chatham House
10 St James's Square
London SW1Y 4LE

EEC Unit
Polytechnic of Central
    London
35 Marylebone Road
London NW1 5SL

The Library
Polytechnic of North London
129/133 Camden High Street
London NW1 7IU

British Library of Political and
    Economic Science
University of London
Houghton Street
London WC2A 2AE

The Library
Queen Mary College
University of London
Mile End Road
London E1 4NS

Official Publications Library
British Library Reference
   Division
Great Russell Street
London WC1B 3DG

Westminster Central
   Reference Library
St Martin's Street
London WC2H 7HP

The Library
The University
Loughborough LE11 3TU

John Rylands University
   Library
The University
Oxford Road
Manchester M13 9PP

The Library
Newcastle Polytechnic
Ellison Building
Ellison Place
Newcastle upon Tyne NE1
   8ST

The Library
University of East Anglia
University Plain
Norwich NR4 7TJ

The Library
The University
Nottingham NG7 2RD

Department of Printed Books
Bodleian Library
The University
Oxford OX1 3BG

The Library
Portsmouth Polytechnic
Mercantile House
Hampshire Terrace
Portsmouth PO1 2EG

The Library
The University
Whiteknights
Reading RG6 2AA

The Library
The University
Salford M5 4WT

The Library
Sheffield Polytechnic
Sheffield S1 1WB

The Library
The University
Highfield
Southampton SO9 4NH

The Library
Wolverhampton Polytechnic
Stafford Street
Wolverhampton WV1 1LY

The Library
Centre for European
  Agricultural Studies
Wye College
University of London
Wye
Ashford TN25 5AH

UNITED STATES

University of Arizona
University Library
Tucson
Arizona 85721

University of Arkansas at
  Little Rock
33rd and University
Little Rock
Arkansas 72204

University of California
Berkeley Campus
General Library
Berkeley
California 94720

University of California
Los Angeles Campus
University Research Library
Public Affairs Service
405 Hilgard Ave.
Los Angeles
California 90024

University of Southern
  California
Von Kleinsmid Library
University Park
Los Angeles
California 90007

University of California
San Diego Campus
Central University Library
La Jolla
San Diego
California 92093

Stanford University
Hoover Institution
Acquisition Department
Central and Western
  European Collection
Stanford
California 94305

University of Colorado
Libraries
Government Documents
  Division
Boulder
Colorado 80302

Yale University
Law Library
Public Documents Room
New Haven
Connecticut 06520

Center for Research and
  Documentation on the
  European Community
The American University
Asbury Building
Massachusetts and Nebraska
  Aves., NW
Washington DC 20016

Library of Congress
Exchange and Gift Division
Washington DC 20540

University of Florida
Libraries
Documents Department
Library West
Gainesville
Florida 32611

Emory University
School of Law
Law Library
Atlanta
Georgia 30322

University of Hawaii
Library
2425 Campus Road
Honolulu
Hawaii 96822

University of Illinois at
  Urbana–Champaign
School of Law Library
104 Law Building
Champaign
Illinois 61820

University of Chicago
Library
Documents Department
1100 East 57th Street
Chicago
Illinois 60657

Library of International
  Relations
660 North Wabash Avenue
Chicago
Illinois 60611

Northwestern University
University Library
Government Publications
  Department
Evanston
Illinois 60201

Indiana University
Library
Documents Department
Bloomington
Indiana 47401

University of Notre-Dame
Memorial Library
Notre-Dame
Indiana 46556

University of Iowa
Libraries
Government Publications
  Department
Iowa City
Iowa 52240

University of Kansas
Law Library
Green Hall
Lawrence
Kansas 66044

University of Kentucky
Government Publications
  Department
Margaret I. King Library
Lexington
Kentucky 40506

University of New Orleans
Department of Political
  Science
Earl K. Long Library
Lakefront
New Orleans
Louisiana 70122

University of Maine
Raymond H. Fogler Library
Orono
Portland
Maine 04473

Harvard University
Law School Library
Langdell Hall
Cambridge
Massachusetts 02138

University of Michigan
Law School Library
Legal Research Building
Ann Arbor
Michigan 48104

Michigan State University
Library
Documents Department
East Lansing
Michigan 48803

University of Minnesota
Walter Library
Minneapolis 14
Minnesota 55455

Washington University
John M. Olin Library
Lindell and Schinker Blvds.
St Louis
Missouri 63130

University of
  Nebraska–Lincoln
University Libraries
Lincoln
Nebraska 68508

Princeton University
Library
Documents Division
Princeton
New Jersey 08540

University of New Mexico
General Library
Albuquerque
New Mexico 87131

State University of New York
  at Albany
University Library
1223 Western Avenue
Albany
New York 12203

State University of New York
  at Buffalo
Lockwood Memorial Library
Buffalo
New York 14214

Council on Foreign Relations
  Library
The Harold Pratt House
58 East 68th Street
New York
New York 10021

New York Public Library
Preparation Division
Grand Central Station
PO Box 1932/RS
New York
New York 10017

New York University
School of Law Library
40 Washington Sq. South
New York
New York 10012

Duke University Library
Public Documents
  Department
Durham
North Carolina 27706

Ohio State University
Library
Gift and Exchange Section
1858 Neil Avenue
Columbus
Ohio 43210

University of Oklahoma
Library
401 West Brooks Room 141
Norman
Oklahoma 73069

University of Oregon
Library
Documents Section
Eugene
Oregon 97403

University of Pennsylvania
Van Pelt Library
3420 Walnut Street
Philadelphia
Pennsylvania 19104

University of Pittsburgh
Libraries
Gift and Exchange
  Department
Hillman Library
Pittsburgh
Pennsylvania 15260

Pennsylvania State University
University Library
Documents Section
University Park
Pennsylvania 16823

University of South Carolina
University Libraries
Columbia
South Carolina 29208

University of Texas
School of Law Library
2500 Red River Street
Austin 5
Texas 78705

University of Utah
Research Libraries
Documents Division
Salt Lake City
Utah 84112

University of Virginia
The Alderman Library
Charlottesville
Virginia 22901

University of
  Wisconsin–Madison
Memorial Library
Madison
Wisconsin 53706

URUGUAY

Universidad de Montevideo
Faculdad de Ciencias
  Economicas y de
  Administracion
Casilla de Correo 5052
Sucursal A.N. 1
Montevideo

VENEZUELA

Universidad Central de
  Venezuela
Faculdad de Derecho
Seccion Integracion
Caracas
Venezuela

YUGOSLAVIA

Institute of International
  Politics and Economics
Makedonska 25
P.O.B. 750
11000 Beograd

ZAIRE

Université Nationale du Zaïre
Campus de Kinshasa
Bibliothèque Centrale
B.P. 125
Kinshasa XI

Université Officielle du Zaïre
Faculté de Droit
Bibliothèque
B.P. 1825
Lubumbashi

APPENDIX III

Further reading on the European Communities

This is a highly selective list of non-official sources of information on the European Communities which might serve to direct the reader in a closer study of policies and events. It is only intended to be indicative.

BIBLIOGRAPHIES

Allen, K. *Regional problems and policies in the European Community: a bibliography*, 2 vols., Saxon House, 1978.

Cosgrove, C. A. *A reader's guide to Britain and the European Communities*. Political and Economic Planning, 1970.

Dahlmanns, G. J. 'European Communities law', *International journal of law libraries*, 3, 1975.

Kujath, W. *Bibliography on European integration*. Europa Union Verlag, 1977.

Siemers, J. P. *European integration: select international bibliography of theses and dissertations, 1957–1977*. Sijthoff & Noordhoff, 1979.

BOOKS

Barber, J. and Reed, B. *European Community: vision and reality*. Open University, 1974.

Brown, L. N. *The Court of Justice of the European Communities*. Sweet & Maxwell, 1977.

Central Office of Information. *Britain and the European Community* (Reference pamphlet 137). HMSO, 1976.

Cook, C. and Paxton, J. *European political facts 1918–73*. Macmillan, 1975

Dagtoglou, P. D. *Basic problems of the European Community*. Blackwell, 1975.

Drew, J. *Doing business in the European Community*. Butterworths, 1979.

Evans, D. *While Britain slept: the selling of the Common Market*. Gollancz, 1975.

Galtung, J. *The European Community: a superpower in the making*. Allen & Unwin, 1973.

Harrison, R. J. *Europe in question*. Allen & Unwin, 1974.

Hodges, M. *European integration: selected readings*. Penguin, 1972.

Jowell, R. and Hoinville, G. *Britain into Europe: public opinion and the EEC 1961–75*. Croom Helm, 1976.

Kerr, A. J. C. *The Common Market and how it works*. Pergamon, 1977.

Lasok, D. and Bridge, J. W. *Introduction to the law and institutions of the European Communities*. 2nd ed. Butterworths, 1976.

Lewis, D. E. S. *Britain and the European Economic Community*. Heinemann, 1978.

Minshull, G. N. *The new Europe: an economic geography of the EEC*. Hodder & Stoughton, 1973.

Paxton, J. *The developing Common Market*. 3rd ed. Macmillan, 1976.

Pryce, R. *Politics of the European Community*. Butterworths, 1973.

Schonfield, A. *Journey to an unknown destination*. Penguin, 1973.

This is your business: a Trade and Industry Guide to the European Communities [in three parts]. HMSO, 1978.

INFORMATION SERVICES

There are a number of periodical publications and information services, some of which are very expensive, which aim to provide current information on the activities of the European Communities. Some of the more important ones are listed below:

Agence Europe (Europe Agence Internationale d'Information pour la Presse)
Common Market Signposts (ECI Services)
Community markets (Financial Times)
Competition law in the European Communities (The Centre for Legal and Business Information)
Euro insight (Metra Consulting group/PPR International)
European digest (Greater London Council)
European information service (International Union of Local Authorities/Council of European Municipalities)
European law newsletter (Financial Times)
European report (European Report, Brussels)

JOURNALS

Agenor
Agra Europe
Common Market law review
Common Market newsletter
Europ
Euromoney
Europa: fatti e idee
Euro Cooperation
European law review
European intelligence
Journal of Common Market studies
Legal issues of European integration
New Europe

REFERENCE BOOKS

European Communities' and other European organisations' who's who, 1978/79. Editions Delta, 1979.
European Communities yearbook, including the other European organisations 1979. Editions Delta, 1979.

ACP States yearbook 1979. Editions Delta, 1979.

Les comités consultatifs communautaires à composition socio-économique. Editions Delta, 1979.

Palmer, D. M. *Sources of information on the European Communities.* Mansell, 1979.

The Times guide to the European Parliament. Times Books, 1980.

Vacher's European companion [quarterly].

Index